# THE WEST HIGHLAND RAILWAY

*Arisaig, the most westerly station on BR, in 1959. K1 2–6–0 No. 62011 is on the train for Mallaig crossing an up service including an observation car converted from former LNER streamlined stock.*

# THE WEST HIGHLAND RAILWAY

## The History of the Railways of the Scottish Highlands—Vol 1

*by*

## John Thomas

*extra material by*

Alan J.S. Paterson
P.J.G. Ransom

*Cover illustration:* NBR Glens 62496 Glen Loy and 12471 Glen
Falloch on 05.45 Glasgow–Fort William train at Ardlui on 9
May 1959. This was the regular train including sleepers from
Kings Cross, but the Glens were provided instead of the usual
locomotives for the BBC Railway Roundabout film Two
Glens to Fort William. *By courtesy of E.S. Russell.*

**British Library Cataloguing in Publication Data**
A catalogue record for this book is available from the British Library

ISBN 1-899863-21 4 (paperback)

First published 1965
Second edition with new introduction 1976
Third edition with new material 1984
Fourth edition with new material and reset index 1998

Printed in Great Britain by Redwood Books, Trowbridge
for House of Lochar, Isle of Colonsay, Argyll PA61 7YR

# Contents

# Acknowledgements (to first edition)

I am greatly indebted to Mr R. M. Hogg, Curator of Historical Records, British Railways Board, Edinburgh, and his staff, and to Mr C. W. Black, City Librarian of Glasgow, and the staff of the Mitchell Library for placing at my disposal most of the material on which this history is based. Mr Alan Cameron, who received me with great courtesy at the office of *The Oban Times*, made available the unique information contained in the files of his newspaper. Robert McAlpine & Sons readily lent me the only pictures of the Mallaig Extension bridges they possess, and Miss Drysdale of the West Highland Museum, Fort William, supplied the rare prints of the sod-cutting and opening ceremonies. The original WHR appointment notices were unearthed by J. Michie, signalman Rannoch, and the map and gradient profile are printed by courtesy of the Editor of *The Railway Magazine*. Alan Paterson not only read the manuscript but gave me a free run of his copious West Highland notebooks with their valuable logs and station diagrams. J. F. McEwan read the page proofs and made several valuable suggestions. And more than one generation of West Highland railwaymen provided a fund of stories.

### THE ILLUSTRATIONS

W. A. C. Smith, plates 5, 28, 47, 48, 49, 52; West Highland Museum, plates 8, 9; W. Hennigan, plate 10; A. J. S. Paterson, frontispiece, plates 12, 15, 32, 51, 52, 53; H. A. Vallance, plates 16, 34; C. Murray, plate 20; D. McMillan, plates 21, 22; J. F. McEwan, plate 27; Robert McAlpine & Sons, plates 29, 30, 31; Boy Scouts Association, plate 33; W. A. Camwell, plates 36, 40, 41; H. J. Patterson Rutherford, plates 37, 45; G. D. King, plate 39; M. Smith, plate 50; Derek Cross, plates 54, 55, 56; P.J.G. Ransom, plates 57, 58 and p.179; the Author, plates 1, 2, 3, 4, 6, 7, 11, 13, 14, 17, 18, 19, 23, 24, 25, 26, 35, 38, 42, 43, 44, 46. The sketches in Chapter 1 were taken from *Mountain, Moor and Loch*, the original guide to the West Highland Railway, published in 1894.

### COLOUR ILLUSTRATIONS

J. M. Jarvis, Colour-Rail, A; W. J. V. Anderson, Colour-Rail, B, C; R. E. Toop, Colour-Rail, D; Derek Cross, E, F, G; Anthony J. Lambert, H.

# From a Carriage Window

*There are many ways of seeing landscape, and none more vivid,*
*in spite of canting dilettanti, than from a railway train.*
—Robert Louis Stevenson.

## BY MOUNTAIN MOOR AND LOCH

Queen Street station, the North British terminus in Glasgow, had seen nothing like it since the day the station was opened in 1842. The date was Saturday, 11 August 1894, the time 8 o'clock in the morning. The polished carriages of the Glasgow gentry arriving in a steady stream were depositing their occupants in the station forecourt, and railway staff were at hand to conduct the distinguished guests to a train of brand-new claret-coloured carriages waiting at the main departure platform.

The visitors were gathering to celebrate an event unique in British railway history. That day there was to be opened ceremonially a main line through one hundred miles of mountain and moorland with not a branch line nor scarcely a village worthy of the name in all its length. For the first time a massive tract of hitherto rail-less country (except for a straggling cross-country line) was being opened up for traffic. At long last the West Highland Railway was ready for service. 'It throws open to the public,' said the *Railway Herald*, 'wide and interesting tracts of country which have been almost as much unknown to the ordinary tourist hitherto as Central Africa was ten years ago to the geographer.' And a guide book in a popular railway series had this to say of the country traversed by the new railway: 'Like England it is situated in the temperate zone, but nearer to the frigid polar regions and hence its climate is relatively cold, dense and moist.'

The passengers who took their seats in the coaches specially built by the North British at Cowlairs Works for the West Highland Railway did not need long to find that a map of the railway was printed on the inside of each window blind. The route was inspected with interest and enthusiasm. The line could be seen leaving the North British Glasgow—Helensburgh line at Craigendoran on the Clyde coast and climbing up beside the Gareloch through Row (later Rhu) and Shandon to Garelochhead. The passengers traced it, still climbing, across to the east side of Loch Long, then followed it all the way up the loch, with one brief deviation inland to Arrochar. A short valley took the railway across to Loch Lomond; then it forced its way up Glen Falloch past Crianlarich and on through Strathfillan to Tyndrum and Bridge of Orchy.

There it started on its long climb to the bleak 400 square miles of the Moor of Rannoch, crossed the very roof of Scotland and then made a swift descent down Loch Treigside and through the gorges of the Spean to a sea-level terminus at Fort William, in the shadow of Ben Nevis. Never before in Britain had such a length of line been opened in one day. Never before had opening-day guests been taken on so spectacular and exciting a trip. Here was a railway fascinating beyond words, every foot of it with a place in the past, a story in every mile.

The West Highland was a railway within a railway. It had its own board of directors and its own capital (later it was to have its own very special atmosphere), but the North British had undertaken to staff and work the line with its own men, engines, and rolling stock. For the privilege of thus extending its influence into the Western Highlands the North British had been willing to guarantee a dividend of 3½ per cent to the West Highland Railway shareholders. By 1894 attempts to build railways into the West Highlands had been going on for fifty years. All the attempts had failed, most of them because of opposition from the firmly established Highland Railway and its natural ally, the Caledonian. The Highland Railway, not without reason, considered that any railway pushed into the West Highlands would harm its own hard-won, precarious line from Stanley Junction up over the Grampians into Inverness. The Caledonian, on the other hand, feared a possible threat to its subordinate the Callander & Oban Railway.

It must have been a source of satisfaction to the North British directors on that opening day to know that it was their bronze-green engines and claret coaches that would enter Fort William and not the blue engines of the Caledonian. The Caledonian had regarded the West of Scotland as its special preserve; thirty years before it had fought tooth and nail to prevent the North British from absorbing the Edinburgh & Glasgow Railway and so gaining access to the west. But the Edinburgh & Glasgow had fallen to the enemy and the North British had become firmly entrenched on the north bank of the Clyde.

Long before that, when the ink on the Caledonian's original Act of 1845 was barely dry, the railway was concerned in bills to promote lines into the West Highlands. And now the North British had triumphed again, albeit through the agency of its foster-child the West Highland Railway, and had penetrated deep into the heart of Caledonian territory. And the fight was far from over. A year earlier, the West Highland had made a bid to take its line on to Inverness, and it was to make another attack on the Highland capital in a matter of weeks. For all that, among the guests on the ceremonial train were representatives of the Caledonian and High-land companies. They were on the way to sup at the enemy's table in Fort William in the moment of his triumph.

Guests of honour on the train were the Marquess and Marchioness of Tweeddale. Behind-the-scenes moves had been made to have Queen Victoria herself honour the great occasion. But it was 1894, people no longer got excited over the opening of a railway, and royalty had long ceased to patronize such events. The West Highland had to make do with the chairman's wife.

### THE THREE LOCHS

At 8.15 the ceremonial train, headed by two of the smart 4—4—0s specially built for the line, started on its journey. It had been preceded 40 minutes earlier by the regular passenger train, for the railway had been open for public services since the previous Tuesday—7 August. One of the press men on board thought it odd that he should have received an invitation to an opening when the line had already been opened. 'But,' he subsequently wrote, 'the guests were not perturbed by the fact that other people had gone before them. It gave them an assurance of safety and they enjoyed the scenery all the better.'

The first stage of the journey—the 1½-mile climb up Cowlairs Incline on the end of the steel cable—took the train to the high ground on the northern fringe of Glasgow.* As soon as the cable was slipped the two 4—4—0s whisked their train round the western suburbs and headed down the valley that carries the Clyde to the sea. On they rattled through suburban stations. Heads turned as passengers waiting for the morning trains to the city watched the unusual spectacle of two flag-decked locomotives with an important-

* See the author's *The Springburn Story*. David & Charles, Dawlish, 1964.

looking train on their tail sail by. At Bowling the railway picked up the broadening river and ran with it through Dumbarton and Cardross to Craigendoran where the river opened out into the firth. And it was at Craigendoran that the West Highland Railway began. From the large windows of their coaches the guests could see the railway diverging to the right from the Helensburgh line of the North British and begin at once to climb sharply into the hills. A curtain of mountain peaks hung on the horizon barely 10 miles away. It was hardly conceivable that in half an hour the train would be deep among those very mountains.

First there was a halt at Craigendoran station to have a hot axle-box given attention. Then the special was off on the curving climb up the hillside, the engines' exhausts crackling, cinders pattering down on the carriage roofs. Within seconds the passengers were looking down on the roofs of Craigendoran pier buildings with the

CRAIGENDORAN · PIER.

pretty North British paddle boats clustered round them like celluloid ducks in a bath. Within minutes the whole panorama of the Firth of Clyde with Port Glasgow, Greenock and Gourock strung out along the opposite shore, opened out below the railway. Two miles of stiff climbing brought the train to Helensburgh Upper station, then followed a relaxed 6 miles as the engines followed the undulating track round the hillside above the Gareloch. Through the gaps in the trees the guests could see the ever-changing views of the loch and the rolling wooded hills that enclosed it. Row and Shandon stations, sparkling in their fresh green paint, slipped behind. Discerning passengers could feel the dip and sway of the coaches as the gradients beneath the wheels changed abruptly. Once on Garelochside the train swung into a great left hand bend and the engines were clearly visible from carriages even in the middle of the train.

A stop for water at Garelochhead, then the train swung out on the hillside, crossing the head of the loch and giving the passengers a fine panoramic view all the way down to Greenock. Suddenly, a high wall of rock blotted out the view, but less than a minute later the train emerged from the cutting and presented the passengers with an entirely different view. The Gareloch with its trim villages and pleasant wooded hills had given place in the blinking of an eye to the lonely, rugged grandeur of Loch Long. The speed of the transition was bewildering. One minute the train was in the Lowlands, the next it was in the Highlands. The passengers might well have entered another country. Far below was Loch Long, thrusting a fiord-like finger far into the mountains of Argyll. The precipitous slopes plunged straight down the rugged peaks into the dark water.

The train wound along the mountain face steadily climbing higher and higher above the water. A mile or two of this and it slipped into Glen Mallin and continued its journey with a range of bare mountains between the railway and the loch. At the top of the Glen was Glen Douglas passing place, the first of several outposts established in lonely places to break the long empty sections—a short platform, a signal box and a simple cottage to house the railway family. Glen Douglas was the first summit of the line— 560 ft above sea level. The train slowed briefly as the fireman of the second engine exchanged tablets with the signalman, then it slewed abruptly to the left, burrowed down through a rock cutting on a reverse curve and came out once again on the mountainside high above Loch Long. It wound along on a ledge stepped out of the mountain and just wide enough to hold the railway. A wall of freshly cut rock rose up outside the right-hand carriage windows; on the left side a precipice dropped more than 500 ft to the water's edge. The guests were thrilled at one place to find themselves looking down the face of a perpendicular wall. Through the large windows of their saloons they could see the engines nosing cautiously in and out of the crevices as they negotiated a continuous series of reverse curves. Often the engines were out of sight of spectators in the middle of the train. At one point, perched on a buttress overhanging the loch was a cottage built to house the surfaceman whose job it was to patrol this spectacular length of railway.

Where Loch Long ended against a barrier of mountain peaks the railway turned to the right into a short valley—an ancient portage connecting salt-water Loch Long with fresh-water Loch Lomond. No sooner was Loch Long lost to view at the left-hand windows than the right-hand windows presented the delighted passengers with the beauties of Loch Lomond; few of them had seen the famous waterway to such advantage. The little-used coach road hugged the shore, but the railway ran high up on the face of the hill giving wide views over the loch. In the years to come many patrons were to glory in this view of Loch Lomond. Writing about it and other West Highland high-level views the Scottish author J. J. Bell said: 'We have, indeed, several stretches of line which in scenic outlook are immeasurably richer than the roads leading to the same destinations, and one of them is the West Highland Railway.'

After a brief stop at Arrochar and Tarbet station, the train steamed off through a birchwood and for the next 8 miles meandered round the hillside, sometimes edging out close to the water, at others swinging back into the recesses of the hillface. Ben Lomond across the loch dominated the scene at first. Then came Inversnaid village with its waterfall plummeting down a

A WEST HIGHLAND STATION (ARROCHAR AND TARBET).

wooded ravine. It was a dullish morning with cloud caps on the highest mountain tops, but for all that the rich colourings of the Loch Lomond scene captivated the guests. The heather patches on the mountains were beginning to assume their autumn purple, and the thick bracken rolled green down to the water's edge, while here and there were rowan trees hanging with scarlet berries.

### UP THE VALE OF AWFUL SOUND

At the head of Loch Lomond came another dramatic change of scene. Direct from the end of the platform at Ardlui the train plunged into the craggy entrance to Glen Falloch, and started on a gruelling climb that was to last for 15 miles and take it over 1,000 ft above sea level. The railway climbed higher and higher up the west

THE WEST HIGHLAND SCENE—1

(1) *Excursion train hauled by* B12 *Class* 4—6—0 *and* LNER *No.* 9695 *above*
*Loch Long*

(2) *Loch Long, showing the railway on the mountainside*

THE WEST HIGHLAND SCENE—2

(3) *Loch Lomond. The* G & NW *would have followed the far shore of the loch*
(4) *Glens doublehead a Glasgow—Fort William train on Glen Falloch viaduct
in* LNE *days*

wall of the glen, twisting constantly left and right in an effort to gain altitude. Glen Falloch became narrower and wilder with each milepost. The steep slopes pitched down to the bottom of the valley along which the Falloch river ran its noisy course, down to Loch Lomond. Waterfalls large and small cascaded into the glen from the surrounding mountains. The passengers had a wonderful view for many minutes of the great Ben-y-Glas Fall, foaming over a precipice and plunging 120 ft to the rocks below with a force that sent a curtain of vapour to the tree tops. The rush and roar of water was the characteristic sound of Glen Falloch. William Wordsworth called it 'the vale of awful sound'. Even Wordsworth the railway hater would have been impressed by the new sound that invaded Glen Falloch that day—the bark and crackle of Matthew Holmes's little West Highland bogies as they struggled to lift their ten coaches up the glen.

Another highlight of the journey was reached when the engines curved, still climbing, on to the Glen Falloch viaduct carrying the line over the gorge of the Black Water—the Dubh Eas—at a height only 7 ft less than that of the recently-completed Forth Bridge. Passengers who looked forward as the engines leaned to the right with the curvature of the bridge could see the flash of their pounding coupling rods. Up they climbed through the remnants of the ancient Caledonian Forest and under the curious triangular hill, Cruach Ardran. After 7 stiff miles the glen opened out, and the

CRIANLARICH.

B

steady beat of the exhausts quietened as the train breasted a minor summit—to become known to generations of West Highland foot-platemen as 'the fireman's rest'—and drifted down into Crianlarich.

The huts and equipment used by the contractor were still to be seen alongside the station. The railway company had established Crianlarich as the halfway posting establishment between Glasgow and Fort William. The engines were groomed and watered for the task that lay immediately ahead and the passengers were given refreshments. Crianlarich hamlet stood in the bottom of a natural bowl set among great mountains, penetrated by three deep passes. The West Highland came up from the south through Glen Falloch, the Callander & Oban Railway came in from the east through Glen Dochart, and both railways shared Strathfillan to continue their way north.

The ceremonial train pulled out of Crianlarich station, crossed the Oban line at right angles on a viaduct, swung through a 90° curve and began the ascent of the eastern side of Strathfillan. The Oban line, keeping to the floor of the valley on the western side, ran on a parallel course with the West Highland for 5 or 6 miles. The train climbed steadily up the strath, rising all the time above

VIADUCT OF WEST HIGHLAND RAILWAY AT CRIANLARICH.

the Oban line. Beyond Tyndrum, the hamlet at the head of the valley, two glens opened out from the main valley like the arms of a Y. The Oban line disappeared through the western pass to run by Dalmally and Loch Awe and Loch Etive to the coast at Oban. The

West Highland line entered a deep V-cut penetrating the mountains to the north. Five minutes more steaming took the train to the county march of Perth and Argyll and at the same time to a summit 1,024·75 ft above sea level.

By consulting their programmes of the day's events and the maps on the window blinds the passengers would have discovered that they were approaching one of the most eagerly-awaited features of the line—the Horse Shoe Curve. Directly ahead of the engines was Ben Doran, by far the most striking of all the West Highland mountains. There was nothing very remarkable about its 3,523 ft of height; it was the symmetry of the beautifully-moulded cone visible at a glance from the base to the summit that made Ben Doran as distinctive and distinguished as the Fuji Yama of the tapestries and lacquered trays.

A broad valley separated the train from Ben Doran, but instead of cutting straight across the valley on a viaduct or embankment the line suddenly swerved to the right round the shoulder of Ben Odhar, until it was heading almost due east. Then it turned north again,

BRIDGE OF DOCHART.

and then struck westward along the side of Ben Doran. The passengers could look across the valley and see the line they had just traversed: above the railway, marking its course round the mountainsides, hung a U-shaped pall of smoke.

Bridge of Orchy proved to be a typical West Highland 'bridge' settlement—a bridge over a river, a few stone cottages, an inn. That day the inn exhibited a flag in honour of the coming of the railway. On the climb northwards away from Bridge of Orchy the sense of adventure aboard heightened. The narrow coach-road that had kept company with the railway from Loch Lomondside diverged to the left and disappeared over the rim of the Black Mount. The line struck north into barren roadless country that only a handful of intrepid travellers had ever seen before. Between Bridge of Orchy and Inverlair lay 30 miles of the most desolate and forbidding country in Europe, and in the middle of it was the Moor of Rannoch.

### THE MOOR OF RANNOCH

Passengers who knew their Robert Louis Stevenson remembered how in *Kidnapped* David Balfour and Alan Breck had caught their first glimpse of the Moor.

> The mist rose and died away and showed us that country lying as waste as the sea; only the moorfowl and the peewits crying over it and far over to the east a herd of deer moving like dots. Much of it was red with heather; much of the rest broken up with bogs and hags and peaty pools; some had been burned black in a heath fire; and in another place there was quite a forest of dead firs standing like skeletons. A wearier looking desert man never saw.

Climbing again on the 21 mile drag that would take it to the summit of the line the train roared up the valley of the Tulla water. Below and to the west lay Loch Tulla and beyond it the Black Mount and the jagged peaks of Glen Etive and Glencoe. The scenery changed perceptibly with every mile that passed. Trees vanished. Vegetation other than scrub and heather became scarcer and scarcer. The bare, stony framework of the mountains protruded in patches through the thin outer covering of turf. Traces of civilization melted away.

After an 8-mile steady climb came Gortan (later Gorton), a West Highland outpost on the edge of the Moor. There was a signal box and a house to shelter the family who had relinquished their former life in a more hospitable region of the North British system to attend to the safety of the trains in their passage over the Moor. The train rolled out into the wilderness. Never before had the passengers witnessed such a scene of desolation. For mile after mile a dun-coloured sea flecked with grey granite stretched from either side of the line to the horizon. The dreary surface of the Moor was blotched with mud-filled ditches and pools of dark water. Black bog lapped at the railway line : in the worst places it was floated over the bog on a raft of brushwood and heather. The Caledonian Forest long ago had covered all of the Moor. Not a tree now remained, but the black roots, pickled for ages in the bog, were everywhere to be seen.

The train wound among the peat hags at never more than 25 m.p.h. It crossed the Gauer Water, a dark stream coursing sluggishly through the bog, and presently the appearance of a distant signal heralded the approach of civilization. Ahead lay Rannoch station, an oasis wrested from the Moor by the railway engineers to house and shelter the men who would pass the trains and service this lonely section of the line. The visitors marvelled at the isolation of the settlement. 'How will they get food supplies? How will their children get to school? What will it be like in the depths of winter?' Such bustling questions must have occupied their minds. The shareholders among them might well have been asking themselves where on earth the traffic was to come from to make the railway pay.

From a re-start at Rannoch the train struggled upwards towards the highest part of the Moor. Through a cutting in the Cruach Rock it went, and soon it was swinging gently on a series of shallow reverse curves as the track sought out the best route through the peat bogs. It was now crossing the great tableland of Scotland. Mountain ranges and peaks ringed the horizon; rain clouds hung on the tops, and intermittent drizzle swept the highest parts of the Moor. One eye-witness at least was unperturbed by the indifferent weather. 'Nobody could have wished a better day,' he was to write, 'except those who were anxious to see every clearly-cut peak outlined against the sky—and then they would have paid the penalty of sweltering in the sunshine. The clouds swathed the mountaintops, but they did not dissolve into more than a few drops of rain.' The red train with its two bronze-green engines made a brave sight as it mounted towards the high north-west corner of the Moor. Then at last it reached Corrour, the third of the railway settlements on the Moor and the summit of the line.

More than three hours had passed since the run at sea level beside the Firth of Clyde at Craigendoran. In that time 72 miles had been covered and 1,347 ft had been climbed above sea level. Now the passengers were faced with an exciting, headlong plunge back to sea level at Fort William in a distance of only 28 miles.

### THROUGH THE GORGES OF THE SPEAN

The carriage wheels drummed faster and faster over the rail joints as the train gathered speed down the valley that led the railway away from the inhospitable Moor. At once the scenery began to change, trees beginning to appear again. At the end of the valley the brakes hissed and the two engines curved slowly out on to the face of yet another mountain. Loch Treig filled a great hollow in the mountains 450 ft below, and across the water rose the massif of which Ben Nevis was the apex. Loch Treig, a hitherto seldom-seen loch, had no roads by its shores. The railway began high above at the western end, and for 5 miles dropped down and down the mountainside until it reached the water's edge. No fewer than 150 bridges were provided to carry it over the innumerable watercourses that poured down the slopes.

At the end of the loch the River Treig leapt and tumbled down a wooded glen, the railway running beside it. Then a mile down the glen the train swung through 90°, passed through Inverlair station, and entered the gorges of the Spean. The coach-road from Kingussie on the Highland Railway came in from the east and ran parallel to the railway. No road had been seen since Bridge of Orchy.

After the long, bleak trip across the Moor of Rannoch and down Loch Treigside, the richly-wooded Glen Spean with its occasional cultivated strips by the river seemed bright and friendly. The railway kept close company with the Spean as it roared through the rocky channels it had cut for itself in the floor of the valley through the ages. The passengers watched the river shoot in a smother of foam through black-walled chasms and froth down to lower levels in a series of cascades. They saw it roar round obstructing boulders and then suddenly broaden out to flow between lush meadows. But never for long. The gorge closed in again and the constricted river surged along in a flurry of amber and white rapids.

At one point a sharp brake application brought down speed to 10 m.p.h., and the engines felt their way through the perfect crescent of the Monessie Gorge. There was just room for railway and river to squeeze through the narrow defile. The line ran on a ledge halfway up the right-hand wall of the gorge and the passengers could look directly down on to the brown water churning over a jumbled mass of granite boulders. There were to be times, and they were not far off, when the floodwaters of the Spean would climb 15 ft up the walls of the Monessie Gorge in an hour.

Once clear of the Spean gorges the train sped steadily westwards through Lochaber. Tablets were exchanged at Roy Bridge and at Spean Bridge, the last station before Fort William. As the last miles dropped behind, the passengers made themselves ready for the ceremonial welcome that awaited them. Many of them admired the mass of Ben Nevis rising close by the railway to the left of the train.

### LOCHABER WELCOME

The first houses of the first town in 100 miles drifted past the carriage windows. Then came the mingled sound of bagpipes and muffled cheering. The train slowed and stopped at a temporary wooden platform on the outskirts of the town. Directly ahead, an ornamental arch flanked by battlemented towers spanned the railway, and closed double gates barred the progress of the train. The whole edifice looked solid and imposing, although it was only a flimsy framework of timber clothed with the green and purple of fern and heather, and adorned with flags and heraldic devices.

Cameron of Lochiel, a director of the West Highland, Provost Young of Fort William, and the Chief Constable of Inverness-shire were among the important local people who greeted the train from the south. Lady Tweeddale stepped from the train—it was her first visit to the West Highlands by any means—and was conducted to the closed archway. She was handed a golden key hung from a gold shield engraved 'W.H.R.' in diamonds. She turned the key in a gold padlock ostensibly securing the gate of the archway, and that was the signal for members of the railway staff hidden among the foliage to pull the gates slowly open. The moment that Fort William had awaited for half a century had come at last. The train steamed into the town as pipers played a merry march on the battlements above.

Some 400 guests repaired to a large marquee near the station. Its interior was decorated with a thousand blooms brought up from Glasgow the previous day. Mr Rupprecht of the North British Hotel in Glasgow presided over a meal worthy of the occasion. There were the usual speeches. The seating arrangements were such that Cameron of Lochiel was sandwiched between a director of the Highland Railway and the vice-chairman of the Caledonian Railway, gentlemen who had done their damnedest to keep the West Highland out of Fort William and who were to fight relentlessly to prevent the expansion of the West Highland into their territories. But Lochiel was in benevolent mood. 'I will let bygones be bygones and never say a word about the past,' he told the company. To which he might well have added under his breath, 'For today only'. A succession of speakers prophesied a bright future for the new railway. The reporter from the *Glasgow Evening News* had his doubts. In the next issue of his newspaper he wrote :

It would be difficult to parallel it (the railway) for sparseness of population. For mile upon mile of its length not a single vestige of human life or habitation is to be seen. Its very stations between Crianlarich and Fort William are at present simply names—oases in the barren moorland. A paying traffic must be a matter of slow growth, and it will test the management severely to make ends meet long years after the present time. All who have the interest of our Highland population at heart will join in hoping that a brighter day has dawned for them, and that with the breaking down of the natural barriers which have so long confined them, there will follow an era of prosperity of which parallels can be found wherever the railway has found an entrance.

# CHAPTER 2

# West Highland Pre-History

### THE MANIA YEAR

*The Great National Direct Independent Land's End to John o' Groats Atmospheric Railway.*

That was one of the headings that caught the eye of the avid reader who scanned the announcements of new railways that filled the newspaper columns in the Mania Year, 1845. 'It will cross Loch Ness on a magnificent viaduct not less than 5,500 feet long,' went on the announcement, 'and a tunnel will pierce through the centre of Ben Nevis. Travellers will thus be enabled in the transit to see two of the finest objects in the North Highlands of Scotland.' It was not until the reader was assured that the proposed railway would proceed from terminus to terminus by the most indirect route and scrupulously avoid all cities and centres of industry that he realized that he was having his leg pulled. Yet the unknown satirist's fake prospectus was hardly less outrageous than some of the genuine prospectuses that appeared alongside it. Promoters were greedy for ground on which to lay their paper railways. No place was too ridiculous to merit their interest.

Of all the wildcat schemes of the Mania Year none were more maniacal than those that envisaged the penetration of the Western Highlands of Scotland. Here was country that was a great mass of mountain peaks cut and cross-cut with deep V-shaped valleys, many of them filled with ribbon lochs. It was raw, barren country without industry, and with hundreds of square miles completely depopulated. It presented a mighty challenge to the railway engineer, yet there was little for a railway to do once it was built.

For all that, in 1845 West Highland schemes with grand-sounding names were legion. There was the Scottish Western Railway and the Scottish North Western Railway, the Caledonian & Grand Northern Railway, the Caledonian Northern Direct, and the Scottish Grand Junction Railway. The language of the prospectuses of some of the projected companies was scarcely less extravagant than that of the mythical Land's End and John o' Groats. The Scottish Grand Junction 'connecting the whole of the Western and Northern counties of Scotland with the Scottish Central and Caledonian Railways' thus described its route through the rugged heart of the Highlands.

> The country to be traversed by the proposed lines has been surveyed and is found to present every facility. For the most part it is a dead level and the surface is so regular that the cost of construction will be much below the average of Railway undertakings. The works are generally light—there are no tunnels—and the bridges will be few in number and of inconsiderable magnitude.

In spite of this farrago of falsehood, the Scottish Grand Junction and its rivals received wide public acclaim and financial support. And it was not by accident that names appeared among the committee members of the West Highland schemes that were already familiar to students of the official literature of the Caledonian Railway. The Caledonian had gained its Act in July 1845. It was one of the most ambitious railways promoted up to that time; it was backed by London financiers, and engineered by men of the highest repute. The Caledonian was destined to be a great railway. Already, with the first sod scarcely turned, the board-room had visions of creating a great national line. There were two northern citadels to be conquered—Aberdeen and Inverness. The Caledonian had an eye on a series of satellite railways that, end on end, were to provide through communication with Aberdeen within fifteen years. With one long tentacle stretching through the rich valleys of eastern Scotland to the Dee, it was natural that the Caledonian should give thought to establishing a complementary line running through the rugged west to a terminus on the Ness. Hence the Caledonian finger in the various West Highland pies.

In the autumn of 1845 Locke and Errington, who had surveyed trunk lines from Birmingham to Castlecary in the Forth-Clyde valley, were in Stirling surveying a route for the Scottish Central Railway, the first of the lines that was to take the Caledonian influence on towards Aberdeen. Fresh from their successes with the Grand Junction and the Caledonian, Locke and Errington were highly esteemed as railway engineers; their names on a prospectus provided the hallmark of respectability. Investors raised their eyebrows when the prospectus of the Caledonian & Grand Northern Railway seemed to indicate that Locke and Errington had transferred their interest from the gentle east to the wild west, and had engineered a major railway from Glasgow through the West

Highlands and the Great Glen to Inverness. But in the same news-paper column that exhibited the C & GN prospectus there appeared this letter.

Stirling 6 Sept. 1845

Sir,

I observe that Parties promoting the above Line of Railway have done Mr. Locke and myself the honour to nominate us Engineers of the Scheme. It is usual to have the sanction of a professional man for placing his name before the public in connection with any project, for the propriety of which he may, to a certain extent, be held accountable. I have received no applications from either of the interim secretaries, or from the Solicitors named in the advertisement, and have no connection whatever with the above line.

I am, Sir,

Your servant,

J. E. Errington.

That was the end of the Caledonian & Grand Northern Railway.

In September 1845 the Scottish Western Railway entered the field. Like most of the West Highland projects of the period, the SWR aimed at providing communication between the western seaboard and the industrial Lowlands. The Scottish Western was to start at Oban and thread its way along lochsides and through glens (by the route taken three decades later by the Callander & Oban Railway) to join at Callander a proposed railway in the Caledonian sphere of influence. From Crianlarich, a branch was to strike south down Glen Falloch and Loch Lomond to make connection at Balloch with another proposed Caledonian-sponsored line, the Caledonian & Dumbartonshire. The Scottish Western therefore had a choice of two routes to Glasgow from Oban, both dominated by the Caledon-ian. The promoters pointed out that if hostile landowners barred their passage down Glen Falloch, they would take the line east through the Trossachs to the Blane Valley, and link up with the Campsie branch of the Edinburgh & Glasgow Railway.

The Scottish Western committee was well sprinkled with names of reputable Scots—landowners, lairds, merchants, and MPs. The scheme had the confidence of the public, and within a few days of the appearance of the prospectus the railway office announced that they 'found it impossible to comply with the requests of many respectable applicants' who indicated their intention to take up the £700,000 in SWR shares.

One, John Lammond, criticized the Scottish Western on the grounds that it was too expensive. He could see no point in building a railway down Loch Lomondside. He had a plan to make a line from Oban to the head of Loch Lomond, and to link this northern line 'by means of strong and powerful steamers' to the Caledonian & Dumbartonshire at Balloch. The estimated cost of Lammond's line was a mere £300,000. His announcement said, 'A full prospectus of the West Highland Railway will appear in a few days.' It never did appear, but the episode is interesting because it introduced the title West Highland Railway for the first time.

The Scottish Western was followed within a few weeks by the Caledonian Northern Direct and the Scottish Grand Junction Railway. The proposed route of the Scottish Grand Junction was almost identical with that of the Scottish Western : Oban to Callander and a branch down Glen Falloch, thence through the Trossachs to a junction with the Caledonian & Dumbartonshire at Milngavie. The Grand Junction also planned a second main line, starting at Tyndrum and passing eastward through Glen Ericht to join up with the proposed Perth & Inverness Railway (later the Highland Railway main line) at Dalwhinnie. The end result would have been a Y-shaped system with Glasgow at the base of the stem, and Oban and Dalwhinnie (later it was hoped Inverness) at the tips of the arms. The Grand Junction was headed by Sir Alexander Campbell and the Scottish Western by Sir James Campbell. The Campbells did the right thing : they got together in Glasgow on 30 October 1845, and as a result the Scottish Western agreed to withdraw, leaving the field clear for the Scottish Grand Junction.

The Caledonian Northern Direct was more or less a repetition of the southern half of the Scottish Grand Junction. Apparently it was promoted to ensure a Caledonian-controlled line of communication should the Scottish Grand Junction get permission for the Callander—Oban, Tyndrum—Dalwhinnie section and be refused the extension. The prospectus said in part :

> It is therefore proposed to form a Company to make a Railway from a point on the Caledonian and Dumbartonshire Junction Line near Milngavie through Strathblane and Strathendrick into the Valley of the Forth, between Gartmore and Buchlyvie, thence by Aberfoyle, Lochard, Lochchon and Loch Katrine, by Glengyle through Glen Falloch and Glen Dochart to a point near Tyndrum, there to form a Junction with the proposed lines from Oban to Callander and from Tyndrum to Dalwhinnie and Inverness.

After informing investors that it would 'be difficult to over-estimate the earning capacity of the line', the prospectus gave the usual assurance that the West Highlands presented no difficulties to the engineers : 'The line will be for the most part along valleys and margins of lakes, the gradients are good and there are no engineering difficulties.' A ruling gradient of 1 in 100 was promised and a tunnel three-quarters of a mile long was to pierce the mountain barrier between the Trossachs and Glen Falloch. By contrast George Marton, engineer of the rival Scottish Grand Junction, proposed to take his line from the Trossachs over the tops of the mountains on gradients of 1 in 40, which he planned to surmount 'by application of the atmospheric principle'.

The Caledonian Northern Direct's proposed capital was £600,000 to be issued in shares of £25 each. The Duke of Montrose was provisional chairman, and his committee was studded with well-known names: John James Hope Johnston, chairman of the Caledonian (significantly); John Orr Ewing, merchant of Glasgow; Peter Denny, the famous shipbuilder and Provost of Dumbarton; Henry Dann, director of the Shrewsbury, Oswestry & Chester Railway; George Whitmore, deputy chairman of the North Kent Railway; and many more. By 28 October 1845 the Caledonian Northern Direct announced that it had allocated all its stock 'from a multiplicity of applications'. *The Glasgow Argus*, which strongly criticized certain railway proposals in England, said of the Scottish projects: 'These lines are all together of a *bona fide* character and as wide apart from what are appropriately termed bubble lines as truth is from falsehood.' But bubble lines they were, and very soon the bubbles burst. The end of the Mania saw the Scottish schemes swept away and forty years were to pass before the idea of a trunk line through the Western Highlands was resurrected.

### LIMITED SUCCESS

In the twenty years that followed 1845 the Scottish railways concentrated on extending and consolidating their lines. By 1865 the Highland Railway had a trunk route to Inverness by Blair Atholl, Aviemore and Forres, and associated companies took the line north of Inverness as far as Bonar Bridge. The Caledonian main line stretched from Carlisle to Perth, and in the following year the absorption of the Scottish North Eastern was to give the Caledonian the long-sought-after through route from Carlisle to Aberdeen. The Highland Railway ran up through the centre of Scotland like a spinal column. The country to the east of the line was well served by railways, but the country to the west was still rail-less.

With their main lines secure, both the Caledonian and the Highland turned their attention to possible conquests in the West Highlands. This time there was no talk of a trunk line from north to south. Instead the respective companies backed schemes which would take what were virtually long branch lines from the parent trunk lines through the glens and over the mountain passes to two points on the western seaboard. The Callander & Oban was authorized to build a line between the two towns of the title by the route favoured by the 1845 promoters, and the Dingwall & Skye Railway was authorized to construct a line from Dingwall across Wester Ross to the coast at Kyle of Lochalsh. The object of both schemes was to tap the trade of the west coast and islands—mainly fish—and route it to the parent lines. The Callander & Oban was to be worked by the Caledonian, the Dingwall & Skye by the Highland. But most of the money for the Dingwall & Skye had come out of the Caledonian's coffers; plainly the Caledonian had not weakened over the years in its determination to control the West Highlands.

Five years of trials and difficulties taught the sponsors of those lines what it meant to take railways into those inhospitable regions. By 1870 the Skye line reached as far as Strome Ferry on Loch Carron, and the plan to take it on to the projected terminus at Kyle of Lochalsh was abandoned. The Callander & Oban had fared much worse. By 1870 the promoters had been able to build only 17 miles of track. Overwhelming engineering difficulties had drained away the company's capital, and the line stuck in Glen Ogle for lack of finance. Enough money was found to take it on another 15 miles to Tyndrum and there, after an Act had been obtained abandoning the route westward to Oban, the Callander & Oban established a railhead. The line as it stood ended in the middle of nowhere. It had failed entirely in its purpose to link the western seas with the Lowlands. Four years passed before a fresh injection of capital gave the Callander & Oban heart to seek a new Act for the extension of the line to Oban, which point was reached in 1880. The Highland did not get to the Kyle of Lochalsh until 1897.

### THE GLASGOW & NORTH WESTERN RAILWAY

By 1880 the public conscience was becoming troubled about the plight of the people of North West Scotland. At long last Westminster wakened to the fact that the population of the West Highlands and Islands were in dire straits. The deliberate and ruthless depopulation of the area during the Highland Clearances, massive governmental indifference and neglect and primitive or non-existent transport had combined to make the area one of the most backward in Europe. The bulk of the people lived on the poverty line. The pride of family that had characterized the clan system had to a large measure been lost and some of the clan chiefs had become grasping landlords, sometimes absentees whose indolent lives in the fleshpots of England had to be supported by rents wrested from their Highland estates. Then came the Crofters' War, when the fisherfolk and crofters rebelled against their oppressors and staged rent strikes. The result was the setting up of the Crofters' Commission, whose members were dispatched to the trouble-spots on a painstaking fact-finding mission, with a mandate to report on the causes of the West Highland malaise and suggest methods of improving the lot of the West Highlanders. It was against this background that the promotion of the Glasgow & North Western Railway was announced.

The Glasgow & North Western was the grandest railway ever to be promoted in the British Isles. It was to stretch for 167 miles from Glasgow to Inverness, taking in vast tracts of new country embracing Loch Lomond, the Moor of Rannoch, Glen Coe, part of the Argyllshire coast, Fort William, Fort Augustus and Loch Ness. Unlike the Highland Railway and the extensions into the West Highlands, the G & NW was not locally financed. London money was behind it, and it was engineered in Westminster by Thomas Walron Smith who had twenty years of experience building railways in Sweden, Wales, and Ireland.

The enterprise was backed, not by the Caledonian, but by the North British who hoped to work it. That was enough to spark off a full-scale railway war in Scotland. The Caledonian and North British were bitter rivals. The North British with its base in Edinburgh had developed the east side of the country, the Caledonian based in Glasgow regarded the west side as its preserve. The Caledonian had suffered a serious setback when in 1865 the North British had absorbed the Edinburgh & Glasgow Railway and gained access to Glasgow and the west. Now the North British was threatening to extend its influence into country long regarded by the Caledonian and its partner, the Highland, as their territory. It was a prospect that neither company could contemplate with equanimity.

The bold new railway was planned to leave the North British Helensburgh branch at Maryhill on the northern fringe of Glasgow and stretch north-west across 20 miles of pleasant, undulating country to the southern shore of Loch Lomond. There were plans to develop this initial length of line—which was double—as a prosperous outer suburban section. It passed just to the west of Milngavie, the terminus of the North British branch from Glasgow, soon to be linked with the stations on the Glasgow District Railway then in course of construction. The G & NW hoped to make a junction with the Milngavie line and send some trains into the new Queen Street Low Level station, serving the GDR suburban stations west of Glasgow on the way.

From Milngavie the line crossed some high ground to the west side of Craigallion Loch, climbed into the hills flanking the Blane Valley (through which passed the North British Aberfoyle branch) and then struck across moorland and hill pasture towards Loch Lomond, crossing a mile west of Drymen another North British possession, the Forth & Clyde Junction Railway. There the Glasgow & North Western proposed a double junction enabling its traffic to reach Balloch and Dumbarton on one hand and Stirling and Alloa on the other. The approach to Loch Lomond was by the Pass of Balmaha. The double line was to end at a railway-owned pier from which boats would ply to various destinations on the loch.

Beyond Balmaha the character of the line changed abruptly. Pastureland and moors gave place to mountains rising in some places sheer out of the loch. The single line continued for some 20 miles up the eastern shore of the loch partly in cuttings but mainly on embankments varying in height from 7 to 35 ft above the water. The line wound round the contours, skirted the base of Ben Lomond, and crossed the garden in front of Inversnaid Hotel, eventually to reach the head of the loch and enter Glen Falloch. Still forging north, it climbed up the eastern side of the glen 200 ft above the existing coach road, and passed so close to the great waterfall Ben-y-Glas that the spray was expected to fall on the rails. At the end of an 8-mile climb the line emerged from the glen to cross the Callander & Oban line at Crianlarich where a 'spacious staircase' was envisaged linking the two railways.

The next stage took the line up Strathfillan through Tyndrum, and on past Glen Orchy and round the shores of Loch Tulla to a summit of 1,077 ft on the Black Mount. Then came a gentle fall over moorland, followed at once by a spectacular 4½-mile plunge down Glen Coe on gradients of 1 in 50 and 1 in 53 to sea level at Ballachulish. Now that the line had won its way over the difficult terrain of the interior, the way to Inverness lay open to it in an almost straight line 76½ miles long. The railway continued across Loch Leven at the Dog Ferry, passed along the shore of Loch Linnhe to Fort William, and went on to cross the Spean at Mucomir Bridge and reach the shores of Loch Oich and Loch Ness. A 19-mile length of dead-level line, partly on a causeway built out into the water, was planned for Loch Ness side.

THE WEST HIGHLAND SCENE—3

(5) 'Loch Arkaig' on a Glasgow—Crianlarich train
(6) Crianlarich period piece, 1938

THE WEST HIGHLAND SCENE—4

(7) *Ben Doran, 3,523 ft. The railway near the Horse Shoe Curve*

The Glasgow & North Western was to reach its own station in South Inverness and take a final sweep round the town to a junction with the Highland Railway, and so gain access to the Highland station. A branch planned to run down to Inverness Harbour was intended to secure for the Glasgow & North Western a share of the east coast as well as the west coast fish trade. The railway was to have twenty-eight stations, seven tunnels totalling 1,336 yd, and five viaducts totalling 498 yd; the whole enterprise was to cost £1,526,116.

### THE BATTLE IN PARLIAMENT

The Glasgow & North Western Railway bill was presented in Parliament in November 1882, and its consideration in committee extended throughout April and May 1883. It was a memorable episode in railway Parliamentary history, and it shed an interesting light on social conditions in the West Highlands. For weeks each side collected potential evidence against the other. Witnesses were interviewed, briefed and brought to London at considerable expense to their sponsors.

Opposition to the Glasgow & North Western was massive: rail interests, steamer interests and private individuals combined to thwart the scheme. The Highland Railway had more cause than most to fear the newcomer. The Highland or its constituent companies had created their railway using local money and talents at a time when their territory offered no attraction to southern speculators. The new venture, which could prosper only at the expense of the Highland, would, they insisted, be unfair. The Caledonian, with an eye to developing the West Highlands through its subsidiary the Callander & Oban, and with more than a passing thought for its capital invested in the Skye line, gave the Highland wholehearted support. The Caledonian Canal Commissioners and the steamboat operators on Loch Lomond abhorred the idea of a railway line running parallel with their steamer routes, and they prepared to fight the bill. David MacBrayne, who had a near-monopoly of West Highland steamer services, likewise protested against the railway. And there were landowners, dedicated to the idea of preserving the West Highlands for deer and sheep, who dipped into their pockets to finance the anti-railway factions.

Nevertheless, there was optimism in the Glasgow & North Western camp. Every day the newspapers reported the proceedings of the Crofters' Commission as it made its slow progress through the West Highlands. and it was plain from the reports that the crying need of the area was *transport*. Despite the opposition, there never had been a time more propitious for the promotion of a railway in the West Highlands.

At the outset the Glasgow & North Western Railway had taken pains to placate possible hostile landowners through whose estates the line was to pass. They were issued with prospectuses and maps to show how the promoters had gone out of their way to avoid what the reports called 'gentlemen's seats'. At Rowardenan the line was diverted from the side of Loch Lomond and screened by a curtain of rocks and trees from an important shooting lodge. In places where the line had no alternative but to cross estates, the owners were promised that it would be decently shrouded in trees and carried over estate roads on pretty ornamental bridges.

The Duke of Montrose was assured that although the line would pass half a mile to the west of the ducal seat, Buchanan Castle, it would not be visible from the castle grounds. But the duke insisted that it *would* be visible from the castle towers and he sent his map back to the G & NW with an acceptable diversion pencilled in—a diversion that entailed an impossible rise to a 1,200 ft summit and an equally impossible fall. Special care had to be taken to avoid Lord Lovat's house: not only was Lord Lovat a hostile landowner, but he was also a director of the Highland Railway.

In order to avoid giving possible offence to the residents of Fort Augustus, the railway was kept a third of a mile away from the town, and Fort William was similarly avoided. But so overjoyed were the people of Fort William at the prospect of getting a railway that they would hear nothing of the proposed detour round the town. The local council invited the G & NW to bring the line straight up the coast and take it across the end of the pier and along the side of Loch Linnhe between the town and the water. That decision was to cause bitter recrimination in the years to come! The disused military fort had been purchased about 1867 by Mr Campbell of Monzie, and his will stipulated that the fort had to be given for the site of a station in the event of a railway reaching Fort William. When the Glasgow & North Western made its survey, it found the old barrack blocks occupied as dwelling houses, but considered that the station could be established without unduly disturbing the occupants.

Not all Highland landowners were hostile to the railway. One George Grant McKay of Glengloy commented: 'At present there is great destitution in some parts of the West Highlands, but there is none near where there is a railway. Destitution flies away from within a considerable distance of a railway.' McKay was in a position to know. He had made a practice of buying estates where railways were due to pass, and selling them after the railway had been established. In this way he bought an estate at Lairg for £50,000 and sold it for £100,000 when the railway came—on his own admission. The fact that the Glasgow & North Western was to cross his land near Loch Lochy troubled him not at all.

### 'THE DEER WILL NOT LIKE IT'

The contestants paraded witnesses ranging literally from peers to ploughmen before the Parliamentary committee, and day after day the glib London lawyers put the Highlanders through their paces. Discussions on fish, sheep and tourists—in that order—occupied many sessions. The G & NW barrister, Mr Littler, made much of the point that while Scotland's 425-mile eastern seaboard from Berwick to Thurso had 44 points from which fish could be carried by rail, the west coast, with 1,200 miles of seaboard from the Mull of Kintyre to Cape Wrath, had only two points. The west coast fishing industry was being stifled for lack of communication with the markets of the south. Fish landed at the small villages in the north-west coast was being carted over the rough mountain roads and down the glens that entered the Great Glen from the north to be distributed in Fort Augustus and Fort William. Such fish, claimed George Grant McKay of Glengloy, could be sent on the railway to Glasgow and the south. Mr Pope, counsel opposing the G & NW on behalf of the Highland, was sceptical.

'What! Would you cart herrings for 30 miles along a mountain road?' he asked McKay. 'Yes,' replied McKay. 'It is done every day. Hundreds of carts pass my door on their way to Fort Augustus.' 'They drive them 30 miles?' persisted the barrister. 'Yes. You seem to think it impossible.' 'Oh, no,' smirked Pope, 'I only laugh at the idea.' 'But you would not laugh if you knew more about it,' countered McKay.

Pope then changed his tactics in an effort to discredit the witness. 'You are going to be a railway director?' 'No, I am not,' said McKay. 'But you said so.' 'I never said anything of the kind.' 'You did not say you were going to be a director?' insisted Pope. 'No, I said if I were asked, but I have not been asked. I am only speaking the truth.' 'But I want to know how far it is based on intelligence. I see no disgrace in it,' continued the lawyer. 'You seem to think it is a

good joke,' complained McKay. 'You don't like to be joked at?'
'Not when I am speaking in earnest on important matters.' 'Surely
you cannot be in earnest about the herrings?' taunted Pope. 'Yes, I
am. There will be no difficulty whatever in getting down the glens.'

'What about Fort Augustus?' inquired Pope, changing his tactics
again. 'Is that a large place?' 'Yes.' 'Is there a monastery there?'
'Yes.' 'Is that the place where the gigantic Highlander used to be?'
'Yes. Gordon Cumming.' 'And it was he who used to charge half a
crown for seeing his museum as the boat passed?' 'Yes, but if you
think Fort Augustus is only a monastery and a museum you are
mistaken.'

'Well,' conceded Pope, 'I agree with you in your description of
the country—it is very pretty, but I don't think it is as pretty as
Perth.'

'Were you ever in it?' asked McKay with exasperation.

'Oh, yes, I have shot all over it,' replied Pope airily.

The evidence continued at this level for hours on end. The
opposition plan was to poke fun at the West Highlands and any
West Highlanders who were naive enough to support the railway.
Pope questioned McKay at length about some of the places the
railway was to pass through. Talking about Dores he asked, 'Is that
simply a public house?' 'It is a small village.' 'Take Tyndrum, which
is marked on the railway map in bigger letters than Edinburgh——'

The committee room dissolved in laughter. When the merriment
had subsided Pope went on: 'Is there only a public house there?'
'Yes,' admitted McKay. 'Then King's House, is that the place where
the man murdered his wife, and was not found for a week because
there was nobody about?' 'Yes. It is as wild a place as you could
imagine,' confessed McKay. 'And that is the *valuable land* which
Lord Breadalbane objects to the railway going through,' he added
as a parting shot.

Fishermen were called to testify that west coast fish were very
inferior to east coast fish. The implication was that money spent on
a railway built to transport west coast fish would be money wasted.
Mr Holmes, a fish dealer of Berwick on Tweed, was brought to
Westminster to extoll the virtues of east coast fish. But in cross-
examination Mr Littler drew from him the admission that much of
the fish landed from east coast boats had been caught in western
fishing grounds.

'What brought you here to give evidence against this Bill?' asked
the railway lawyer. 'I don't know,' admitted Holmes. 'I was asked
to give evidence.' 'You wanted a nice trip to London, perhaps?' 'It

has been a nice trip.' 'I hope you will go back none the worse for it,' commented Littler.

There was endless talk about sheep. The Clearances had converted the country north of the Caledonian Canal into a series of sheep farms, and every year there was a mass movement of sheep from Sutherland and Ross and Cromarty down to the southern markets. Until recent times the sheep had been driven down a well-defined system of drove roads all the way to Glasgow, Edinburgh, Falkirk, Stirling and other towns in the south. With the coming of the railways, collecting-points had been established at Dalwhinnie on the Highland line and Tyndrum on the Callander & Oban, from whence the journey south was made by train. The G & NW planned to establish sheep stations in the Great Glen and so greatly shorten the distance covered by the drovers. The North Western's prospectus gave the sheep population north of the Great Glen as 470,000, but the Highland, which gave the impression of having been round counting the beasts, said there were 214,759 sheep precisely. Whatever the figure, the transport of sheep was a vital factor in the economy of any railway, existing or projected, and the Highland and Callander & Oban were determined not to lose the traffic to a rival.

Throughout the hearing much solicitude was shown for the animals of the West Highlands. A landowner in the Glencoe area who could not get to London in person sent this message to a friend who was a witness:

> I am quite in favour of the Glasgow and North Western Railway. The station at King's House would save our sheep the long walk to Tyndrum and place our glen in direct land communication with Glasgow which would greatly increase the value of my property. I shall be glad if you would say anything on my behalf before the Committee.

The impact of the railway on the deer population of the area was discussed in detail. When the Glasgow & North Western told the Parliamentary committee of its plans to erect special deer fencing where the line passed through the deer forests, an opposition spokesman objected, 'The deer will not like it.' Lord Abinger, who was generally favourable towards the railway and whose territory straddled the proposed line in Lochaber, suggested that the line should be unfenced in the deer forests. But Walron Smith said that he could provide a fence that the deer would get over with ease. Lord Abinger confessed: 'I have had a rare rough time of it with Lady Abinger and some others about the railway.' For some reason the ladies of the West Highlands, like the deer, did not like the railway.

When the fish and the sheep had been disposed of, talk in the committee room turned to tourists. Ever since Queen Victoria had made her famous tour of the Highlands in 1848, tourism had brought welcome revenue to the area. The all-water 'Royal Route' took its patrons in stages from Glasgow to Inverness by way of the Firth of Clyde, the Crinan Canal, the Firth of Lorne, Loch Linnhe and the Caledonian Canal. For those who could spare the time and expense involved it was a magnificent trip, but the Royal Route had its limitations. The Highland Railway had opened Inverness to a new class of tourist, and the North Western proposed to do the same for the West Highlands. The Caledonian Canal Commissioners feared that once a railway was built alongside the canal the revenue they derived from Royal Route steamers would dwindle.

The lawyer appearing for the canal was at pains to point out that the railway would serve the communities on the south side of Loch Ness only and that should the steamers be driven out of business the people on the north side of Loch Ness would lose their transport. The railway countered this accusation by presenting its plan to connect the stations on Loch Ness side with the communities across the loch by means of ferries. The canal spokesman was of the opinion that 'it would be impossible to have a ferry across the loch to the railway stations because Loch Ness is very stormy. The steamers go up and down the loch easily, but going across they would meet a very stormy sea.'

As the spring days of 1883 passed, the long-drawn-out arguments for and against the railway unfolded. In the effort to defeat it, the Highland went to the trouble and expense of employing D. M. Crouch, C.E., of Crouch & Hogg, Glasgow, to re-survey the whole of the North Western's route and submit plans to it. The Highland then came to the committee with the accusation that the North Western had underestimated the difficulties and costs of construction. Crouch put the overall cost of the line at £2,118,000, which was £645,000 more than Walron Smith's estimate.

It had been the hope of the Glasgow & North Western promoters that in the course of the hearing they would be able to announce a North British—North Western agreement over the financing and working of the line; meetings with North British officers were taking place in the background. But then came a shock. The North British looked askance at the North Western's plan to urbanize and develop the territory within 30 miles of Glasgow—with the consequent threat to existing or planned North British residential branches—and withdrew support from the North Western. But the North British had no sooner withdrawn than the Glasgow & South Western Railway offered the G & NW running powers over the City of Glasgow Union Railway into St Enoch, the G & SW terminus in Glasgow, in return for certain running powers over the North Western. In its letter to the North Western, the South Western described St Enoch as 'the best possible home that could be provided'.

The two-month Parliamentary hearing ended on 31 May, and the committee room was cleared to allow the members to debate the case and reach a conclusion. Not ten minutes later someone came rushing to Littler, who was relaxing in a lounge in the House of Commons, with the news that the railway case was lost. Dumbfounded, the barrister hurried back to the committee room to find the members preparing to leave. They had taken only five minutes to decide that there wasn't enough traffic to warrant another railway in the Highlands. The Highland Railway's plea had been upheld.

Then followed a dramatic scene when Littler pleaded to be allowed to speak. The committee, impatient after listening for weeks on end to dissertations on herrings and sheep, urged the lawyer to say what he had to say and be gone. But Littler insisted that his argument was of the highest importance, and he asked time to prepare a speech for presentation the following day, a Saturday. Reluctantly, the committee agreed to meet then.

But Littler was only playing for time. On the Saturday morning he made a last desperate bid to retrieve something from the wreck. He pointed out that Fort William was eager for a railway, and that the G & NW would be willing to content itself with a line from Fort William down through Tyndrum to Ardlui and was prepared to abandon the rest of the scheme. 'That would give Fort William and the district their communication with the outer world,' explained Littler,

> and would form a connection with the Callander and Oban Railway to which in these circumstances it would form a feeder rather than a system which would detract from the traffic of that railway. We should, if the Committee were willing, be content to accept that part of the scheme, and I may say it is a part which in no way affects the Highland company, on whose opposition the scheme has failed.

The committee was unsympathetic. 'I think,' said the chairman, 'it would be very much more regular if such a line was applied for in another session of Parliament.'

'Very good, Sir, and I say no more,' replied Littler.

Thus ended the story of the Glasgow & North Western. It would have been a magnificent railway. Its winding course up Loch Lomond would have presented superb views, the descent of Glencoe would have been something without parallel on Britain's railways, and the high-speed sweep along the water-level causeway on Loch Ness side would have made a thrilling approach to Inverness. The station names would have looked exciting on a timetable: Rowardenan, Inversnaid, Inveroran, King's House, Pap of Glencoe, Glencoe Bridge, Onich, Falls of Foyers. What would have happened if the G & SW and not the North British had worked and perhaps eventually absorbed the North Western makes fascinating speculation. The Glasgow & South Western would have stretched all the way from Stranraer to Inverness skirting miles of glorious coastline both north and south of the Clyde. What would have been the name of that grand railway? Scottish Great Western?

Such dreams evaporated on that Saturday morning in June when the doors of the committee room finally closed and the contestants strolled out into the London streets. Victor and vanquished alike went back to Scotland a lot lighter in the pocket. But the London lawyers made a fat killing.

EARLY DAYS

(8) *Lord Abinger cutting the first sod*
(9) *The ceremonial arrival of the first train at Fort William*
(10) *Fort William station, interior*

WEST HIGHLAND STATIONS
(11)  *Whistlefield*
(12)  *Ardlui*

WEST HIGHLAND BRIDGES

(13)  *Glen Falloch viaduct with Ben More, 3,843 ft, in distance*
(14)  *Craigenarden viaduct, Loch Lomond*

IN GLEN FALLOCH

(15) *A Class 5 heads a Glasgow—Mallaig train at the entrance to Glen Falloch*

# CHAPTER 3

# *Plans Win Through*

In its issue of 19 January 1889 *The Railway Times* printed a trenchant editorial under the above heading:

> As a field for the extension of railway enterprise we fail to understand the special fascination which the Western Highland districts seem to possess for the promoter. That portion of Scotland is certainly not well supplied with railway communication, and the fact that there are people living 50 miles from a railway might well be regarded as evidence of necessity, but the check to development which has allowed this condition of things to prevail—the small prospect of securing sufficient traffic to pay—exists with as much force now as heretofore, and the introduction of renewed efforts in that direction might well give rise to a suspicion that other influences than the power of the country to furnish remunerative traffic have operated on the minds of those who have promoted the Bill.

In other words the North British was making another attempt to establish itself in the West Highlands. In spite of the fears and strictures of *The Railway Times* the latest West Highland scheme was the one that succeeded.

Four years separated the failure of the Glasgow & North Western Railway and the launching of the West Highland Railway, and in those four years the social and political climate had changed. The publicity given to the findings of the Crofters' Commission had smoothed the way for the promoters of the West Highland. The members of the Commission were unequivocal in their insistence that lack of transport was at the root of the West Highland troubles. Parliament, and even some of the hostile landowners, realized that something *must* be done.

The West Highland Railway was conceived in a mail coach rumbling along the rough road from Fort William to Kingussie one morning in the mid-80s. In those days the people of Lochaber had to travel 50 miles to Kingussie on the Highland Railway to reach a railhead. The mail coach left Fort William every weekday at 6 a.m. and did not reach Kingussie until 12.20 p.m. The fares were 13s 6d second class and 16s 6d first class, plus 1s driver's fee in each class. A Mr Boyd of Fort William was a passenger in the coach that morning. Boyd had been very disappointed over the recent failure of the G & NW and as the Kingussie coach made its slow way eastward he reflected on the handicaps of life in rail-less Lochaber.

'It was at Kingussie,' he afterwards said,

> that I first thought of doing all that lay in my power to get a railway to Fort William. I had been on a journey to Banffshire and was the only passenger by coach that morning. On going to the hotel at Kingussie I was surprised to find *The Scotsman* for that day already there. For a moment I thought of Fort William and Lochaber and said to myself, 'Well, it may be 5 o'clock, it may be 8 o'clock before the letters and papers reach Fort William, and if it is stormy they may not arrive until the following day.' In soliloquising thus I thought of the backwardness of Lochaber, how far behind Kingussie, Inverness and Oban it was, and I might tell you frankly that when I thought of these things I wept.

On his return to Lochaber, Boyd got in touch with George Malcolm, the factor of Invergloy, and propounded his scheme. This time there was to be no attempt to reach Inverness; the new railway was to link Lochaber with the south and give an outlet to the western sea. Malcolm shared Boyd's enthusiasm, and the two men obtained the moral and financial support of local landowners. According to Boyd the Caledonian was invited to build the railway, but would have nothing to do with it. The North British, when sounded, showed a lively interest. *The Scotsman* said of the venture:

> We have here an endeavour to mark an era in the development of the Highlands. Access to markets has heretofore been deemed the one thing needful to raise into activity our island populations who live near seas teeming with fish. The people of these districts—whether the lairds, the tenants or the crofters—are too poor to provide capital for such works, and the return in dividend is so doubtful (though perhaps not hopeless) that the subscription lists might be viewed askance on the Stock Exchanges.

The West Highland Railway, like its predecessor, was backed by the North British who proposed to operate it, but in many other ways it differed from the Glasgow & North Western. The West Highland was to leave the existing North British coastal line to Helensburgh at Craigendoran, and pass by the Gareloch and Loch Long and Loch Lomond to Ardlui—a route not hitherto considered by the railway promoters. At Ardlui the line was to join the proposed route of the G & NW, but the West Highland was to keep to the west side of Glen Falloch whereas the North Western had been planned to climb up the east wall of the glen.

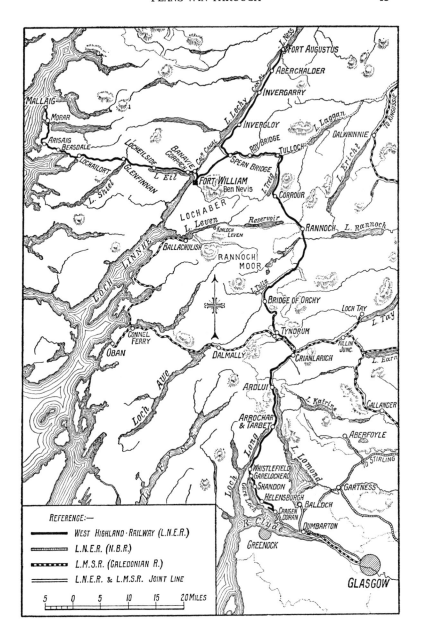

REFERENCE:—

West Highland Railway (L.N.E.R.)

L.N.E.R. (N.B.R.)

L.M.S.R. (Caledonian R.)

L.N.E.R. & L.M.S.R. Joint Line

5  0  5  10  15  20 MILES

From Crianlarich the West Highland was to follow the route of the North Western up Strathfillan to Bridge of Orchy, but instead of continuing westwards over the Black Mount and down Glencoe to the coast, the West Highland was to strike north through 30 miles of elevated, depopulated country which included the Moor of Rannoch, and drop down Loch Treigside into the heart of Lochaber. It was then to thread its way through the gorges of the Spean and enter Fort William from the east. The last stage of the route was round the end of Loch Eil and on to Roshven on the coast where a terminal and pier were to be built to service the island steamers and the fishing fleets. There was no mention of a foray in the direction of Inverness.

In the 100 miles of route between the Firth of Clyde and Fort William there were only five main proprietors—the Colquhoun Trustees, the Marquess of Breadalbane, Sir Robert Menzies, Sir John Stirling Maxwell and William Frederick Scarlett, Baron Abinger. All of them, if not actually connected with the railway, at least assented to its passage. Lord Abinger became the first chairman, and several clan chiefs joined him on the board, among them Cameron of Lochiel, Mackintosh of Mackintosh and Colquhoun of Luss.

It was a different story north and west of Fort William. Feudal landowners, still dedicated to the idea of keeping people out of their domains, opposed the scheme with such tenacity that the West Highland Railway was forced to abandon the extension to Roshven, and with it the hope of terminating at a vital fishing port. In fairness to the Highlanders, some Lowlanders were the bitterest opponents of the railway. Professor Blackburn, Emeritus Professor of Mathematics at the University of Glasgow, owned 60,000 acres at Roshven and the new harbour was to take shape under the windows of his mansion house. 'The whole thing is abominable,' he said. He was supported in his protest by his eminent colleague at Glasgow University, Sir William Thomson, Professor of Natural Philosophy, who told of the difficulty he had of getting into Roshven in his yacht. The committee considering the bill seemed to place more faith in Sir William's words than in the Admiralty sailing charts which described Roshven as the best harbour on the west coast of Scotland.

### LOST ON RANNOCH MOOR

On the evening of 29 January 1889 seven gentlemen gathered in the hotel at Spean Bridge. On the following day they were to set

---

(A) *BR Class 5 4-6-0 No 73077 and K2/2 2-6-0 No 61792 head a Fort William to Glasgow train around the horseshoe curve at Tyndrum in March 1956*

out on a walk that was to take them across the Moor of Rannoch to Inveroran nearly 40 miles to the south. It was a walk that was to become a West Highland legend.

The party consisted of three men from the Glasgow firm of civil engineers, Formans & McCall—Charles Forman himself, James Bulloch his chief engineer and a young assistant engineer, J. E. Harrison—with Robert (later Sir Robert) McAlpine, head of the contracting firm of Robert McAlpine & Sons, John Bett, the 60-year-old factor of the Breadalbane Estates, Major Martin of Kilmartin, factor of the Poltalloch Estates, and N. B. McKenzie, solicitor, of Fort William, the local agent for the West Highland Railway bill. Of the seven, only James Bulloch had been across Rannoch Moor before. The purpose of the expedition was to obtain additional information about the route across the Moor and in particular to meet Sir Robert Menzies of Rannoch Lodge to discuss some minor deviations where the line passed through his land. It was an intrepid, not to say foolhardy, journey for such an odd assortment of men in the depths of winter.

At daybreak on 30 January the party left Spean Bridge by coach. It was a grey, cold morning with lowering clouds and a threat of sleet. By mid-morning they reached Inverlair Lodge where—after having their last substantial meal for two days—they set off on foot on a track that led 2½ miles to the north end of Loch Treig. The shores of Loch Treig were trackless and Lord Abinger had arranged that a boatman would meet the party and row them 6 miles up the loch to its southern end where they would be given food and shelter for the night at his shooting lodge, Craig-uaine-ach. On the following day they were to cross the Moor of Rannoch.

The expedition must have presented an incongruous sight as its members walked in single file along the mountain-girt track in the gathering darkness of the January afternoon. Old John Bett wore his high-sided felt hat and carried his umbrella. McKenzie, tall, polished and dignified as became a gentleman of his profession, also carried his umbrella. Forman, who was not too robust—he was to die later of consumption—must have had qualms about the venture, but McAlpine, who was described as 'stout, full-blooded and loquacious', was in high spirits.

From the outset things went wrong. A guide whom Lord Abinger had sent to conduct the party along the track to Loch Treig failed to turn up. When the men reached the loch they were well behind schedule and there was no sign of either boat or boatman. Eventually they found a decrepit boathouse which they proceeded to

(B) *Former North British Railway Class C15 4-4-2T No 67474 leaves the siding at Arrochar & Tarbet to back into the platform with the stock for the local service to Craigendoran. Taken in May 1959, the service was withdrawn in 1964*

break down. The noise of their activities brought an irate Highlander on the scene, but when they explained who they were the Highlander revealed that he was the boatman and that the boat was hidden in bushes by the lochside. An ancient tarred craft was duly launched and all eight men squeezed into it and set sail up the now dark and stormy loch. Very soon night enveloped the party and squalls of sleet assaulted them. One can picture that strangest of railway ménages sailing up the loch in the darkness, the younger members helping with the rowing, others using their boots to bail out the water that constantly seeped into the vessel, and the solicitor and the aged land agent sheltering as best they could under their umbrellas.

The boat was kept close into the eastern shore. Once when they went to investigate a light they grounded on a patch of gravel. There was a great deal of shouting and arguing and the commotion aroused two lochside gamekeepers who came out in their own boat, rescued the railway party, and conducted them to Lord Abinger's shooting lodge, which they reached about midnight, hungry, wet and cold. Another disappointment awaited them. A messenger who had been dispatched by a mountain track to warn the lodge-keeper of the party's approach had not appeared, and neither food nor beds were ready. However, the keeper provided a meal of sorts and produced blankets under which the travellers huddled, listening to the beat of the rain and hail on the roof.

By the morning a strong wind was driving the rain and sleet across the loch. In these conditions the seven men set off to climb a track that was to ascend in 3 miles to a height of 1,300 ft and was to take them to the northern edge of the Moor of Rannoch. Ahead of them stretched 23 miles of utterly desolate, trackless, stormswept waste. The keeper took them to the end of the track and pointed out the direction they had to take. Then he went back, no doubt thankfully, to the shelter of the lodge.

For hour after hour the seven men squelched through the morass, jumping from tuft to tuft to escape the worst of the bog. Rain alternated with sleet squalls. It was slow, exhausting work. The incredible thing was that they were heading for a business meeting due to be held in the middle of the wilderness about noon. Sir Robert Menzies had arranged to come out from Rannoch Lodge, some 4 miles to the east of the line of the proposed railway, and meet them on the north bank of the River Gauer. Guided by James Bulloch, the party came within sight of the Gauer after four hours of trudging across the Moor, and the figure of a man could be seen

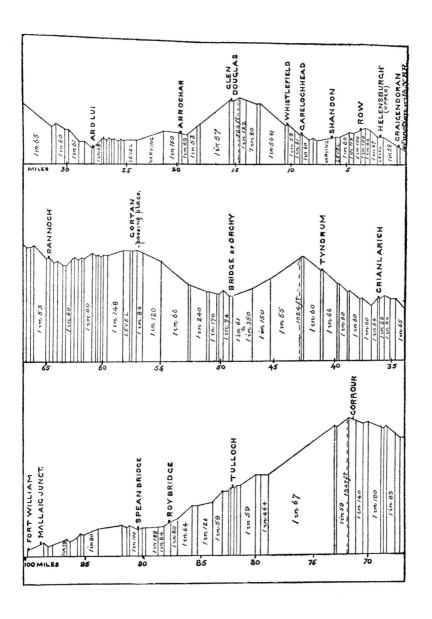

standing by the river. But when they reached the spot they found that he was Menzies' head keeper, who invited them to go with him to Rannoch Lodge for the night. About three hours of daylight remained; the nearest cottage was 8 miles away and their ultimate destination was still 14 miles distant. They decided to carry on.

It did not take them long to realize that they had made a mistake, but it was too late to turn back. They had passed the point of no return. As the going became rougher the men straggled across the Moor in ones and twos seeking the best footholds. When dusk fell in the early afternoon they could no longer distinguish the relatively dry spots and they plunged and floundered in the bog, sometimes falling full length. Bett and McKenzie became tired and dispirited, and the younger men helped them by carrying their kit. At length Bett collapsed, protesting that he could go no further. Major Martin and young Harrison stayed with him and did what they could to comfort him, improvising a tent using his umbrella. Forman and McKenzie stumbled on, but very soon they had to admit exhaustion and sought shelter behind a large boulder. McAlpine, although he did not know the Moor and had little sense of direction, decided to carry on alone in the hope of reaching Inveroran, where he could get help for the others. Bulloch set off independently, trusting that his limited knowledge of the Moor would enable him to locate the cottage at Gorton where he had called when making a survey of the line.

Bulloch had been wandering through the darkness for several hours when he tripped over a fence and fell so heavily that he lay stunned on the ground for four hours. When he regained consciousness he realized that fences were scarce on Rannoch Moor and that this one must lead somewhere. He groped his way along it until he found himself on a track. He followed the track, and out of the darkness loomed the Gorton cottage.

Meanwhile, far out on the Moor, Bett had lapsed into unconsciousness. Martin and the young engineer tried to keep warm by running round in circles, and once during the process they lost Bett. When they found him again they tied a handkerchief to his protecting umbrella so that it would be easily recognizable in the dark.

From time to time Martin and Harrison lit matches to see the time on their watches. Then, about 2.30 in the morning, they saw lights bobbing on the Moor and heard the distant bark of dogs. Matches were lit, this time as flares. Eventually two men appeared and explained that they were shepherds from Gorton cottage. They had been roused by Bulloch and told of the plight of the party.

CRIANLARICH IN THE THIRTIES

(16) *A Glen taking water on a wintry March day in 1930*

(17) *Morning break in the mid-thirties. The train is composed entirely of North British stock*

(18) *Crianlarich station in 1937. The station buildings were burned down on 30 March 1962*

(19) *Trains crossing in* LNE *days. Note the railway carriage school*
(20) *January* 1963

Shouts in the distance revealed the whereabouts of Forman and McKenzie, and soon the shepherds had gathered the remaining five members of the party together and guided them towards safety. John Bett, still semi-conscious, had to be half carried, half dragged. The rescuers knew of a small hut 2 miles away, and not without difficulty they found it. Inside was a rusty stove, with a heap of wet peats. Some dry peats were extracted from the centre of the heap and the shepherds soon had a fire roaring with such purpose that the entire stove and chimney glowed red-hot. Steam from the clinging wet clothes of the refugees mingling with the acrid fumes of peat reek filled the hut.

Once they had made their guests comfortable the shepherds returned to their cottage where they had left the sleeping Bulloch. By daybreak they were back at the hut with supplies of hot food and drink. By 10.30 the railway party had revived sufficiently to make the journey to Gorton, which they reached about mid-day. They were glad to find Bulloch safe and well, but they were anxious about McAlpine about whom nothing had been heard. Almost at once news was received that he was safe in a cottage three miles down the valley of the Tulla Water. He had reached the place early in the morning, hatless, soaking wet and covered in mud after having spent 14 hours alone on the Moor.

John Bett was put on a cart and the party set off to cover the remaining 8 or 9 miles to Inveroran. They picked up McAlpine on the way, and that evening all were made welcome by the host of Inveroran Inn. As they slept, a blizzard broke over the West Highlands and next morning as they made their way down to Tyndrum station on the Callander & Oban Railway they had to climb over deep snowdrifts. If the blizzard had come 24 hours earlier the outcome of the expedition might have been tragically different.

### OPPOSITION

The usual opposition to the West Highland bill came from the now traditional quarters. The Highland Railway fearing (rightly) that the West Highland would at some future date be used as a jumping-off point for a renewed assault on Inverness fought determinedly. But its case had no substance. As described in the bill, the West Highland's nearest approach to the Highland was at Inverlair and that was 32 miles away from Highland metals. There was no mention (on paper) of any intention of taking the line on to Inverness.

**D**

The Caledonian Railway for its part considered that it had a potentially better route from Glasgow to Fort William and, moreover, it was already two-thirds built. The Callander & Oban reached the west coast at Connel Ferry. The Caledonian proposed to build a line up the coast through Ballachulish to Fort William, entering the town from the south as the G & NW would have done. The Caledonian's case was that it could complete the Glasgow—Fort William link at a third of the cost and in a third of the time needed for the West Highland. It undertook, too, to build the line the moment the West Highland bill was thrown out of Parliament. It further argued, with justification, that the Appin coast was well populated (by West Highland standards) whereas the Moor of Rannoch was desolate and barren. The Caledonian made much of the wisdom (or lack of it) of attempting to cross Rannoch Moor by rail. The story of the lost survey party got around, the counsel for the Caledonian questioning Forman pointedly about it. Forman, telling a diplomatic lie, denied that the episode had taken place. But his young assistant, Harrison, afterwards wrote that the story was 'guaranteed and free from varnish'.

There was no doubt that the West Highland offered the most direct route to Lochaber. Moreover, it was the one that the people of Lochaber wanted. In April 1889 the preamble to the bill was proved. G. B. Weiland, the secretary of the North British, was also secretary of the West Highland, but the North British took immediate steps to strengthen its position by replacing Lord Abinger as West Highland chairman with its own chairman, the Marquess of Tweeddale. It also undertook to contribute £150,000 towards the cost of construction of the line and to guarantee $3\frac{1}{2}$ per cent to the holders of the £800,000 of West Highland stock. It further agreed to staff and work the line when it was ready. 'This is really a North British scheme propounded as an attack on Caledonian territory,' said *The Railway Times* when these terms were announced. The journal was full of foreboding for the future of the enterprise, and described it as

> owing more to misdirected ambition than to its own merits. We do not say, if the shareholders of the North British through their directors express their willingness to throw away their money into a scheme from which they are likely to derive little if any benefit, that they should be prevented from so doing; but we doubt much whether they have not like many others before them, been deceived by overcoloured pictures.

## JUBILATION

A very different atmosphere prevailed in Fort William. When news of the passing of the preamble reached the town the population was jubilant. There were processions and music in the streets, and after nightfall bonfires were lit on the heights commanding the town. Each successive phase of the bill's passage through Parliament was greeted with enthusiasm.

When the bill passed its third reading in the Commons on 3 July 1889 the news reached the town shortly after 5 o'clock, and the town crier was sent round the streets to announce the glad tidings. Fort William decided on a night of rejoicing. The centrepiece of the festivities was to be a torchlight procession through the town, but in those northern latitudes there was still a trace of daylight left at 11 p.m. It was, therefore, decided to delay the start of the procession until 10.30. Meanwhile, hotels and villas were decorated and lit up, and the townsfolk gathered together all the fireworks they could find. By 10 o'clock the crowds were gathering at the prescribed collecting point. What happened after that was described in the local paper.

> Punctually at 10.30 p.m. a torchlight procession started from Captain Peter Cameron's monument in Fassifern Road and marching to the strains of the bagpipes by Bank Street it proceeded along the High Street to the West End of the town. Everywhere along the route the people lined the streets and the windows and vigorously cheered the processionists whose numbers rapidly increased as they moved along. The effect was extremely picturesque. The night was calm, the light was "tween the gloamin' and the mirk' and Loch Linnhe lay placid as an inland lake. Coloured Roman lights shot up at intervals from among the torches and rockets flashed brilliantly across the sky. The distant report of the ships' guns on the Corpach side of the loch heightened the effect of a display which was really very fine.

The people gathered on the foreshore near the pier. There were speeches galore. 'This is a profound night for Lochaber and Fort William,' declared one speaker, and he was roundly cheered. More rockets were fired off and the merry evening ended with a 'liberal distribution of refreshments'. The railway was coming to Lochaber.

The Caledonian intruded with a parting shot. Its protégé the Callander & Oban promoted a branch line down Glen Falloch from Crianlarich to Ardlui 'to obviate the present coach journey'. The C & O line was to take the eastern side of the glen on what was substantially the route of the G & NW, and the cost was estimated at £50,000.

There was more to this move than met the eye. The hitherto privately-owned Loch Lomond steamers had just passed into North British control. The North British not only had the steamers, but had rail access to the south end of Loch Lomond at Balloch, and the new West Highland Railway would give it access to the northern reaches of the loch. The Caledonian saw itself being excluded from one of Scotland's most lucrative tourist assets by its keenest rival. Already the Caledonian was bidding for a stake in the Loch Lomond traffic by seeking rail access and a pier of its own at the south end of the loch, and the Crianlarich—Ardlui branch was intended to give it a railway-served pier at the north end. The preamble to the bill was not proved, and the absurdity of having two railways serving the same depopulated valley was avoided.

# CHAPTER 4

# Construction of the Line

### THE CONTRACTORS

The engineers of the West Highland were Formans & McCall of Glasgow, a firm founded in 1828 which had been responsible for some of the earliest Scottish railways. The title was adopted when Charles Forman, son of the Scots-Canadian founder, became a partner. The contractors were Lucas & Aird, a famous Westminster firm with strong Scottish connections. The dominant figure was John Aird, a Member of Parliament, whose crofter father had emigrated from the Highlands to London early in the 19th century to found and develop a contracting business with international ramifications. John Aird and Charles Forman were the key figures in the construction of the West Highland Railway.

Charles de Neuville Forman deserves to be better remembered as a railway engineer. He was born on 10 August 1852 and died on 2 February 1901. During his 48 years he signed his name to the plans of many important railways and he put more railway mileage on the map of Western Scotland than any other railway engineer. Among his projects were the intricate Glasgow Central Railway built under the streets of the city, the Lanarkshire & Ayrshire Railway, the line from Glasgow to Clydebank *via* Yoker, and the Strathendrick & Aberfoyle Railway. He took time off from the West of Scotland to engineer the Foxdale Railway in the Isle of Man, and in a moment of aberration he built a *coach road*: it was the exciting one from Aberfoyle over the hills to the Trossachs. Among projects of his that did not come off were the Glasgow, Berwick & Newcastle direct railway and the Fort Augustus to Inverness railway.

On 23 October 1889 a party of railway and contractors' men went to a spot outside Fort William opposite the Glen Nevis distillery. There, in the presence of at least half the populace (all the shops had been closed at noon), John Aird handed Lord Abinger the silver spade with which he dug the first sod. That was the end of ceremonial for the time being; the gruelling task of building the West Highland began, and it was to continue for five years.

Lucas & Aird's men must have felt at home with the West Highland contract. The firm had specialized in colonial railways, and the West Highland had many of the characteristics of a colonial-type railway. In view of the sparse traffic likely to be offered the directors wanted it built as cheaply as possible; it was intended to carry light loads at moderate speeds. The territory which the contractors set out to master was as tough as any they had encountered overseas. There were passes over 1,000 ft above sea level through which the railway had to be led. There were innumerable gorges to be spanned, rivers to be bridged and miles of boggy moor to be crossed.

The inaccessibility of the country was its most daunting feature. First of all the great army of navvies required for large-scale civil engineering enterprises in the days before universal power tools and earth moving machinery had to be assembled and camps established for them and their equipment in remote places. It was perhaps unfortunate that the contract started at the onset of winter, when nights were long and the weather restricted use of the limited daylight.

For administrative purposes the work was divided into Railway No. 1 from Craigendoran to Crianlarich and Railway No. 2 from Crianlarich to Fort William. Construction began at five points. The southernmost camp was at Craigendoran with easy access both by rail and sea. Arrochar at the head of Loch Long was the site of the second camp, and the third was at Inveruglas on Loch Lomondside, 3 miles south of Ardlui. A pier was built at the lochside to which heavy materials were brought in boats and barges. A smaller pier at Ardlui was used to accommodate light materials and personnel. Crianlarich was the location of the next camp, served by the Callander & Oban line. The fifth camp was on the shore of Loch Linnhe at Fort William. Work over the entire route was in charge of G. M. Tarry of Lucas & Aird. Railway No. 1 was divided into three sub-sections, each with its own resident engineer, inspectors and labour force. The sections were: 1, Craigendoran to milepost 12; 2, milepost 12 to milepost 24; 3, milepost 24 to Crianlarich.

Railway No. 2 was divided into two, Crianlarich to Gorton and Gorton to Fort William. On Railway No. 1 no point was more than 8 miles from a base camp, but on Railway No. 2 at first there was no permanent camp between Crianlarich and Fort William. At an early stage a large base camp was established at Inveroran, the northernmost point reached by the coach road. (This was also known as Achallader Camp.) All the camps were linked to head-quarters at Helensburgh by private telephone so that a close check could be kept on progress.

Among the materials ordered for delivery by sea at Helensburgh and Fort William and by rail to Tyndrum were

| | | | |
|---|---|---|---|
| 12,000 | tons of 75 pound steel rails at | £6.5.0 | per ton |
| 5,500 | tons of chairs | £4 | per ton |
| 450 | tons of spikes | £8 | per ton |
| 450 | tons of fish plates | £7.17.6 | per ton |
| 110 | tons of fish bolts and nuts | £11 | per ton |
| 30,000 | Scots fir sleepers at 2s 5d each | | |
| 51,000 | Scots fir sleepers at 2s 6d each | | |

### THE NAVVIES

The itinerant Irish navvies who flocked to the building of the West Highland were a rough, motley crew. They did not take well to the lonely, isolated camps, and many of them left after a few weeks for the lusher pastures of Lancashire where the Manchester Ship Canal was being cut. With the onset of winter Lucas & Aird's labour troubles increased.

The navvies' pay varied according to the type of work they did and where they did it. South of Ardlui the average weekly wage was 15s, north of Ardlui it was 21s. Part of it was paid in basic foodstuffs, which the navvies cooked for themselves. This appar-ently was an attempt to prevent them from spending all their money on liquid sustenance. First aid posts staffed by permanent nurses were set up at all the camps, and the men contributed a small amount each week to an insurance fund which entitled them to disablement benefit if they were injured on the site.

Remembering that the West Highland railway was intended to bring prosperity to the Highlanders, local clan chiefs and public men pressed the contractor to employ Highland labour. But there were few able-bodied men available along the route, and men in the more remote parts and in the Western Isles were too poor to pay their fares to the sites. Again, the Highlanders were not accus-tomed to working in large organized groups. Nevertheless, Lucas & Aird advertised for Highland labour, and the following is a typical announcement.

In order to afford work for Highlanders, and acting on the suggestion of Maclaine of Lochbuie, Messrs Lucas & Aird, Contractors for the

West Highland Railway, desire again to state that they are prepared
to employ at piecework or day's wages a large number of competent
rock men or labourers. Comfortable hutting is provided, but Messrs
Lucas & Aird will gladly give every facility for those who prefer it to
erect Turf Dwellings. Every information can be obtained by application
to the Head Office at Helensburgh or the following Agents . . .

In order to attract more Highlanders, Lucas & Aird then offered
to pay the fares of applicants who were destitute, and in a short
time succeeded in building up a considerable force. A report on
recruitment sent by the contractors to Maclaine of Lochbuie on
30 June 1890 throws light on the quality and behaviour of the
Highland railway navvy.

*Helensburgh and Arrochar Section*
Passages paid 34, no passages paid 46; total 80.
Appear contented to stay, work steadily and compare very favourably with other labourers. A large proportion are good rock
quarriers, and none as yet has given any trouble.

*Inverarnan Section*
Passages paid 33, no passages paid 28; total 61.
Sixty-seven arrived all together, but 6 have left during the month.
Furnish good and steady labour, useful with the shovel, but only a
few on this section are good rockmen. As a class they are very
steady.

*Tyndrum Section*
Passages paid 42, no passages paid 43; total 85.
There are some youths and elderly men, but the great proportion
are strong, hard-working men who quite hold their own with the
labourers from the South. They are very steady, and can be depended on for being at their work all through the week if the
weather is favourable.

*Fort William Section*
Passages paid 69, no passages paid 5; total 74.
Good labourers, many of them excellent rockmen. They are frugal,
living mostly on oatmeal, and saving all the money they can.
Total of men employed on above, 300.
   That the qualities of the Highland navvies were appreciated
beyond their homeland was shown when railway enterprises in
other parts of the country began to compete with Lucas & Aird for

their services. A rival advertisement in *The Oban Times* ran :

> Forfar and Brechin Railway. Wanted. Good Navvies. Comfortable quarters. Subs daily.

'Subs daily' meant that the navvies could draw their weekly wage in daily instalments.

To their credit the civil population of the West Highlands took the welfare of the temporary navvy invasion very much to heart. Churches, clubs, councils and groups of many kinds co-operated to make life easier for the railway builders. The Rev Mr Elder, minister of Tarbet, built a reading room and canteen on the church glebe and undertook to provide coffee at any hour of the day. In Fort William the Rev Canon MacColl established a reading and recreation room and headed the committee of townsfolk delegated to run it. One of the rules barred the entry of 'intoxicated or swearing men'. Even amid the lonely wastes of Achallader Camp, a group of public-spirited enthusiasts presided over by the Marquess of Breadalbane formed the Blackmount Literary Association, which had as its object 'the intellectual improvement of the members and to excite a spirit of inquiry combined with healthy amusement among men employed upon the West Highland Railway during the winter season'. A concert given by the Blackmount Literary Association was thus described in *The Oban Times*:

> The first part of the programme consisted of choice selections on the bagpipes by Mr. D. MacLachlan, Argyll and Sutherland Highlanders, whose steady playing evinced his proficiency, while Mr. Cropper, Inverarnan, led the second part with pianoforte selections of no mean order, and played the accompaniment to the vocalists, after which a service of fruit took place.

Not quite traditional navvy fare!

The Highland Temperance League's agent went round the camps on pay days and hard on his heels was the representative of the Post Office Savings Bank. The Home Mission of the Free Church of Scotland sent missionaries. One of these reported:

> In prosecuting the more direct mission work among them (the navvies) it is found necessary to visit the men in their respective huts on the Sabbath, and to conduct services in such—an undertaking which, while it involves considerable effort on the part of the visitor, is found to be productive of encouraging results. While the men do not care to come out to services in a church, or even in a hall, they are usually ready to respond to the invitation to join in one conducted in their own temporary dwelling. But for such attentions on the part of those who seek them out the men would be almost destitute of the means of grace.

PROGRESS

As the railway progressed the labour force rose to 5,000. Month after month the navvies pushed the lengthening permanent way round the mountainsides and through the glens. 'The unhallowed hoof of the iron horse is beginning to show traces on the hillside', reported a summer visitor to Loch Lomond in 1890. The quiet passes echoed to the bark of explosives. For the most part the rock through which the contractors had to hack their way was old, twisted mica-schist interspersed with veins of quartz. It was impervious to drills and dynamite had to be used to remove it. Steam shovels were used in making some of the earth cuttings, but there was frequent trouble due to the scoops encountering large boulders among the soil.

Wherever possible, and remembering the need for economy, the line was taken in wide sweeps round projecting spurs. In this way tunnels and some of the heaviest excavations were avoided. In 100 miles of mountainous country the engineers found it necessary to build only one tunnel—that on Loch Lomondside 47 yd long.

The broad policy was to balance embankments against cuttings and to use excavated stone to build the piers of bridges. The West Highland was thus saved the cost of purchasing and transporting the materials. The first two miles from Craigendoran to Helensburgh Upper involved a 1 in 58 climb, partly on a mile-long embankment 30 ft high and partly in a deep cutting. Some 140,000 cubic yards of material were required to form the embankment and of this 74,000 cubic yards of earth and 32,000 cubic yards of red sandstone came out of the corresponding cutting. Three parallel lines of light railway, with two engines working on each, were used to convey the filling material from the cuttings to the embankment. The operation was in charge of a Mr Bloomfield Smith.

A few miles further on the promoters, if they hadn't had to count every penny, would have taken the railway across Whistler's Glen on a viaduct. Instead the contractors put down two long culverts and used the many thousands of cubic yards of material taken out of the Gareloch hills to fill the depression. Rail level was 57 ft above the culverts, one of which was lined with bricks from an old wall demolished near the site. Nature co-operated, and the stone taken from the cutting at Rhu could be carried a few miles along the line and used to build the piers of the Garelochhead viaduct. Masons dressed the newly-cut stones on the spot. When the contractors

(C) *Class K2/2 2-6-0 No 61764* Loch Arkaig *at Fort William shed in March 1959 with BR Class 5 4-6-0 No 73077 in the background*

found their way into Crianlarich from the south barred by a great mound of mountain clay, they cut their way through it and used the spoil to make an embankment across Strathfillan at the north end of Crianlarich station. Stone for the piers of the viaducts at this point—one across the Callander & Oban Railway, the other across the Fillan—was brought down the Callander & Oban from the Ben Cruachan quarries.

Above Loch Long where a shelf had to be gouged out of the mountainside to carry the rails the incline was too steep to support the contractors' equipment. Temporary piers were built at the loch-side, and plant and material brought in by sea were passed up to the railway builders on inclined roads worked by steam winches and wire ropes. The inclines varied from 1 in 3 to 1 in 15.

The movement of material for bridges and the erection of the bridges on difficult sites called for much ingenuity. The bridge contract was let to Alexander Findlay & Company of Motherwell. In all, 4,000 tons of steel had to be moved into the West Highlands to go into 19 viaducts with three spans or more, 102 bridges of one and two spans, and numerous cattle creeps. The contractors employed different techniques to suit varying conditions. Three miles north of Ardlui the deep gorge of the Dubh Eas called for a viaduct of seven spans, the centre span being 118 ft long. The piers were founded on rock and built up in concrete layers 9 in. thick. Access to the tops of the piers was obtained by building a light service bridge over the gorge and suspending it by means of union screws and sheer legs on either slope of the gorge. The metal work for the Dubh Eas viaduct was landed at the Loch Lomond pier and conveyed 6 miles to the site, where the sections were riveted together and launched out over the piers. Findlay & Company charged £16 per ton for the bridge work. This included cost of shipment to a base camp and erection on the site, but it did not include transport from the base camp to the site. That item normally accounted for another £2 per ton.

A different technique was used in the construction of the viaducts on the Horse Shoe Curve. Economy dictated the building of the Horse Shoe in the first place. Three mountains stood almost shoulder to shoulder immediately east of the railway, Ben Odhar, Ben a Chaistel and Ben Doran, with Ben a Chaistel recessed about a mile to the east of its two neighbours. The mountains were separated by two glens running in from the east. If cost had not been a prime consideration, the railway would have been taken direct from the slopes of Ben Odhar across the valley to Ben Doran on a long (and

(D) *Period piece at Fort William: Class K2/2 No 61787* Loch Quoich *at the old station with a MacBrayne AEC lorry and Morris 8 GPO van. The MacBrayne Pier is to the left. The old Station has been demolished and resited nearer Mallaig Junction*

expensive) viaduct. But the slimness of the West Highland's purse resulted in the line being carried in a U formation round the flank of Ben Odhar, across the face of Ben a Chaistel and back along the side of Ben Doran. The railway clung to the mountainsides all the way round the U except where it crossed the two intervening glens and at those points curved viaducts were necessary, one of five spans and the other of nine spans.

The girders for the five-span viaduct were built on the site and temporary rails were fitted to the bottom booms. Corresponding wheels were fixed in small frames securely anchored in the ground, and the girders were lowered so that the rails under the booms fitted on to the wheels. The five spans were linked together and tackle was used to pull what was virtually a train of girders out on to the tops of the piers. Once the spans had been built and placed on the wheels the launching of the bridge was completed in a matter of hours.

The engineers found that a viaduct was required at Craigenarden, one of the prettiest spots on Loch Lomonside, and fearing that a lattice girder erection would be a blemish on the landscape they designed the only arched viaduct on the line. Craigenarden Viaduct, 6 chains long and with eight arches of 36 ft span, was built of whinstone. To enhance the scenic effect the parapets were castellated and balusters were run up the piers.

## CRISIS

Progress at the northern end was slower than in the south because the Fort William section could be served from only one point. The West Highland bought a strip of the foreshore at Fort William for £25 an acre, and began clearing the site for a station and approach lines. A minute recorded on 5 March 1890 said:

> It has now become necessary to displace certain persons of the labouring classes from their present houses in Fort William and the Engineers were instructed to prepare drawings for the necessary new houses in compliance with the provisions of the Act on the most economical plan possible.

By the end of June 1891 the railway had reached the northern end of Loch Treig, and to celebrate the event the board invited merchants, landowners and other supporters in Lochaber to a complimentary dinner at the new hotel at Invergloy. The guests were taken from Fort William to Inverlair by train and then by four-in-hand to Invergloy. Representatives of railway, contractor and engineer combined to make the day memorable for the visitors, yet that must have been a day of tension for the hosts. Just beneath the surface a serious crisis was bubbling.

Less than three weeks after the dinner the crisis broke. At every camp from Helensburgh to Fort William Lucas & Aird began to pay off men. At the beginning of the month the labour force had been close on 5,000; by the end of the month there were only 1,200 employed on the line, and they had been retained to maintain plant. All construction work ceased. Wild rumours swept the West Highlands. The railway had been abandoned! Construction had proved too difficult! The West Highland had run out of money! *The Oban Times* commented:

> It is, of course, known that only reasons of the gravest possible urgency would induce a firm of such high standing and exhaustless resources as Messrs Lucas & Aird to take the extreme step of recalling their employees while their contract is as yet only about half finished.

The stoppage was the culmination of a dispute that had arisen between the West Highland board and Lucas & Aird in 1890. By the terms of their contract Lucas & Aird had agreed to construct the railway for the lump sum of £393,638 4s 2d payable in monthly instalments. The practice was for Formans & McCall's inspectors to survey the work in hand month by month and submit a certificate of work done to the West Highland board. The amount on the monthly cheque handed to Lucas & Aird was based on the engineer's certificate. The dispute arose because excavated material was classified as rock or soil, and the contractor found that he was dealing with material that was neither rock nor soil, but soil mixed with boulders. The removal of this took more time than the removal of soil, but since it was classified as soil the certificates recorded less work done. The contractor put his case to the West Highland board and asked for a review of prices. But in January 1891 he was informed that the West Highland directors were not prepared to depart from the terms of the original contract. Lucas & Aird made several attempts to get better terms and it was when these attempts failed that they withdrew their labour.

The West Highland was brought face to face with an ugly situation that could have been avoided by the exercise of a little tact. Its first move was to rush to court for an interdict against Lucas & Aird to prevent them removing their plant from the railway. The magistrate granted an interim interdict pending a full hearing of an action which the railway now brought against the contractor.

The case was heard in August 1891 at Dumbarton Sheriff Court. The West Highland case was that the contractors had agreed to build the railway for a fixed sum after they had examined the proposed route and assessed its difficulties. If they could work within this amount they were entitled to all the profit they could make, but if they discovered snags during the construction they had no right to demand more money. Lucas & Aird's case was that

> the line as actually laid down and constructed has been so materially altered by the pursuer's engineer from that shown in the original plan that it is substantially an entirely different railway from that which the defenders contracted to make.

The Sheriff of Dumbarton decided for the railway. An independent engineer was appointed to assess the work done by Lucas & Aird up to the time of their withdrawal, and the West Highland opened negotiations with another contractor for the completion of the line. Meanwhile the fine summer months passed without a foot of permanent way being laid. Worse still, the labour force was dissipated. Particularly unfortunate was the fact that the Highland navvies returned to their distant homes and many of them did not come back to the railway.

Before long common sense prevailed. Lucas & Aird, Charles Forman and the West Highland chairman did some hard bargaining round the boardroom table, as a result of which the original contractor agreed to carry on. Work was resumed throughout on 14 October 1891, on the understanding that the contractors would be paid £10,000 in addition to their agreed fee on the completion of the line. A formal agreement to this effect was signed on Christmas Eve 1891. The set-back had proved costly for the West Highland. The navvies were reluctant to return to the moors and mountains in the middle of winter and it was the spring of 1892 before full-scale working was resumed.

### TROUBLE ON RANNOCH MOOR

The great new railway took shape. The lengths of line built out from the base camps merged—with one exception. By the end of the third year a continuous line (except for some of the heavier bridges) ran all the way from Craigendoran to a bleak spot on the fringe of the Moor of Rannoch, some 60 miles from the Clyde. The northern section built out from Fort William had been pushed through the Spean gorges and up Loch Treigside to end in the wilderness at the northern edge of the Moor.

In June 1892 Charles Forman and John Aird conducted a party of West Highland directors and their friends by special train from Fort William to the end of the line. But in the middle between the two broken-off ends of the line was a gap of nearly 20 miles in which little work had been done, and filling the gap was a sombre morass of peat moss and heather. Telford in his day had surveyed a road across the Moor of Rannoch by the almost identical route taken by the railway, but he had abandoned the project. How the railway engineers conquered the Moor is one of the highlights in the West Highland story.

John Aird employed the technique that Stephenson had used on Chat Moss 60 years before. He decided to float the railway across the worst of the bog. First of all the contractors dug longitudinal ditches on either side of the railway 40 ft from the centre line of the track; then at intervals of 30 ft they cut cross-drains. Tons of turf and brushwood were brought to the edges of the Moor and taken out to the workings on the contractors' light railway.

First a layer of turf, then a layer of brushwood, was laid along the line of the railway, followed by further layers. Often the filling sank out of sight at once, and many applications were required before something resembling a permanent way appeared above the level of the bog. All the soil and mountain till that could be obtained from cuttings along the route were tipped on to the path across the Moor, and when no more material was left thousands of tons of ash were brought up from the industrial south to help consolidate the roadbed. The work trains which brought the spoil from all parts of the system were taken out over the Moor on a temporary standard-gauge light railway.

North of Rannoch station a depression nearly 1,000 ft across gave the railway builders a lot of trouble. The bog was 20 ft deep and it was not practicable to find the great volume of material that would be required to fill it and raise an embankment to a height of some 50 ft above it. A viaduct was the only answer, and the engineers decided on a nine-span steel structure, each span being $70\frac{1}{2}$ ft long. The area of the pier foundations was timbered and the soft moss was scooped out down to the firm boulder clay. Granite for the piers was obtained from the convenient Cruach Rock cutting, less than a mile to the north of the site. Rannoch Viaduct, 684 ft, was to be the longest on the line.

The Moor swallowed everything that was offered. Progress was slow at the best of times, and in the depths of winter when work was impossible not a foot was gained for days on end. And the

Moor was swallowing money as well as material. By the summer of 1893 the promoters in their office at 4 Princes Street, Edinburgh, realized that the authorized capital would not cover the construction of the line. The financial crisis that ensued had become acute when Mr Renton, one of the directors of the West Highland, gave part of his private fortune to save the situation. With the help of a fine summer, saved it was. The brushwood no longer sank. A dry, springy carpet stretched across the Moor and on this elongated raft the rails were laid. The last length of rail was dropped into position on 5 September 1893 and Mr Renton was given the privilege of driving the last spike. The railway navvies manhandled a huge boulder to the north end of Rannoch station and out of it sculptured an excellent head of Renton, using only the tools of their trade.

At the half-yearly meeting of the West Highland Railway, held on 28 September, the shareholders were told that 95 per cent of the earthworks and 88 per cent of the mason work was complete. All but 2½ miles of permanent way had been laid, 95 per cent of the track had been fenced and 90 miles of telegraph poles had been erected. 'Given a favourable winter,' said the Marquess of Tweeddale, 'we hope to open in the spring.'

But the winter was far from favourable, and the spring of 1894 found the contractors still wrestling with problems. The railway was like a large liner that had been launched and towed to the fitting-out basin; a lot of fitting-out remained to be done. Station buildings had to be finished, signalling installed, fencing completed and minor bridges built before the inspecting officer from the Board of Trade could be invited to give his accolade.

There were fifteen stations: Craigendoran, Helensburgh Upper, Row (later Rhu), Shandon, Garelochhead, Arrochar and Tarbet, Ardlui, Crianlarich, Tyndrum, Bridge of Orchy, Rannoch, Tulloch (Inverlair), Roy Bridge, Spean Bridge, and Fort William. There were passing places at Glen Douglas, Gorton and Corrour. (The decision to establish a station at Whistlefield had not yet been made.) The longest distance between stations was 18 miles between Rannoch and Tulloch, but this was divided into two sections by Corrour passing place. All the stations except Row, Tulloch, Roy Bridge and Spean Bridge, which had side platforms, had island platforms. The station buildings were finished after the style of Swiss chalets, overhanging roofs and exterior walls faced with wooden shingles brought from Switzerland adding to the atmosphere. Originally the stations were painted in two shades of green and the platforms were covered with red blaize—an attractive combination.

RANNOCH

(21)  *Rannoch station, looking north*
(22)  *Cruach Rock snowshed*

FROM THE FOOTPLATE

(23) *A J36 on Rannoch Moor*

(24) *A J37 heading south towards Gorton*

(25) *A West Highland driver in* LNE *days*

(26) *A typical West Highland footplate scene. Tablet on the handbrake handle, milk for delivery at lineside cottages*

Single-line tablet was installed throughout by Saxby & Farmer. The tablet instruments usually were situated in the stationmaster's office, the signalboxes at the ends of the platforms containing only the lever frames. A technical journal had this odd comment to make about the West Highland inter-station telephones.

> One of the peculiarities of the instrument is that the tone of voice undergoes a change in the course of transmission and when heard resembles nothing more than the shrill and unmusical tone of voice used by the manipulator of puppets in the Punch and Judy show.

The telephones were said to amplify the voice to such a degree that the speaker could be heard clearly 10 or 15 ft away from the receiver.

The animal population of the West Highlands had to receive special consideration. No fewer than 200 creeps were built, ranging from simple wooden sheep-creeps 4 ft wide, costing £70, to plate girder cattle-creeps costing £230. Where the line passed through deer forests a special fence, 6 ft high, was devised, the lower wires of 7 gauge being 5½ in. apart and the upper wires of 6 gauge being 10 in. apart. In addition a single strand of barbed wire ran 42 in. above the ground. Otherwise 4 ft wooden fencing was used.

Throughout the late spring and early summer of 1894 strenuous efforts were made to have the line ready in time for the fast-approaching tourist season. Coloured posters extolling the new railway appeared in North British stations. A press announcement gave 12 July as the opening date and added that Princess Louise, Marchioness of Lorne, would perform the opening ceremony. But July came and went and the line remained unopened.

Meanwhile staff were recruited from all over the North British system, and railway families moved into their West Highland homes to embark on a life very different from that which they were leaving. William Arnott, district superintendent at Perth, was appointed district superintendent of the West Highland, with an office in Fort William. P. Jamieson, agent at Longwitton in Northumberland, became agent at Rannoch—at a salary of £65 per annum. A signalman was appointed at the same station for a wage of 16s per week. Wages on the West Highland were lower than those for the same job on the North British but, as a contemporary railway journal pointed out,

> To be a clerk in Glasgow on £80 a year is to be a nobody; to be a stationmaster with £60 per annum, free house coal and gas is to be a notable figure in a small community.

The last stages of construction were marred by a number of

E

unpleasant incidents. In June a labourer was knocked down and killed by a light engine at Gorton. A few days later, at 6.15 on the morning of 25 June, a ballast train consisting of two engines, thirty-five wagons and a van left the rails at a contractors' service siding in Glen Falloch. A permanent-way inspector was seriously hurt and the two engine crews were lucky to get away with light injuries. The derailment turned out to be the work of three labourers who had pulled over the hand points 'just to see what would happen'. The men were taken to court and subsequently sent to prison.

Heavy rain in July brought about the collapse of earthworks near Tyndrum and an engine rolled down the embankment, killing its fireman and injuring the driver. In the following week a driver was killed on Garelochside. 'Recent accidents,' said a press report, 'have suggested the safe and prudent course of not opening the line for traffic till every part of the works has been minutely examined.'

Political as well as physical difficulties beset the West Highland in the last hectic weeks before opening. When the engineers proposed to supply Bridge of Orchy station with drinking water by tapping a nearby mountain stream the noble owner objected. He went to court in Edinburgh and was unsuccessful in an effort to prevent the West Highland from entering his land and taking the water. But in an appeal to the House of Lords his fellow-peers overturned the Edinburgh decision. All this for a few gallons of water in country where water was anything but a scarce commodity! The gentry in an Upper Helensburgh street complained that they could *see* the railway from their gardens and asked the West Highland to heighten their garden walls. Three years later the railway gave them £110 between them and told them to build up the walls themselves.

Then there was a last-minute dispute between the people of Fort William and the railway. The West Highland had been allowed to bring its line along the shore of Loch Linnhe to the pier which stood at the south end of the town. It was the route, indeed, which the townspeople had invited the Glasgow & North Western Railway to use. Too late they realized that the railway cut the town off from the shore, as it ran parallel to and immediately behind the buildings of the main street. It was a monumental blunder in town planning. In the years to come Fort William was to think of the beautiful lochside esplanade it might have had if the town fathers had kept the line away from the water. In 1894 a special meeting of the Police Commissioners in Fort William pointed out that the railway had cut off access roads to the shore and that the station and signal box were not in the places indicated in the original plans. The company poured some oil on the troubled waters by providing wicket gates and level crossings at certain of the shore access roads.

## 'THE FORT'

When the railway engineers came to Lochaber in 1889 they found Fort William a small, backward town. It had developed a modest tourist trade partly because it was on the Royal Route from Glasgow to Inverness, partly because it nestled at the foot of Britain's highest mountain, Ben Nevis. The town had its origin in the days when William of Orange had many enemies in the Highlands; it was established in 1690 as one of a chain of military installations guarding the Great Glen. Cameron of Lochiel, William's most formidable opponent in these parts, was recovering from a sword wound at the time, and McKay of Killiecrankie notoriety seized the opportunity to establish a fort unmolested on Loch Linnhe on the site of an older fort. The entire fortifications on the landward side were completed in a fortnight and a man-of-war sailed up the loch and delivered a score of guns for its defence. McKay climbed to the battlements, unfurled the standard of the King and insulted the Highlanders by naming the place Fort William.

It was a name that stuck in the throats of the men of Lochaber, and several attempts were made to change it. In a span of 200 years the town was known variously as Duncansburgh, Maryborough and Gordonsburgh, and in comparatively recent times there was a move to have it re-christened Invernevis. Local folks spoke of it as *an gearasdan*—the garrison; today it is known colloquially as 'the Fort'. In the end the entire fort except one building was blown sky-high by a London-based railway contractor, and it fell to a London-based railway company to deliver the *coup de grace* forty years later.

The route of the West Highland into Fort William passed through the disused fort. The railway surveyor found the walls unbreached and entry to the fort was still gained through the archway that McKay had built two centuries earlier. The barrack blocks were occupied as dwelling-houses, and cabbages grew in the fosse. The site was wanted for an engine shed, and John Aird set about demolishing the ancient fortifications. Cannon balls were dug out of the walls, coins were unearthed and a male skeleton was found in the ramparts. The entrance archway, on the instruction of the

West Highland directors, was dismantled and rebuilt at the gateway to the town cemetery, which was the spot where the first Cameron Highlanders had been sworn in.

Thus the gateway to a fort built largely to suppress the rebel Camerons became a monument recording the service given by the clan to the Crown. Within the fort, the building that had been Government House was retained, and the railway company took special steps to preserve the Governor's Room intact. It had been in that room on 12 February 1692 that Colonel Hill had signed the order for the Massacre of Glencoe. The West Highland and its successors provided a caretaker to look after the historic apartment and for over forty years it remained undisturbed amid the bustle of a busy locomotive depot. When the LNE at last demolished the old building, the panelling of the Governor's Room and the stairway leading up to the room were removed to the West Highland Museum in the town.

# CHAPTER 5

# *The Early Years*

## THE LINE IN SERVICE

Major Marindin took several long looks at the West Highland on behalf of the Board of Trade, suggesting improvements and alterations. On his final visit on 3 August 1894, he rode in state in one of the new first-class saloons hauled by two of Matthew Holmes's West Highland bogies. At long last authority to open the line was received on 7 August. The directors had organized their ceremonial opening for Saturday 11 August 1894, but in order to squeeze as much revenue as possible from the ebbing tourist season they opened the public service on the very day permission was received from the Board of Trade.

The first revenue-earning train left Fort William for Glasgow at 6.10 a.m. on 7 August. In spite of the early hour the townsfolk turned out in large numbers to watch its departure. Many of them bought tickets for Spean Bridge and Roy Bridge with the intention of returning on the first down train, and for some it was their first journey by rail. Such was the demand for places that extra coaches had to be added. Charles Forman was among the important guests, and several of Lucas & Aird's navvies were passengers. Groups of people were watching at all the stations; time was kept as far as Ardlui, where it was held to await the down train which had been delayed at Craigendoran for the detachment of a vehicle with a hot box.

The first timetable showed three passenger trains each way between Glasgow Queen Street High Level and Fort William, timed as follows:

| | | | | |
|---|---|---|---|---|
| Queen Street | dep. | 7.30 | 12.40 | 4.50 |
| Fort William | arr. | 12.15 | 5.20 | 9.40 |
| | | | | |
| Fort William | dep. | 6.10 | 11.15 | 4.25 |
| Queen Street | arr. | 11.00 | 4.00 | 9.08 |

The trains normally consisted of two third-class and one first-class

West Highland saloons, except for the first down and the last up train which normally carried one through carriage each for Edinburgh and King's Cross. This service was maintained for three months, then on 1 November the timetable was recast to suit the requirements of the winter traffic. On the same day steam heating was introduced—and not a moment too soon! The winter timings were:

| Queen Street | dep. | 7.55 | 3.50 |
| Fort William | arr. | 12.47 | 8.47 |
| | | | |
| Fort William | dep. | 7.20 | 3.55 |
| Queen Street | arr. | 12.52 | 8.43 |

One freight in each direction was sufficient to handle all the traffic offered.

The West Highland published its timetable showing the new through London—Fort William service in the press on the day it opened for business. Not to be outdone, the Caledonian Railway

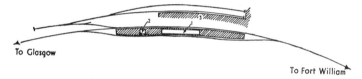

To Glasgow

To Fort William

Tyndrum Upper station. Example of standard 'island' station
1.  main station offices
2.  signal box
3.  cattle loading bank
    Sidings to loading bank are on much lower level than main
    passenger platform and running lines

published its own London—Fort William service alongside the rival announcement. The West Coast service was from Euston to Oban and then by MacBrayne steamer to Fort William. Oddly enough, in spite of the boat journey, the West Coast combine could have their passengers in Fort William right on the tail of those who had travelled in the through coach from King's Cross.

The West Highland had high hopes of developing a local service between Craigendoran and Garelochhead serving Helensburgh Upper, Row and Shandon. Garelochside was a residential area highly favoured with the cream of the Glasgow professional and business community. Passengers to town hitherto had travelled either by private coach or by North British steamer to Helensburgh to join the trains. Now the West Highland offered four trains a day between Craigendoran and Garelochhead, with connections for Glasgow at Craigendoran. The innovation was not a success, mainly because the West Highland stations were sited high on the hills behind the lochside villages and were approached by long, steep roads. As the local correspondent of the *Railway Herald* put it, 'Sound heart and lungs and experience in hill climbing are essential to a man who hurries from the breakfast table to catch a train at one of the lochside stations. It is easier to go to a pier.' Potential passengers complained that the first up train left too late and the last down train left too early.

To increase the scope of the service, railway tickets were made interavailable with steamer tickets. Greenock Town Council petitioned the North British for a restoration of the Greenock—Helensburgh steamer service (which had been abandoned by the North British because it did not pay) so that people on the south shore of the Clyde estuary could have easy access to the West Highland. But when the Greenock merchants were sounded on the prospects of their sending freight over the West Highland, they stated bluntly that the new railway was of no use to them; it was cheaper to send freight to Fort William by boat.

The Garelochside train service won unwanted publicity on 4 September 1894, when 14-year-old Helen Hamill, a servant girl, placed a stone in the path of the 7.35 from Helensburgh at Woodend Farm Crossing. The engine and two coaches finished up in a cornfield. The delinquent Helen was removed to Dumbarton court where 'she emitted a declaration' and was sent to prison.

Tourist tickets on the West Highland were made available for travel on the Loch Lomond steamers. Southbound passengers could detrain at Ardlui or Arrochar and Tarbet and continue their journey by boat to Balloch, thence by rail to Glasgow. The same facility was available in the reverse direction.

By the West Highland Railway Act of 1889 the railway undertook to build a station at Portincaple. This was a hamlet beside Loch Long, opposite Loch Goil and several hundred feet below the railway where it emerged from the cutting above Garelochhead. It was further intended to operate a ferry between Portincaple and Loch Goil. When the railway was built and there was no sign of Portincaple station materializing, the handful of local people protested. The West Highland then announced that a decision on the station would be postponed until the line was opened. A further memorial was dispatched to the railway office whereupon the secretary was 'instructed to intimate to the Memorialists that the

Company were not prepared at present to erect a station at that place'. The station—named Whistlefield—was eventually opened on 1 May 1896.

The West Highland, in company with other lines that had built railways through sparsely-populated territory at high cost, charged fares at the full Parliamentary rate. But it was quick to introduce cheap excursions. Weekend fares to all stations were offered before the end of September, the return fare from Glasgow to Fort William being 9s 2d and from Edinburgh 11s 8d. On 13 September 1894, a local holiday in Glasgow, the first day-excursion was run to Fort William. The train started from Bridgeton Cross (now Bridgeton Central) at 6.30 a.m. and called at Queen Street Low Level and various suburban stations west of the city centre, thereby setting a pattern for almost all day-excursion traffic in the future.

Tulloch, a two-platform station

1. station buildings
2. signal box
3. water tank

The official opening of the West Highland was on 11 August 1894 —a significant date. August 12—the Glorious Twelfth—was still a key date in the British calendar of social events, and the trunk lines from the south to Scotland still carried their heaviest passenger traffic on 10 and 11 August each year. With many thousands of acres of grouse shooting along its metals, the West Highland hoped to make capital out of the shooting season. The sport was first class, but its development was limited by the lack of accommodation in these barren regions for the potential sportsmen. Nevertheless the traffic developed sufficiently to justify the employment of temporary clerkesses at the Moor of Rannoch outposts—Corrour and Gortan as well as Rannoch station—whose duty it was to handle the administration of the shooting season traffic. This involved the dispatch of grouse to the markets in the south as well as the reception of the sportsmen. The girls were employed from 12 August until 12 October at a wage of 12s per week.

In order to facilitate sporting and other traffic the West Highland had the foresight to build a road from Rannoch station eastward across the Moor to Loch Rannoch. The contract had been given to

ON THE ROAD TO THE ISLES

(27) *Lochailort station showing concrete construction of platforms*
(28) *Two Lochs head a Glasgow—Mallaig train out of Glenfinnan in 1958*

(29) *Glenfir*

(30) *Morar viaduct*

*duct*

(31) *Borrodale bridge*

IN THE FAR WEST

(32) *A K1 crosses Loch nan Uamh viaduct on a Glasgow—Mallaig train*

Lucas & Aird originally, but was later transferred to William Wilson of Kirkcaldy who built the road for £4,896 3s 9d. The West Highland was obliged to pay Lucas & Aird 10 per cent of this amount. A venison slide was erected at Rannoch. This device, which was like a children's chute, extended from the road (which was at a higher level than the railway) to the loading bank. Deer carcases were brought by cart to the road end and slid down the chute to the waiting vans.

Additional passenger traffic came from an unexpected source. When the West Highland opened there was, 15 miles or so west of the line where it crossed the Moor of Rannoch, a community as wild and lawless as a pioneer settlement in the Yukon. This was Kinlochleven, a motley town that had sprung up at the end of Loch Leven and was the base for the construction of the first of the great Highland hydro-electric schemes. It was an incredible place of saloons and gambling dens, where men flocked to work like gold prospectors of old. There were no policemen in Kinlochleven, except the two who came to escort the postman on his once-weekly round. Nor were there in those days any roads into Kinlochleven. The navvies had to go in by boat or trudge round the unmarked shore of Loch Leven from Ballachulish.

With the coming of the West Highland Railway the navvies found that they could go by train to Corrour and walk by an ill-defined path across the Moor to Kinlochleven. It was a dangerous and foolhardy journey. Some of the men who went there were refugees from justice who hoped to lose their identity in the rough and ready colony in the west. On one occasion the Glasgow police traced a wanted man to Corrour station, but a search of Kinlochleven revealed no sign of him. When the Moor was combed the searchers found not only the body of the wanted man, but the skeletons of three others.

### THE FIRST WINTER

It was unfortunate that the West Highland's first winter was the worst of the nineteenth century. The great frost that ushered in 1895 was long remembered. Contemporary newspaper headlines tell their own story : *Seas and Lochs Icebound. Railways and Roads Obliterated. Coldest Days of the Century. Many Deaths in the Great Storm.* The severe weather came in three phases. The first dated from 29 December 1894 until 11 January 1895, when a snowstorm of exceptional severity was followed by a lull and a rapid rise of temperature. On 29 January a second storm even more violent than the first swept the country. Another brief period of calm was followed on 5 February by a terrifying blizzard that reached a climax on 6 February.

If conditions were bad in the cities of Britain they were unspeakable on the Moor of Rannoch. The West Highlands were ravaged daily by scouring blizzards that made a mockery of time-tables. Day after day the trains that left Glasgow for Fort William got no further than Tyndrum or Bridge of Orchy. Southbound trains rarely covered more than the first 18 miles of their journey. Tulloch was about their limit; the difficult miles between Tulloch and Rannoch were impassable for days. Gangs of railwaymen reinforced by civilian labourers were sent out to attack the drifts on Loch Treigside but to little avail. As a drift was cleared the storm piled up new ones.

On the first Monday of 1895 the district superintendent at Fort William took the precaution of sending out an engine and plough in advance of the first up goods. The engine got as far as Tulloch, and the goods following it came to grief in a newly-formed drift near Tulloch Farm. The 7.30 passenger train reached Roy Bridge, where it was held until mid-day and sent back to Fort William. Meanwhile the first down train, which should have reached Fort William, was still 75 miles short of its terminus, held fast by big snowslides in the hills above Loch Lomond.

In the lull between the first and second phases of the storm some headway was made in clearing the line, but with the renewal of the blizzard the work of a week was undone in an hour. Snow dug out of the cuttings and piled up by the lineside was swept back into the cuttings and layers of fresh snow drifted over it. By now the district superintendent had pin-pointed the danger spots and concerted attacks were made on them by ploughs and diggers. The worst spot of all was Cruach Rock cutting a mile and a half above Rannoch. On a wild Sunday night forces were sent out from Fort William and from Glasgow to tackle the Cruach region simultaneously from both ends. The engine and plough from Fort William climbed all the way up to Corrour only to be caught and held immovable in a huge drift. Two engines from Glasgow struggled as far north as Tyndrum, where they ran into a big drift and became derailed somewhat precariously on the brink of a snow-covered slope. During Monday the engines were re-railed and succeeded in getting through to Rannoch.

Then, when the successful clearing of the line was in sight, came the final and worst phase of the storm. The renewed blizzard was followed at once by a gale-force wind and intense cold. The whole country found itself encrusted in a tough skin of ice. The drifts that filled the cuttings and covered the tracks froze into a solid rock-like mass. The position for the West Highland was serious. There were booking offices on the line where not a penny-piece had passed through the windows for days. Revenue from passengers and freight had dwindled to vanishing point. *The Engineer* commented:

> The experience of the present severe weather on the new West Highland line connecting Helensburgh with Fort William has been anything but pleasant, and the cost entailed in digging trains out of the snow has been very great, and certainly not of a nature to encourage promoters to carry through additional Highland railways.

The railwaymen could do nothing else but continue their effort to clear the line. A relief unit out of Fort William was battling its way up Loch Treigside when the engine left the rails at a bridge over a gully. A ballast train following it was lost in the snow for several days. In the south the snow fighters met with more success, and before long the line was clear from Craigendoran to beyond Bridge of Orchy.

In the midst of all the anxiety came a piece of comic relief. The roaring game of curling was a popular one in the West Highlands and a Fort William curling team, taking advantage of the new railway, arranged a match between themselves and a team from Dall, Loch Rannoch. The match was due to take place on a small loch near Rannoch station on 6 February, the day the whole series of storms reached a grand climax. Undaunted by the frightful weather the curlers went out from Fort William by the morning train and managed to get through to Rannoch on the recently cleared line. But they had no sooner gained the shelter of Rannoch station than the storm broke in full fury, and the line over which they had travelled was blocked. The Dall team had already arrived by the moorland road. In spite of the weather, neither team would agree to abandon the game. Even when the loch on which they had intended to play was found to be unusable, they trudged through the blizzard for a mile to Loch Laidon, and there in the partial shelter of Cruach Hill the game began. But they were soon glad to seek refuge in Rannoch station.

There was no news of any train anywhere. The curlers were marooned on the Moor. Lucas & Aird had not got around to dismantling their hutments at Rannoch and the players found shelter in a large store hut which still, fortunately, contained stores of

# NORTH BRITISH RAILWAY.

s*31/8*

District Traffic Superintendent's Office,
GORDON SQUARE,
FORT-WILLIAM, *31st Aug* 189*4*

Mr. *Whitfield*
*Rannoch* Station.

DEAR SIR,

My *L 16/8* of *16th inst*
*Walter Lumsden*
having been tested by an Inspector and found competent
for the duties of **Block Telegraph Signalman** at
*Rannoch Station*
you may allow him to assume duty in that capacity *vice*
*Spare Signalman Jardine*
who *send home as soon as*
*the workmens trains are altered*
*which will be in a day or so.*
Please acknowledge receipt on the annexed form.

Yours truly,
*Wm Arnott*
*per Murray*
District Traffic Superintendent.

foodstuffs and supplies of fuel. There was no drinking water, but several cases of lemonade were broached; it had frozen solid, but the refugees soon had the bottles thawing in front of a blazing fire. The men passed the long hours of the night by holding a *ceilidh*, a Gaelic sing-song.

During Thursday forenoon an engine with a gang of 30 men arrived from the south. Conditions were still bad on the heights of the Moor and the engine was held at Rannoch to await an improve-

*Mary Robertson*

(1942)

**NORTH BRITISH RAILWAY.**

3/5466

District Traffic Superintendent's Office,

FORT-WILLIAM, 9th Aug 1901

Mr. Hogarth

Rannoch Station.

DEAR SIR,

Miss Mary Robertson

Supernumerary clerk

Please enter the above-named in Paybill at 12/-

per week from 12th August

to 12th October.

Yours truly,

*Geo Innes,*

*District Traffic Superintendent.*

ment. The men joined the curlers in the store hut. Later in the day a second relief train arrived from the south, and by nightfall two more trains had arrived in Rannoch with no hope of being able to continue their journey northwards.

The population of the moorland settlement was now about 200, and there was anxiety about dwindling food and drink supplies. Fortunately Friday brought an improvement in the weather, and the gangers were able to reach the south end of Cruach Rock cutting. They had to quarry out the ice and frozen snow in blocks. Before the end of the day they met the gang working from the north end, and the line was open again. For several weeks trains crossing the Moor passed through a series of clefts cut in the snow. Smooth white walls rose on either side of the carriages, and it was not until spring was well advanced that the snow buttresses crumbled and disappeared. Meanwhile the West Highland took the precaution of advancing the departure time of the 3.50 Glasgow— Fort William passenger train to 2 p.m., so that it would pass the Cruach Rock danger spot in daylight.

The lesson of that first winter was not lost on the West Highland. North British engineers set about designing permanent snow defences. These took the form of continuous sleeper fences erected on hill faces above the railway where experience had shown that drifting was likely. Danger spots on the Moor of Rannoch were lined with snow fences. Later, at the worst place, Cruach Rock, a snow-shed was built: for a length of 205 yd corrugated sheeting was placed over the notorious cutting. The roof principals were made of old rails spanning the 27 ft 6 in. between the walls. The centre sheets of the snow-shed directly above the rails could be removed in summer. Over the years the defences have worked reasonably well; there have been snowblocks, some of them serious, but none has been on the scale of those of the first winter.

### THE BANAVIE BRANCH

The West Highland Railway Act gave the promoters powers to build a branch from near Fort William to Banavie on the banks of the Caledonian Canal. The branch was not ready for the official opening of the main line, largely because of difficulties involved in building a substantial viaduct over the Lochy. The branch left the main line at Banavie Junction a mile east of Fort William, and ran 1¾ miles to a station and pier on the Caledonian Canal. The West Highland hoped to establish passenger and freight business with the vessels plying on the canal. The pier was alongside the station but a considerable distance above it, and wagons were taken through the station and back-shunted up a gradient of 1 in 24 to the canal bank.

The first train set off from Banavie on its 2¾-mile journey to Fort William at 5.40 on the morning of 1 June 1895. By southern standards it was a modest occasion, but the railway-conscious West Highlanders had other ideas. The diminutive branch was opened with due ceremony, and the engine that brought the first train into Fort William in the dawn light was decorated with bunting.

The West Highland had no intention of stopping at Banavie. The great aim was to get westwards to the shores of the Atlantic and north-east to Inverness. In spite of the bland assurances of friendship given to the Highland Railway representatives on the day of the West Highland's opening, the West Highland had surveyors in the Great Glen only a week or two later. They were searching for a route to Inverness. It was odd that the Highland Railway should have *its* surveyors in the Great Glen on the self-same Saturday morning. They were looking for a Highland route to Fort William.

In 1894 the West Highland tried to put a branch across from Inverlair (Tulloch) over the 32 miles to Kingussie on the Highland Railway, but the Highland had no difficulty in thwarting the attempt. The West Highland contented itself by exhibiting at Tulloch what was perhaps the most optimistic notice ever erected on a railway station: 'Tulloch *for Kingussie.*' The timetable designated Tulloch 'for Loch Laggan and Kingussie'.

### MINOR MANIA

A minor railway mania seized the West Highlands with the coming of the railway. Railways were projected hither and thither, and more often than not the indefatigable Charles Forman was behind them. He surveyed an extension of the West Highland down the east shore of Loch Linnhe from Fort William to Ballachulish, over the route that Walron Smith planned for the G & NW. At the same time he planned a Caledonian-sponsored branch from the Callander & Oban at Connel Ferry up through Appin to Ballachulish.

Other Forman enterprises within a 30-mile radius of Ben Nevis included a line from the West Highland at Spean Bridge to Fort Augustus in the Great Glen, and a continuation up Loch Ness to Inverness. Of Forman's projected grand cross-country route from Oban to Inverness, all the links between Oban and Fort Augustus were authorized. The Spean Bridge to Fort Augustus line was built by an independent company (of which we are to hear more), the Callander & Oban built the Connel Ferry—Ballachulish link, but the West Highland did not use its powers to take its branch from Fort William to Ballachulish.

Meanwhile, further south two Forman schemes came into direct conflict with each other, which was not surprising considering that he simultaneously engineered a Caledonian and a North British scheme to reach the same objective. Inveraray, the county town of Argyll, lay isolated among mountains near the head of Loch Fyne, and attempts were made to get railways to it from two directions. On behalf of the Callander & Oban, Forman planned a line running south from a junction with the parent system at Dalmally, a distance of 14½ miles; the cost of £142,568 was to include a pier at Inveraray, through which the railway hoped to benefit from the then intensive Loch Fyne herring-fishing trade.

At the same time Forman surveyed a West Highland branch that was to leave the main line at Arrochar, pass round Loch Long, and cross to Loch Fyne by the Rest and be Thankful, so to reach St Catherine's opposite Inveraray. From Glasgow to Inveraray by the West Highland route was 54 miles, by the Caledonian and Callander & Oban 107¼. Inveraray was a feudal enclave dominated by the castle. The Duke of Argyll favoured the West Highland scheme if only because it decently kept out of his preserves. But the Dalmally line passed under the castle windows and the duke had no difficulty in inducing Parliament to throw out the bill. The West Highland had enough on its plate in the north-west without adding the Inveraray branch. It was never built.

The wave of optimism that swept Lochaber when the railway came spawned two transport schemes, one basically sound, the other plausible but with more than a touch of fantasy. From time to time schemes had been proposed for building a railway to the summit of Ben Nevis. The Ben was the highest mountain in Britain and already very much a 'tourist' mountain. Moreover, since 1883 there had been a permanent observatory on the summit, inhabited all the year round and connected with the base by an easily negotiated pony track. Much more difficult peaks in Europe and elsewhere had been given rack railways that had paid their way and brought prosperity to their base towns. Everybody who climbed Ben Nevis wrote his or her name in the visitors' book at the observatory, and these books provided a ready-made census of potential traffic for a mountain railway.

In 1893 Charles Forman considered building a railway up Ben Nevis. When the West Highland was opened, a London company took up the challenge and planned to construct a line starting near the West Highland station and, following the pony track for the first 2,000 ft, reach the summit by striking east round the shoulder of the mountain. The line was to be 4¾ miles long and have a maximum gradient of 1 in 2.62 for 600 yd. The company expected to spend £30,000 on the venture (the price inclusive of a large hotel on the summit), and estimated that the revenue from 15,000 passengers a year at fares of 1s 6d return and 1s single would enable 6 per cent to be paid on the capital. The scheme was revived several times between 1894 and 1913, but nothing came of it. If ever a mountain was ready for a railway it was Ben Nevis. It was a pity both for the future prosperity of the West Highland Railway and Fort William that the line was not built.

The other transport scheme that engaged the attention of the West Highlanders and others envisaged the establishment of an Atlantic terminus at Fort William. At that time the steamship route from Liverpool to Quebec was 2,625 miles and the time taken on the voyage was 6 days 12 hours. From Fort William to Quebec *via* Skerryvore and the Ross of Mull was 2,083 miles and the estimated time of the voyage was exactly 5 days. From London to Liverpool was 5 hours by rail, London to Fort William was 14 hours by rail, so that the Fort William—Quebec route was 1 day 3 hours shorter than the existing Liverpool—Quebec route.

And Fort William had other claims. Loch Linnhe was a large

F

natural harbour with a bottom of firm blue clay and no rocks. It was deep enough to take the largest liners at any state of the tide, and it was safe and perfectly sheltered by the surrounding mountains. Loch Eil nearby was available as an additional anchorage. Furthermore, there were 1,200 acres of flat ground by the lochside, and plenty of local stone for the building of wharves and warehouses. On paper Fort William looked a likely choice for a new Atlantic port. The big ships went to Southampton, but it is intriguing to picture the *Queen Mary* arriving at Fort William and her 2,000 passengers trying to make their way down the West Highland, perhaps in December with Rannoch Moor not on its best behaviour..

### TWO DERAILMENTS

On 14 October 1895 an alarming accident involving the 4.20 p.m. from Fort William occurred at Shandon station. The train was double headed, with Driver Thornton in charge of the leading engine and Driver Thomson on the train engine. A storm had been gathering in the West Highlands that afternoon, and by the time the train got to Garelochhead the night was wild and black. Thomson picked up the Garelochhead—Shandon tablet and the train steamed off on the next stage of its journey. The line curves through deep cuttings and dense woods at this part and somewhere in the featureless blackness of the 2½-mile section Driver Thornton became disorientated. He did not know where he was. Thornton had been 11 hours and Thomson 14 hours on duty, and it may have been that the faculties of both men were impaired. Thornton strained through the darkness for a sight of the Shandon up distant, but he never saw it for its lamp was unlit. Presently the up home came into view, but Thornton took it to be the distant (distant and home both exhibited red lights then), and he made only a slight reduction in speed.

Thornton could not have chosen a more inopportune night on which to lose himself, for John Crawford, the Shandon signalman, had been very remiss in his duties that day. Before dusk he should have trimmed all his signal lamps, but he considered that the top of a signal ladder on a windswept hillface was no place for him when he could be making himself comfortable at the porter's room fire. The result was that the up and down distant lamps went out, and in those days there were no repeaters in the cabins to indicate that a lamp had failed.

To complicate matters, after the last down train had passed Crawford had been unable to tear himself away from the fire to reset the road for the next traffic move—the 4.20 up train. Even after he had received the train-entering-section signal from Garelochhead and he knew the 4.20 was on its way, he remained in the staff room. It was only when he heard the train rumbling round the hillside that he hurried along the platform to the box. First of all he had to reverse the points at the south end of the station. By that time the train was running into the down (wrong) side of the island platform, but Crawford did not see it and he pulled the points under it.

Then under the bemused signalman's nose followed a disconcerting spectacle. The train split in two. The two engines and one coach ran round the right side of the island platform and the rear half of the train ran round the left side; and the two portions between them dragged the second carriage up the ramp on to the platform where it overturned. Thornton's engine was 164 ft past the points when it stopped. Luckily the train was lightly loaded, and only one passenger required hospital treatment. But the West Highland had to face a heavy repair bill that it could ill afford.

On 6 May 1896 Thornton was involved in another derailment of a very different kind. His train was the 7.35 a.m. from Glasgow and he had reached milepost 97¼ safely and was steaming easily along the last lap towards Fort William. It was an exceptionally hot day, the sun temperature a foot above the grass in Fort William being no less than 128 deg. F. Suddenly Thornton noticed a bad kink in the rails in front of him. Before he could do anything the tender and entire train, but not the engine, left the rails. The Board of Trade report on the accident trounced the West Highland for badly maintained track; which was disconcerting for the owners of a new railway.

## DISAPPOINTMENT

That the West Highland had made life easier for the people of Lochaber was beyond doubt, but the line was not the panacea for the ills of the Highlands that its promoters had thought it would be. The tourist trade boomed, and summer passenger traffic was even better than the directors had anticipated. But in winter there were few travellers in the West Highlands and the trains ran for the most part with only a handful of passengers. The meagre freight traffic developed very slowly and the pattern remained almost static for over 30 years; then the British Aluminium Company changed the face of Lochaber (see page 128).

The West Highland cattle and sheep farmers had been assured that the new railway would give them direct access to the markets of Perth and Stirling, *via* the Crianlarich spur to the Callander & Oban Railway. Cattle traffic to those destinations was indeed secured, but it was routed *via* Glasgow, because the Crianlarich spur was not ready. After the autumn cattle sales of 1895, the town authorities of Perth and Stirling protested to the West Highland over its failure to provide the promised direct (and cheaper) route. The Crianlarich spur was brought into use on 20 December 1897. Round about the same time the people of Oban agitated for a direct service to and from Oban and Glasgow *via* the West Highland and the Callander & Oban. They eventually got it—in 1949.

Crianlarich became the main servicing point for all trains and their passengers. It was a standard island station, but in addition to having the usual building for the station offices, and a signal box, it was provided with a privately-owned refreshment room that became famous in the annals of the railway. Here originated the celebrated breakfast and luncheon baskets which were supplied to passengers during the Crianlarich stop. On the up side of the island platform were a short siding, a turntable and a small engine shed. On the down side were three sidings, one of which served a cattle

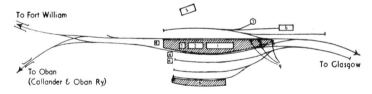

Crianlarich Upper station

1. main station offices
2. refreshment rooms
3. signal box
4. water towers
5. main water reservoir
6. engine shed
7. turntable
8. cattle loading platform
9. water columns

(E) *The most spectacular of many viaducts on the West Highland: Glenfinnan, with North British Locomotive Co Class 29 Bo-Bo D6101 crossing in April 1967*

loading bank. Immediately north of the platform end the spur to the Callander & Oban diverged to the left. It was worked by tablet, a North British instrument being housed in the C & O box. Special attention was paid to the watering of the engines. Before the end of the steam era, when it was common to see two double-headed trains in the station at one time, all four engines taking water simultaneously, a large main reservoir on the hillside overlooking the up road fed three water towers at rail level. At both ends of the platforms water columns were arranged in pairs, so that both pilot and train engine could take water at the same time.

It very soon became apparent that Fort William station was cramped and unable to cope satisfactorily with the peak summer traffic. But there was nothing the West Highland could do about it, for the station was crushed between Loch Linnhe and the buildings of the High Street. There were three platforms, two of which were docks. The third platform line ran alongside the sea wall, carried on beyond the station, crossed the end of MacBrayne's pier and terminated on a jetty just beyond. The three platform lines converged on to the single main line immediately beyond the platform ends. The short trains of the early days were easily accommodated, but increasing traffic brought longer trains and one of these at any platform completely bottled up the station and prevented all movement. Things became really hectic when trains ran out of course and Fort William had a Glasgow—Mallaig and a Mallaig—Glasgow to handle at the same time. Both had to reverse in and out of the station and usually a certain amount of 'topping and tailing' was called for. Much time was lost in conducting these operations in the cramped space available.

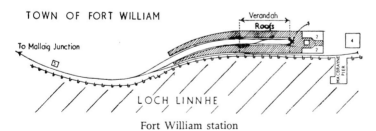

Fort William station

1. bookstall
2. main offices
3. signal box
4. MacBrayne depot
5. lever frame controlling crossover points in station

(F) *Crianlarich was the most important station between Craigendoran and Fort William, having a refreshment room, engine shed and junction with the Callander & Oban line. NBL Class 29 Bo-Bo D6107 is seen at the head of an Oban-Glasgow train in May 1968*

In the early years the revenue of the line showed a steady rise. Here are the combined passenger and freight traffic receipts for the years specified.

| | | | |
|---|---|---|---|
| 1896 | £45,146 | 12 | 10 |
| 1897 | £54,703 | 14 | 9 |
| 1898 | £62,553 | 4 | 10 |
| 1899 | £69,626 | 3 | 4 |
| 1900 | £89,760 | 16 | 4 |
| 1901 | £92,260 | 8 | 4 |

But the line never climbed out of the red. Once working expenses had been paid the North British had to dip into its own coffers to make up the interest on the guaranteed West Highland stock.

In 1899 the North British had to find £34,000 to pay interest due to West Highland stockholders. Maintenance costs on the new railway were light at first but these increased with the passing of the years. North British shareholders became restive over the West Highland. 'I would not venture to prophesy,' lamented the parent company's chairman in 1907, 'whether it (the West Highland) will *ever* pay an adequate return.'

# CHAPTER 6

# The Road to the Isles

## THE MALLAIG EXTENSION

The West Highland Railway as planned had an outlet to the western seas. When feudalism robbed the railway of that outlet the West Highland lost one of the main reasons for its very existence—to provide communication with the far-west fishing and crofting communities and with the peoples of the Western Isles. True enough Fort William was on salt water but, by an accident of geography, Loch Linnhe was far from the fishing grounds. The fishing villages of the west were 40 miles overland from Fort William but close on 100 miles away by water. The West Highland, if it were to survive, could not let its terminal remain at Fort William. The railway had to get to the sea, if only to channel to the main line the fish traffic that alone would give the line a chance of paying its way.

John Aird and Cameron of Lochiel had a look at the country west of Fort William. They liked Loch Nevis as a base for a port; it was deep and sheltered by surrounding mountains and it was close to Skye. But south of Loch Nevis was a tough mountain barrier that would be costly to pierce, so they settled on Mallaig Bay, 4 miles south of Loch Nevis. A railway from Mallaig to the nearest point on the West Highland would be 39 miles and 53 chains long.

In March 1892 the Government sent a committee consisting of Major-General Hutchinson, Rear-Admiral Sir G. S. Nares and Mr Henry Tennant to the West Highlands to inquire into the need for transport and harbours. These gentlemen found that the landowners who had been so obstructive in the recent past were now inclined to modify their views. The more progressive among them even offered their land for a railway at below market prices. The crofters were so enthusiastic that 400 of them offered to work on the construction of the line and devote one-sixth of their wages to the purchase of shares in the railway.

The investigating trio also picked Mallaig Bay as the best place for a railway terminal. They suggested that a breakwater be built to enclose 30 acres of water and that a connecting line be constructed to the West Highland at Banavie. They considered that such a railway built through extremely difficult and sparsely-populated country would have no chance of paying its way and suggested the payment of a £100,000 grant to the builders. Meanwhile the North British railway separately had reached the conclusion that the Mallaig Extension would not pay and the directors were not prepared to recommend its construction to their shareholders unless the Government gave adequate financial guarantees.

The West Highland promoted its West Highland Railway (Mallaig Extension) Bill in January 1894, with the object of building a railway from a point on its Banavie branch to the coast at Mallaig. At the same time the Lords Commissioners of Her Majesty's Treasury were empowered to pay certain grants and dividends to the builders and to holders of Mallaig Extension stock. This gave rise to the quite separate West Highland Railway (Guarantee) Bill. The position was that the promoters had to get their West Highland Railway (Mallaig Extension) Bill passed in the usual way and then await Parliament passing the West Highland Railway (Guarantee) Bill, which would guarantee some of the finance for the project. Without the Guarantee Bill the Extension Bill was useless, and the railway could not be built.

The West Highland Railway (Guarantee) Bill required the promoters of the Mallaig line to satisfy certain conditions. First of all they had to present their bill to Parliament and have it passed. In addition they had to submit plans for the harbour at Mallaig and have them approved by the Government. They were further required to enter into an agreement with the North British Railway whereby that company would maintain and work the line in perpetuity in return for half the gross receipts. Now that Government backing was assured the North British stood behind the West Highland and the promotion of the line was pushed with vigour.

The Highland Railway opposed the Mallaig Extension. It was about to take its Dingwall—Strome Ferry line out to the coast at Kyle of Lochalsh, some 20 miles north of Mallaig, and wanted at all cost to avoid competition from a rival line. Moreover its existing mail contract was worth £27,000, and it visualized losing part of this traffic to the newcomer. As on similar occasions in the past, fish featured prominently in the arguments for and against the line. Cameron of Lochiel spoke of west coast fish being dumped into the sea because there was no means of transporting them south. But Lord Portman told the House of Lords that the fish were thrown back because they were too small! The west coast crabs, the committee were assured, were pathetic creatures compared with the robust crabs handled by the Highland Railway. There was no lack of witnesses to prove that Mallaig would be a dangerous place for a harbour. Donald McDonald, whom the Highland Railway introduced as the man who knew more about Skye than anyone else, declared, 'Mallaig is no harbour at all. It is just a pretty wee bay.'

The committee listened patiently to the arguments, but they were not impressed. The truth was that the time had come when the people of the west must get their railway. To save useless legal expenses the Highland forthwith withdrew its opposition and as a goodwill gesture the North British gave it £500 towards its Parliamentary expenses. The West Highland Railway (Mallaig Extension) Act was passed on 31 July 1894.

Not all dealings between railway promoters and landlords were rancorous. Lord Lovat had been a relentless opponent of the Mallaig Railway but, when the fight was over and the railway was victorious, Lord Lovat's solicitors, Macdonald & Graham of Inverness, wrote in these terms to the secretary of the WHR :

> Before allowing the settlement which has just taken place to pass out of memory, we hope you will not take it amiss if we send you a private expression of our appreciation of your uniform courtesy and ability throughout the whole course of the negotiations. Keen and tenacious to a degree over what you considered your just rights you never pushed your views too far but, after due discussions, met ours in a fair and broad spirit. Without reflection upon others who have to do with railway affairs, we must say that so far as our experience goes your methods formed a pleasant contrast to the narrower and obstructive tactics which we sometimes observed elsewhere. It will be a pleasure to us to meet you again and fight as keenly as ever with the same happy results.

### A POLITICAL PAWN

Meanwhile, the vital Guarantee bill was having a rough passage in the House of Commons. Unhappily, the Mallaig Railway became a pawn in the game of party politics, a political issue of some magnitude. The urgent need of the people of the West Highlands for a railway was forgotten amid the squalid arguments of the politicians. Mallaig was a long way from Westminster. The gist of the situation was that the Tories approved of public subsidies for transport, the Liberals did not. The anti-subsidy faction set them-

selves up as guardians of the public purse and expressed horror at
the 'free gift' being handed over to the railway promoters and their
shareholders.

The principal architect of the opposition to the bill was a Scottish
radical member, J. H. Dalziel, who represented Kirkcaldy. Dalziel
hated the North British. His constituency was wholly in North
British territory, and he maintained that the company used its
monopoly to hold the district to ransom. In the Guarantee bill
Dalziel saw a plot by the rich and rapacious North British to exploit
the West Highland and so extend its own influence at the taxpayers'
expense. Unfortunately, the chairman of the North British played
into Dalziel's hands by delivering an incredibly tactless speech at a
shareholders' meeting. Here are the fatal words:

> It is of the utmost importance that that company (the West
> Highland) should be connected with the coast, and the directors of
> the North British believing it to be of paramount importance in their
> interest that this extension is made have agreed to work the line. If
> the Government carry out their promise the company as a matter of
> fact will obtain a railway 40 miles in length for the moderate sum of
> £100,000. In any case we think this is a gift one should not look
> askance at, but rather is an opportunity to take full advantage of the
> generosity of the Treasury.

With relish the radicals seized on those careless phrases 'in their
interest' and 'a gift'. There were members from comfortable English
constituencies who could not have pointed out Mallaig on the map
if their lives depended on it, who now thundered against the Mallaig
Railway. It was a heaven-sent stick with which to beat the Government. 'The plain truth,' insisted Dalziel,

> is that from the moment of its inception the Bill has been a flagrant
> political manoeuvre. The only interest the taxpayer is to have in the
> undertaking is to be allowed to pay. Notwithstanding that the capital
> is to be subscribed on the strength of the Government guarantee no
> provision is made for the Government having any voice upon the
> board of management as is the case in regard to the Caledonian Canal,
> or having any substantial guarantee that the company's affairs shall be
> wisely and economically conducted. As it is not pretended, even by
> the promoters, that the line will be a commercial success we have the
> spectacle of public funds being pledged to the extent of a quarter of
> a million of money without even providing for a report as to the
> operation of the company to whose exchequer we are so liberally to
> contribute.

An election in Inverness was fought with the Mallaig Railway as
a main issue. At campaign meetings candidates were questioned on
their attitude to the railway, and there was no mistaking the fact

that audiences favoured the candidate who pledged support for the Guarantee bill. The Tory candidate even managed to produce at the last minute that hoary electioneering device, the 'stunt' letter. This particular letter was said to have been written by the Tory Chancellor of the Exchequer to the secretary of the West Highland Railway, and in it he stated that he fully recognized the importance of the Mallaig Railway. The implication was that the return of the Government candidate would ensure the passing of the bill. The rival candidate complained, 'I doubt whether the records of Parliamentary elections provide a more shameless and open-faced political bribe to the electors.'

The efforts of Dalziel and his friends forced the withdrawal of the Mallaig bill. There was anger and dismay in the Highlands. Anticipating that the Guarantee bill would be passed with alacrity, many of the men who had built the West Highland had stayed on in Lochaber. Lucas & Aird, confident that the contract for the Extension would be theirs, put both men and equipment into a proposed base camp at Corpach, overlooking the spot where the first sod would be turned.

When news of the failure of the bill reached Lochaber, the navvies marched from Corpach into Fort William, where they joined the townsfolk in a demonstration against the railway wreckers. Effigies of Dalziel and another Scottish M.P. who had opposed the bill were made and labelled respectively *Kirkcaldy Brat* and *Highland Traitor*. The effigies were kicked through the main street of the town at the head of a procession some hundreds strong to the public refuse dump where they were ceremonially burned. Lucas & Aird struck camp and took their men and equipment to a new railway venture in the south of England.

The set-back to the railway could only be temporary. The Guarantee bill came up in Parliament again in 1896 and this time it was passed. By the terms of the Act the Treasury undertook to guarantee the shareholders 3 per cent on £260,000 of the West Highland (Mallaig Extension) capital, and to make a grant of £30,000 towards the £45,000 pier at Mallaig. The new railway was given preferential treatment in the matter of rating. Section 2 of the Act said:

> The railway shall not be assessed to any local rate at a higher value than at which the land occupied by the railway would have been assessed if it had remained in the condition in which it was immediately before it was acquired for the purpose of the railway.

Under the terms of the Act the railway's annual rate bill was

£147 1s 11d. If it had been assessed *as a railway* the amount payable would have been about £9,000. English members were aggrieved by the benefits conferred on the Mallaig Extension promoters. English railways, they protested, had to find their interest out of their earnings, whereas the Highlanders who had done nothing to help themselves (*sic*) were being mollycoddled.

But English spleen did not prevent the Highlanders from getting the railway for which they had fought for so long. Lady Margaret Cameron of Lochiel cut the first sod in a field at Corpach on 21 January 1897. The Act specified 31 July 1902 as the time-limit for the completion of the line, so that the contractors had 5 years 6 months and 10 days in which to build 40 miles of track.

### 'CONCRETE BOB'

A fresh team embarked on the construction of the Mallaig Railway. The engineers were Simpson & Wilson, and the contractors were Robert McAlpine & Sons, both of Glasgow. The head of the firm of contractors was the same Robert McAlpine who had walked across the Moor of Rannoch in 1889. He was known in civil engineering circles as 'Concrete Bob'.

He was an enthusiastic advocate of the relatively new building medium, mass concrete, and on the Mallaig Extension he was given a glorious opportunity to do wonderful things with concrete. For the next five years McAlpine was to be the central figure in the greatest concentration of concrete construction in the world. The Mallaig line had to be built on the cheap, and concrete was from 10 per cent to 30 per cent cheaper than masonry. (Even if he had wanted McAlpine could not have repeated Lucas & Aird's tactics and used local stone for his bridge piers, for the stone on the Mallaig Railway was virtually unworkable.) Again, the flooring of a concrete viaduct did not have to be painted or replaced; there was no ironwork to rust. And concrete bridges were more in keeping than steel bridges with the scenic splendour of the west.

McAlpine appointed his son Robert, aged 28, to take full charge of construction, and his younger son Malcolm, aged 19, was made his assistant. The route of the Mallaig line was much more accessible than had been the main line. The first 12½ miles along Loch Eil were approachable at every point by sea. A pier was built at Locheilhead and workshops established beside it, and further camps were set up at Mallaig, Morar Beach, Lochailort and Arisaig. The labour force consisted of Irishmen, Lowland Scots, Highlanders,

Scandinavians and men from the islands who spoke only Gaelic.

The largest camp was established at Lochailort; eventually it housed 2,000 of the 3,500 navvies who worked on the line. The old schoolhouse was converted into an eight-bed hospital, staffed by two nurses and a resident doctor; it was the first hospital to be set up on a construction site in Britain. The navvies were housed in huts with beds for 40. They did their own cooking over a hotplate situated in the middle of a large central hut. The navvy's favourite cooking utensil was his shovel, which he kept spotlessly clean and brightly polished when not in use. A large, well-stocked provision shop was provided at Lochailort and a chain of 18 local shops was established along the line. These were supplied by Cooper & Co., a high-class Glasgow firm of provision merchants, and their contract with McAlpine required them to sell only the best quality foodstuffs. The camp bakery provided fresh bread daily. The navvies were paid 4½d or 5d per hour, but a bonus system based on actual work done augmented their earnings.

A writer in McAlpine's house magazine gave this picture of the navvy of the Mallaig line era.

> The regular navvy was proud of his calling and a good man was never out of a job. If their methods were old-fashioned they were skilled in a way which is fading in fashion to-day. They were without many of the mechanical aids known so well to the modern contractor, but as tunnellers, timbermen, platelayers, horse handlers, or in the plain use of a pick and shovel many of them were artists in their own way. Even in their dress they stood out from other men—cloth cap, silk muffler knotted round the neck, heavy grey flannel or checked shirt, corduroy trousers and stout leather hobnail boots. The trousers were supported by at least one stout belt instead of braces which would constrict shoulder movement, and fastened under the knee with leather 'Yorks' to keep them up out of the mud. The more prosperous navvy sported a real moleskin waistcoat.

The navvy's lot on the Mallaig Extension was not an easy one. By 5 a.m. Lochailort camp was a buzz of activity, with men streaming out of the huts to wash in cold water pouring directly into the wash basins from mountain burns. Then came the surge round the hotplate as breakfasts were prepared, followed by the trudge to the working area. Often the weather was wet and disagreeable. It is little wonder that McAlpine, in spite of the good conditions offered, could not retain labour. Navvies came for a few weeks, and left again for the more hospitable south. Tradesmen were particularly difficult to obtain. At one time a force of over 400 joiners was needed for the concrete work, and great difficulty was experienced in attracting and retaining good men. There was a shortage of labour, too, at Locheilhead pier, and supplies were held up because ships could not be unloaded. The owners of a steamer that brought a cargo to Loch Eil in the winter of 1896-7 claimed £314 8s 4d demurrage. The half-yearly reports submitted to the West Highland board by Simpson & Wilson regularly lamented the slowness of progress due to shortage of labour.

At the outset McAlpine had been confident that the line would be ready for the summer traffic of 1900, but unforeseen difficulties slowed construction. On the stretch of line along Loch Eil the track rose no higher than 32½ ft and the contractors' materials were taken by boat to the exact spot where they were required. It was when the railway left Loch Eil that the skill of the builders was taxed, for it had to be taken through rough country calling for stretches of gradient at 1 in 48 and 1 in 50 as well as constant severe curvature. The engineers had hoped to get through to Mallaig with only two tunnels; in the end they needed eleven.

The hard rock encountered greatly slowed progress. Many experiments were carried out to find out the best type of steel drill. At times the steam-operated air compressors could not produce enough air to drive all the drills working in the tunnels and cuttings.

A solution to the problem came to young Malcolm McAlpine in the best Archimedes-in-the-bath tradition when he was sitting in a dentist's chair in Helensburgh. He noticed that the dentist made the drill work by pressing a knob on the floor with his foot. On asking how the device worked, Malcolm was told that the knob operated a valve in a water pipe under the floor, causing a flow of high-pressure water to impinge on a Pelton wheel which provided the rotary motion for the drill. A water turbine! Malcolm asked Andrew Reid, his chief engineer, if a water turbine could be used to provide power for the air compressors. The engineer decided that this was feasible, and an Edinburgh turbine specialist was invited to supply suitable machinery with a compressor coupled to it.

To obtain water for the turbine a dam 7 ft high was built across Loch Dubh. A 21 in. steel pipe carried the water from the dam for 140 yd to the turbine which revolved at 900 r.p.m. The air produced was then conveyed to the workings by a system of cast iron or malleable iron screwed pipes. By the end of 1897 the turbine was working night and day and the air was powering rock drills over two miles of cuttings and tunnels. The engineer reported that the turbine was doing four times the amount of work of the steam compressor it replaced.

It was ironical that young Malcolm McAlpine should have been one of the few serious cases admitted to the hospital at Lochailort. He was superintending a blast in a rock cutting when a sudden explosion showered him with shrapnel-like fragments of rock. He fell to the ground seriously wounded. The doctor at the hospital found that the youth had a fractured pelvis, broken ribs and serious internal injuries caused by rock fragments penetrating his body. That afternoon a telegram was dispatched to his father in Glasgow telling him of his son's grave injuries and adding that he was not expected to live.

Robert McAlpine (senior) got in touch at once with Glasgow's most distinguished surgeon. Professor Sir William Macewen, who agreed to go to Lochailort. By that time the last West Highland train had long since left Glasgow, so the contractor ordered a special. When it reached Craigendoran with its two passengers it was found that the West Highland was closed from end to end and no apparent arrangement had been made to open it. The engine driver had been instructed not to proceed beyond Craigendoran without further orders. Robert McAlpine argued and pleaded with him and eventually, when the contractor said that he would take full responsibility for what happened, the driver set off. Tales have been told about the train's night-long journey. It is said that it covered the length of the West Highland without the benefit of a single tablet and with the driver and fireman manipulating point levers where necessary. What is certain is that the train reached Fort William about 5 a.m. The doctor and contractor roused a coachman, and after seven hours of jolting over the terrible road to the Isles, they reached Lochailort in the early afternoon.

By that time Malcolm was very low. With none of the refinements to which he was accustomed in his own operating theatre, Macewen performed a major operation. Then he sat by his patient for four days and nights. At length he decided that the only hope of saving Malcolm's life lay in getting him to Glasgow. And the transport of the sick man highlighted graphically the lack of communications that the railway was planned to alleviate. Malcolm could not be taken by road; the jolting would have killed him. There was nothing for it but to take him by stretcher to the still distant railhead. Professor Macewen trained eight railway navvies in the art of stretcher bearing and on the morning of the fifth day after the explosion the men set off bearing their injured employer over the rough country. At the end of 2 miles they came to the shore of Loch Eilt, where the stretcher was placed on a boat and towed 3 miles to the other end of the loch. Then followed a gruelling 4 miles overland to Glenfinnan where a halt was made for the night. A window had to be removed in the Glenfinnan hotel to allow the stretcher to be taken into the building.

The stretcher party set off next morning at first light. Two miles took them to the westernmost point reached by the railway, where an engine and wagon were waiting. A long chain coupling was provided between the engine and the vehicle. Navvies sat facing each other in two rows, one on the buffer beam of the engine, the other on the frame of the wagon, their legs touching and braced to take shocks during the slow, careful journey. At Locheilhead the stretcher was transferred to a steamer and taken down the loch to Banavie where a special was waiting to rush the patient to Glasgow. His navvies travelled with him and when the train reached the city they carried him on his stretcher through the streets to Professor Macewen's nursing home. Sir Malcolm McAlpine celebrated his 87th birthday on 19 June 1964.

### BORRODALE BURN

The Mallaig line bridges were built of concrete, most of them in standard spans of 50 ft. The most spectacular viaduct was the one at Glenfinnan which used twenty-one standard spans. There was another at Arnabol Glen, and at Loch nan Uamh there was a viaduct of eight 50 ft arches. A 90 ft span was required to take the line across the River Morar almost under the Falls of Morar. At Borrodale Burn 'Concrete Bob' faced his biggest challenge. The defile in which the burn ran was wide, and the original intention was to put piers in the stream and build a series of standard arches. The owner agreed to this provided that McAlpine clad the piers in granite. Since that was a highly expensive procedure the contractor decided to cross the gap in a single span. Never before had a mass concrete span of such dimensions been built.

Borrodale Bridge has a clear span of 127 ft 6 in. and two side spans of 20 ft each. It is 86 ft high and has a rise of 22½ ft. It created world-wide attention. The American *Engineering News* featured the bridge in an article in 1899. In 1909 an American civil engineer, H. Gratton Tyrell, published a table putting Borrodale Bridge in its proper perspective. The table, which listed major mass concrete bridges built between 1893 and 1909, showed that in the five years before Borrodale only three concrete bridges had been built, all of them road bridges and all the design of the German

RAILWAY PIERS

(33) *Banavie Pier station in 1935. The embankment of the Caledonian Canal is behind the station. The station itself was not renamed. Notice the original West Highland name board*

(34) *Fort Augustus Pier station when in use about 1905*

STATION SCENES

(35) *Rolling stock of the 'big four' companies at Arisaig in 1938. The goods train has been divided to make a passage for the sheep*

(36) *Panorama at Mallaig, 24 May 1952. The engines, left to right, are 'Loch Laidon', 'Loch Eil', 'Loch Rannoch' and 'Loch Sheil'. Steam crane in the centre*

engineer Leibrand. In the eleven years following the building of Borrodale fifty-two concrete bridges were built.

Labour troubles and bad weather continued to hinder progress. In the engineer's report to shareholders on 4 July 1899 it was stated, 'The Contractor has not made good progress owing to the difficulty of getting men.' By January 1900, 33 miles of track had been laid and of the remaining 7 miles 6 were formed ready for the rails. But that same month the engineer again reported: 'We regret to state that in spite of all our efforts there is not a sufficient force of men on the works to insure the completion of the line in time for next summer's traffic.' The last winter was the worst of all for weather. In December 1900 the rainfall in the district was 29 in. above normal. With each delay the radicals began sniping in Parliament. The President of the Board of Trade was frequently under fire about progress on the line, or lack of it. But even in the middle of 1900 he was able to take refuge in the fact that the time limit for completion was still two years away.

In all McAlpine had to excavate 100 cuttings. In complete contrast to the rock work, he had to use the Rannoch Moor floating technique to get the line across bog at Keppoch Moss, north of Arisaig. Mallaig harbour was also his responsibility, the harbour works being constructed of concrete blocks. Stations were built at Banavie, Corpach, Locheilside, Glenfinnan, Lochailort, Morar, and Arisaig, and there was a private station—Beasdale—for Arisaig House between Lochailort and Arisaig. The station platforms and buildings were of concrete. Banavie, Corpach, Locheilside and Morar had one platform only and no loops. In the double platform stations the station buildings were on the down side only, the up side being provided with a small wooden shelter. In the interests of economy sleeper crossings were provided at the platform ends instead of the conventional overbridge. The signalling was by the Railway Signal Company, which also provided wooden signal boxes of its own design.

Mallaig station alone had an island platform. The station was built on a shelf of rock jutting out into the water, and a stout stone wall was erected on the seaward side to protect the platforms from the gales that would at times sweep in from the western seas. The point where the Mallaig railway left the Banavie branch was named Banavie Junction, and the original Banavie Junction was re-named Mallaig Junction. This had the effect of shortening the Banavie branch to three-quarters of a mile. The original Banavie station became Banavie Pier: the name was changed in the timetables and official documents, but not on the station itself. It still exhibited its original West Highland name-board 'Banavie' forty years after a new station of the same name had been provided less than 1 mile away.

VICTORY AT LAST

When the steamer *Clydesdale* cleared Stornoway harbour just after 11 o'clock on the night of 31 March 1901, she had on board the first passengers ever booked through from Lewis to Glasgow and Edinburgh by the new iron road to the isles. At daybreak when the vessel entered the brand-new harbour at Mallaig the passengers crossed to the waiting train where they were joined by people just in from Portree in the *Lovedale*. At 7.20 a.m. the first ever up train on the Mallaig Extension departed for the south. Some two hours later it crossed the first down train, the 5.55 a.m. from Glasgow bringing passengers for their first experience of the new railway.

The train from the south had stopped only at Arrochar and Tarbet, Crianlarich and Spean Bridge, and arrived at Fort William at 9.50, where a fresh engine was attached at what had been its rear. At 10 a.m. the train pulled out to Mallaig Junction, rumbled over the Lochy Viaduct and at the new Banavie Junction ran on to the metals of the Mallaig Extension. As the train worked its way round the elbow bend of Loch Linnhe and Loch Eil, and crossed the Caledonian Canal on a swing bridge pivoted on one bank to leave the whole channel clear for shipping, the passengers had excellent views of Ben Nevis towering in all its brute mass above Fort William. A stop at Corpach was followed by a lively sprint along the shore of Loch Eil on track unaccustomedly straight and level for the West Highlands.

But at the end of Loch Eil mountains closed in on the railway, and the engine's exhaust became more and more laboured as the track pushed its way up a narrow glen and into the heart of some of the most glorious scenery in the world. Within ten minutes the train burst out of the confines of the pass into the natural amphi-theatre at the head of Loch Sheil, encircled by mountains except where the long tongue of Loch Sheil pushed its way in from the west. The railway entered dramatically from the right and crossed the arena on a gracefully curving and dazzling white viaduct of twenty-one arches. Down below by the lochside the passengers could see the lighthouse-like monument that marked the spot where Prince Charlie unfurled his standard in 1745.

---

(G) *The attractive canopy at Mallaig station has been demolished, leaving a stark plat-form. Here, before such depredations, Class 27 D5356 waits to leave with a Glasgow train on 6 April 1971*

Glenfinnan Viaduct curves in a crescent of 12 chains radius for 1,248 ft across the Finnan Valley. The track is supported on slender white pillars 100 ft above the ground, each pair being surmounted by a semi-circular arch with a span of 50 ft. The concrete that went into the making of the viaduct (see page 96) had as one of its constituents crushed rock from the cutting through which the railway passed to enter the valley. It is a beautiful structure, but it is best seen from high up in the surrounding mountains. Then it looks like a Roman aqueduct in a remarkable state of preservation. The Scottish author, J. J. Bell, a staunch friend of the West Highland Railway, described the viaduct as 'a thing so delicate that the fairies might have built it'.

In Glenfinnan they tell a story (perhaps apocryphal) about an incident at the building of Glenfinnan Viaduct. Some of the vertical pillars had hollow interiors, and before the superstructure supporting the rails was built the tops of the columns were open to the sky. It is said that a horse which was being led with a cart over planking resting temporarily across the top of a column slipped into the interior; animal and cart plunged 100 ft down the hollow shaft. Because of the difficulty of removing the carcase the remains were buried inside the pillar.

A brief halt at Glenfinnan station and the train was off again through a narrow wooded glen that took it to the shores of Loch Eilt. The railway began high above the loch and dropped rapidly on a series of reverse curves until the train was running at water level.

The Mallaig Railway is never far from water, salt or fresh. From Loch Eilt it follows the river Ailort to the point where it meets Loch Ailort. Then it crosses the wooded peninsula of Ardnish, past little Loch Dubh and across Glen Mamie on a viaduct to emerge at Loch nan Uamh—the Loch of the Caves. It is when the line meets the Atlantic at Loch nan Uamh that the climax of the journey is reached. In high summer a mass of luxuriant growth sweeps down the hillsides to the edges of the sea. The trees are almost tropical in their brilliance. Where the belt of lush green meets the contour of the many bays is a fringe of rock covered with bright orange seaweed, and beyond that an expanse of blue water ribbed with green. There is a hint of the South Seas about the scene. The islands sparkling out on the polished surface of the ocean might well be Pacific islands; Eigg with its unreal, block-shaped Sgur has a volcanic look about it. Further up the coast at Arisaig palms flourish and there is a garden full of sub-tropical plants.

It is hard to believe that the wilderness of Rannoch is on the

(H) *LMS Class 5 No 5407 leaves Fort William with the SLOA West Highlander railtour for Mallaig on Sunday 27 May 1984, the first public steam working over the West Highland for twenty-two years*

**0419233**

same railway line three hours away. The Gulf Stream, bringing its warmth direct to the west-coast bays, confers many benefits on the Mallaig Extension. There are winters when the villages on the Mallaig line have dawn-to-dusk sunshine for days on end. It is not uncommon for the morning up train to begin its journey in mellow warmth and amid fields sprouting spring flowers and end it six hours later in a city still firmly in the grip of winter.

The first down train on that April opening morning made its way to Lochailort and Arisaig and then on to Morar of the silver sand. The train rattled along rocky galleries and plunged through short tunnels emerging in the intervals into a world ablaze with colour. Each twist of the line revealed enchanting new vistas. That stretch between Lochailort and Arisaig accounted for a disproportionate share of the half-million pounds that went into the making of the Mallaig Extension. In 8¼ miles there were no fewer than nine tunnels. From Morar the train slipped round the toothed coast with the mountains of Skye looming up ahead, to stop at 11.45 in Mallaig station. The *Clydesdale* and the *Lovedale* were waiting to receive their passengers. By 4.30 that afternoon the *Lovedale's* were disembarking at Portree, having taken 10 hours 35 minutes to travel from Glasgow to the capital of Skye. Travellers who had come all the way from London, leaving King's Cross at 8.15 the previous night, were landed at Stornoway at 8 p.m.—not quite a round of the clock.

In the first summer timetable Mallaig was given through-carriage and sleeping-carriage services with King's Cross, but these were not continued in subsequent years. Fort William became the terminus of the sleeping cars. An early innovation was a *weekend* return fare from Mallaig to London, 60s 6d for the 1,202 miles. This compared with the tourist return of 70s 6d and the ordinary return of 83s 8d. The ordinary return fare from Mallaig to Glasgow was 23s 7d, but mindful of its duty to the fishing community, the company issued a special fisherman's ticket at 18s 6d.

An immediate result of the opening of the Mallaig Extension was that it put Fort William and its amenities within easy reach of the people living in the 30 mile stretch of country between Locheilside and Mallaig. Before the railway came the district's transport consisted of one coach, which left Arisaig for Fort William on Tuesdays, Thursdays and Saturdays and returned on Mondays, Wednesdays and Fridays. The journey from Arisaig to Fort William took 7½ hours, and the single fare was 10s plus 1s driver's fee. The potential traveller had now a choice of from two to four trains a day (according to the time of the year); the journey time was under 90 minutes and the fare a fraction of the cost by coach.

*Fish* had been the magic word in all the long arguments leading up to the completion of the Mallaig Railway. Fish became and remained a staple item of West Highland freight, and for many years the red North British fish vans at the tail of a passenger train were a familiar sight on the line. But the traffic never attained the volume that the promoters had expected, and the east coast's supremacy was never seriously challenged. The best prices for prime fish in top condition were obtainable at Billingsgate and the fish dealers aimed at getting their fish shipped to London with all speed. To get fish caught on Friday night and Saturday to the London market for Monday morning meant that it had to be sent over the West Highland Railway on Sunday. What southern economists failed to understand was that Sunday working was completely unacceptable to the Highlanders, railwaymen and civil population alike. So powerful was religious feeling in these areas that the people, notwithstanding their desire for a railway, would have organized a boycott of the system if the company had transgressed their religious code. So weekend fish had to wait until Monday.

Militant Sabbatarianism was one hazard of railway operating in the Highlands that was not mentioned in the various prospectuses. What happened at Strome Ferry on Sunday 3 July 1882 is part of the story of the Highland Railway, but it is worth telling here if only because it gave a pointer to any railway company that attempted to handle the fish traffic of the district. On the last Sunday in May 1882 a fish train was loaded up at Strome Ferry on the Dingwall & Skye line and dispatched to London. When the fact became known there was rage and consternation in the area. On the following Sunday the railway company, aware of the popular feeling, arranged somewhat clandestinely to load and dispatch a train from Strome Ferry in the early hours of the morning. About 1 a.m. two vessels, the *Harold* and the *Locheil*, with 6,700 boxes of fish between them, slipped up Loch Carron and berthed at the railway pier. What happened next was described in the following day's *Glasgow Herald*.

> At that moment a body of about fifty natives armed with clubs and bludgeons presented themselves on the quay and stated they would not allow the unloading of the vessels to go on. It was the Lord's Day and they would not permit such a desecration of the Sabbath for fear of a judgement from heaven. The crowd forcibly ejected a man in

charge of the steamers and, on the crews of the steamers and the railway officials persisting in unloading the fish, threatened them with personal violence. A fight ensued and those belonging to the steamers and the railway company were completely overpowered and compelled to give up hope of unloading the vessels.

Later that morning, when Highland Railway headquarters in Inverness were informed by telegraph of the situation at Strome Ferry, a special train was sent out, stopping at Dingwall on the way to pick up six policemen. They found Strome station and pier invested by some 150 angry and determined men. The police charged the crowd six times and were beaten back to stand cowed and impotent outside the station door. The Highland Railway then requested the military authorities for 'a detachment of bayonets' but the request was refused. Strome stayed in rebel hands until someone shouted 'Twelve o'clock', whereupon the demonstrators disappeared into the darkness. The fish, no longer fresh, left for London.

On the following Sunday the company ran three fish specials out of Strome while 300 policemen (sixty of them brought specially from Glasgow) held the rebels in check. At Fort George a troop train stood ready to rush the local garrison of Cameron Highlanders, reinforced by Gordon Highlanders brought in from Edinburgh the previous day, to the trouble spot. The lesson of the episode was plain to see. Fish, the mainstay of the economy of all the West Highland lines, could not be carried on these lines on a Sunday with impunity.

### THE £ S D OF THE MALLAIG LINE

The railway brought immediate tangible benefits to the inhabitants of the district. There was a substantial drop in the prices of the necessities of life. Coal imported on the railway was cheaper than local peat, and coal supplanted peat as the almost universal domestic fuel. The tourist trade was good in that first year. There was a large-scale international exhibition in Glasgow in 1901, and some of the visitors made their way to the newly opened northwest. One visitor in 1902 was the general manager of the SE & CR and he has left this comment:

> I visited Fort William, Banavie and Mallaig. I found between these stations a very sparse population, and for some years to come there is very little chance of an increase in receipts. The company will have to look to the summer and excursion traffic which at the most can only last about three months. The beauties of the district seem to be

well advertised, and the traffic will no doubt be much augmented when the splendid scenery through which the line passes becomes better known.

Eleven years later Lt-Col E. Druitt, after making the annual inspection of the line on behalf of the Government which the West Highland Railway (Guarantee) Bill required, reported as follows:

> The work in formations, banks, cuttings and tunnels is standing well, and shows no signs of weakness. The permanent way is in good order. Station buildings and passenger accommodation are well maintained. Generally speaking the maintenance and upkeep during the past twelve months have been very satisfactory. The North British Company continue to advertise the attractions of the railway with a view to developing the tourist traffic and endeavour by every reasonable means to promote the earning power of the line.

In spite of the uproar caused by the opponents of the Guarantee bill the Treasury was never called on to pay more than £4,000 under the terms of the guarantee in any one year between 1901 and 1914. The following table sets out the profit and loss account on the railway year by year, and shows the amounts paid by the Treasury.

| Year | Receipts | | | Expenses | | | Loss | | | Paid by Treasury under guarantee | | |
|---|---|---|---|---|---|---|---|---|---|---|---|---|
| | £ | s. | d. | £ | s. | d. | £ | s. | d. | £ | s. | d. |
| 1901-2 | 8,525 | 1 | 7 | 19,385 | 9 | 8 | 10,833 | 8 | 1 | 3,789 | 19 | 9 |
| 1902-3 | 8,465 | 7 | 7 | 14,789 | 11 | 8 | 6,324 | 4 | 1 | 3,790 | 9 | 10 |
| 1903-4 | 8,856 | 13 | 8 | 15,606 | 17 | 3 | 6,750 | 3 | 7 | 3,594 | 6 | 10 |
| 1904-5 | 9,233 | 10 | 5 | 15,518 | 18 | 9 | 6,285 | 8 | 4 | 2,537 | 19 | 11 |
| 1905-6 | 9,126 | 13 | 1 | 15,113 | 5 | 0 | 5,986 | 11 | 11 | 3,228 | 18 | 11 |
| 1906-7 | 9,567 | 11 | 0 | 15,227 | 6 | 3 | 5,659 | 15 | 3 | 3,010 | 8 | 11 |
| 1907-8 | 9,602 | 6 | 10 | 15,477 | 15 | 3 | 5,874 | 8 | 5 | 3,033 | 10 | 7 |
| 1908-9 | 10,360 | 2 | 0 | 13,954 | 11 | 7 | 3,594 | 9 | 7 | 2,696 | 10 | 3 |
| 1909-10 | 9,983 | 7 | 9 | 13,195 | 10 | 7 | 3,212 | 2 | 10 | 2,852 | 9 | 9 |
| 1910-11 | 10,892 | 9 | 0 | 15,202 | 4 | 7 | 4,319 | 15 | 7 | 3,431 | 19 | 4 |
| 1911-12 | 11,044 | 3 | 8 | 13,061 | 15 | 8 | 2,017 | 12 | 0 | 2,325 | 6 | 8 |
| 1912-13 | 12,126 | 5 | 6 | 16,163 | 13 | 9 | 4,036 | 8 | 3 | 1,780 | 7 | 10 |
| 1913-14 | 9,691 | 1 | 4 | 17,469 | 3 | 8 | 7,778 | 2 | 4 | 1,600 | 11 | 4 |

During the period, the railway showed a trading loss of £72,672 10s 3d. The contribution made by the Treasury was £36,672 19s 11d. The following tables show an analysis of the receipts and expenses in two consecutive years.

*Receipts from the Banavie Jc—Mallaig Sec*

|  | 1912-13 |  |  | 1913-14 |  |  |
|---|---|---|---|---|---|---|
| Passengers | £5,644 | 8 | 5 | £3,175 | 3 | 2 |
| Parcels | £3,164 | 9 | 5 | £2,842 | 12 | 2 |
| Goods and Minerals | £2,753 | 8 | 5 | £3,180 | 2 | 5 |
| Livestock | £259 | 11 | 9 | £211 | 9 | 4 |
| Mails | £160 | 0 | 0 | £160 | 0 | 0 |
| Parcel post | £137 | 17 | 2 | £116 | 3 | 5 |
| News contract | £6 | 11 | 4 | £6 | 11 | 4 |

*Expenses*

|  | 1912-13 |  |  | 1913-14 |  |  |
|---|---|---|---|---|---|---|
| Loco. dept | £5,281 | 1 | 0 | £5,904 | 13 | 3 |
| Maintenance | £7,942 | 19 | 2 | £8,472 | 9 | 2 |
| Traffic | £2,939 | 13 | 7 | £3,089 | 11 | 3 |

In 1902 the North British Railway (General Powers) Act abolished all West Highland railway debenture and other stock guaranteed by the North British, and it was replaced with 3 per cent North British debentures. The West Highland thus became a railway without shareholders. Then the North British Railway Confirmation Act of 1908 gave the North British authority to absorb the entire West Highland undertaking. On 31 December 1908 the 142 miles of track comprising the original West Highland line, the Mallaig Extension and the Banavie branch passed to the ownership of the North British Railway. The system represented an investment of £2,370,000.

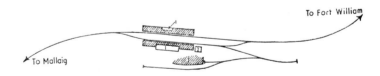

Glenfinnan station

1. station buildings
   On all Mallaig Extension stations with two platforms, the main buildings were on the down side, the up platform having only a hut
2. signal box
3. loading bank—end-on only to short siding
   No passenger footbridges; sleeper crossings only, at platform ends

# CHAPTER 7

# The Battle for Inverness

### THE REMARKABLE VALLEY

'Strange as it may seem to you this day,' prophesied Conneach Odhar, the Brahan Seer, early in the seventeenth century, 'the time will come, and it is not far off, when full-rigged ships will be sailing eastwards and westward by Muirtown and Tomnahurich.'

The Seer was saying that sea-going vessels would be crossing the dry mainland of Scotland from Fort William to Inverness. The country between the two towns seemed to have been made by nature for a canal. It was as if the Creator had rolled back the mountains, as Moses had rolled back the Red Sea, to form a 60-mile valley stretching diagonally across the country from sea to sea. Telford, when he came to look at it, frequently wrote in his notes the phrase, 'this remarkable valley'. Over the years its inviting geographical features lured transport men to it. But it was to become a valley of lost transport causes, a glen of weeping for the people who set their hearts and fortunes on its conquest.

The Caledonian Canal was begun in 1804 and it was then designed to take the largest ocean-going ships. There was a heavy timber traffic in those days from the Baltic to Liverpool, and the timber ships were sometimes wrecked or delayed for weeks on end by contrary winds as they rounded the storm-swept north of Scotland—even if they escaped being harassed and destroyed by the French fleet. The Caledonian Canal was to provide a short, safe and easy passage for the Baltic timber boats as well as for traffic between Britain's east and west coasts.

Telford said he would make the canal in seven years for £350,000. But eighteen years passed before a partially completed channel was opened for traffic and nearly forty years before the canal was fully completed, and it had absorbed a million of money. By that time, steam, unknown when the canal was begun, was triumphant on land and sea. Anyway, the much bigger sea-going ships of 1843 could not even enter the canal conceived four decades earlier. Baltic timber was now taxed 300 per cent and Britain was importing timber from Canada. Above all, Waterloo had been fought and won and the French were no longer a menace on the seas. What had been planned as a great national highway had become a secondary shipping channel of use only to fishing vessels and small coasters. The Caledonian Canal was obsolete before it was opened.

Two years after the canal came into full operation the railway engineers were in the Great Glen seeking a route to Inverness. They might have got it and been first into Inverness from the south had the financial crash of 1845 not put paid to their schemes. In 1882 the Glasgow & North Western Railway engineers came to the remarkable valley. But by then the Highland Railway was established in Inverness and Highland policy was to resist every attack on its citadel. As we have seen in an earlier chapter, it easily defeated the North Western's attempt to reach Inverness. Ever after the Highland, realizing how vulnerable it was to attack up the Great Glen, was specially vigilant when any rival railway showed interest in the route. It had been suspicious when the West Highland Railway was promoted, and its suspicions, despite protestations of innocence, were justified. *Inverness* was the name engraved on the North British chairman's heart.

### TEMPORARY TRUCE

The first West Highland—North British sortie into the Great Glen took place in 1893, when the Edinburgh-based consortium sought to take a line from Fort William to the Highland capital. The Highland Railway's immediate answer was a proposed line of its own from Inverness to Fort William.

It is possible that these were little more than claim-staking exercises. Neither side could have wanted to embark on a Great Glen railway, for both were heavily committed elsewhere. The North British had its West Highland line still to finish and the Mallaig Extension was in prospect. The Highland was in the process of building its very costly direct line from Aviemore to Inverness *via* Carr Bridge, and further developments were maturing in the Far North. The Aviemore—Inverness line was a by-product of the G & NW attempt to get to Inverness ten years earlier. The strongest argument for a West Highland route to Inverness was that it was shorter than the existing Highland route. By building the Aviemore cut-off the Highland was shortening its route and at the same time robbing future Great Glen schemes of what had been their main advantage.

Nothing came of the 1893 plans, but as soon as the West Highland Railway was open in 1894 the Highland and West Highland again produced rival schemes. The Highland looked for widespread local support in its defence against attack from the south. The railway considered itself a truly *Highland* railway, with its headquarters in Inverness, and with a duke and a brace each of marquesses, barons and baronets as well as local landowners on its board. The Highland Railway considered that the Highlanders owed it a debt of gratitude for having given them a railway, even if they had to pay the highest permitted fares for the privilege of using it. That this view was not universally accepted was made plain by Highlanders who welcomed the possibility of another company coming to Inverness.

Contemporary correspondence in the press—much of it anonymous—painted the Highlands as a feudal domain dominated by the big landowners, some of them directors of the Highland line. 'Against the Highland Railway scheme from Inverness to Spean we cannot organize opposition here like the people of the South,' lamented *Sutherlandshire* in the *Glasgow Herald*.

> Our landlord is sure to be a director, and we must keep quiet or suffer. We depend on the free south in its own interest and ours to see that the Highland Railway Company do not command every avenue to the Highlands. If the Highland Railway Company gain their ends the progress of the North and South will be retarded for a century.

This correspondent thought that the lot of the Highlanders would be easier if the West Highland pushed on not only to Inverness but into Highland Railway preserves in the Far North. 'Let there be a junction ten miles or so south of Inverness and from there let the railway extend northwards to the Muir of Ord (for the markets) and on in a straight line to Bonar Bridge and over the Oykel to Dornoch.'

Another correspondent had faith in neither the North British nor the Highland. He wrote:

> I have a strong sympathy with the people of Inverness who are of the opinion that it would be an advantage to the whole district if another company was to come in and provide competition. The history of the Highland Company has been that of close conservation to what might be termed aristocratic ideas of management. They have not catered in any popular sense for the million.

Of the North British he added, 'The policy that guides it gives with a most grudging hand any benefits the public obtain. It does not seem to me desirable that the future extension of the railway enterprise in the Highlands should be kept to either of these two companies.' This correspondent saw the solution to the north's transport problems in a *Caledonian* invasion of the Highlands. The Caledonian, he said, should build a grand scenic line from Oban round the coast by Ballachulish to Fort William and on through the Great Glen to Inverness.

The 1894 phase of the struggle for the Great Glen was short-lived. It ended when in December, William Whitelaw, chairman of the Highland Railway, received a letter from Lord Tweeddale, his opposite number on the North British, suggesting that the parties concerned should meet 'in an amicable spirit' to discuss their problems. Only eight members of the Highland board attended the Highland Railway meeting at which the North British letter was discussed, and the diehards wanted to continue the fight. But reason prevailed and representatives of the Highland, West Highland and North British met in Edinburgh in February 1895. As a result, both sides withdrew their current bills from Parliament, and undertook not to promote railways in the Great Glen during the next ten years. The Caledonian and the Callander & Oban entered into the spirit of the thing and in the same month withdrew a bill by which they had hoped to reach the southern end of the Great Glen from Oban.

BURTON'S FOLLY

The peace of the Great Glen was shattered in 1896 by the appearance of a private company calling itself the Invergarry & Fort Augustus Railway, which proposed to build a railway linking Spean Bridge with Fort Augustus. This was a perfectly genuine local line with no association financially or otherwise with the two big contenders for power in the glen. It was to some extent a one-man show; the principal instigator and chairman was Lord Burton, and he put up more than half the capital. His supporters were wellmeaning but foolhardy local patriots (and their friends in the south) who were devoted to the idea of giving their district a railway.

The Invergarry & Fort Augustus was an incredibly ill-conceived venture, the classic example of the railway that should not have been built. The line, 24 miles long, was to run from Spean Bridge, where there was nothing but a bridge and a few cottages, to Fort Augustus, which boasted a Benedictine monastery, a handful of houses, and a pier on the Caledonian Canal. The intervening country was devoid of industry and supported only a few hundred people. Of Fort Augustus itself a local guide book said: 'It may not be without interest to note that it is exactly in the centre of the deer forest country and that, if the very fertile land east of Inverness be excluded, 99 per cent of the country within 50 miles is deer forest and only 1 per cent arable.' And that was the country through which the Invergarry & Fort Augustus hoped to build an expensive railway—and make it pay.

Although the Invergarry & Fort Augustus was purely a local promotion, the very fact that it had a physical connection with the West Highland at Spean Bridge was enough to raise the Highland Railway hackles. All the West Highland had to do was to acquire running powers over the Invergarry & Fort Augustus to Fort Augustus and it was halfway up the glen and within 30 miles of Inverness. The Highland Railway attacked the Fort Augustus bill vehemently, and the North British and West Highland, bound as they were by the treaty of the previous year to oppose any railway in the Great Glen, also fought; but less vehemently.

The usual dreary, protracted Parliamentary battle ended on 14 August 1896 with victory for the Invergarry & Fort Augustus. The intrepid Lord Burton was free to build his railway. Commenting on the new situation in the Great Glen, a financial journal said:

> . . . the Highland Company forgot that independent promoters might do what the North British, *père et fils* had promised not to do, and although the West Highland and its parent in obedience to treaty arrangements, opposed the Fort Augustus project, their grief at the success must have been a good deal less poignant than that of the Highland.

Formans & McCall were the engineers of the Invergarry & Fort Augustus and James Young of Glasgow was the contractor. The line was to have intermediate stations at Aberchalder, Invergarry and Gairlochy. Not content with reaching Fort Augustus village, the promoters were determined to set up a port of their own on the Caledonian Canal, itself by now partly moribund. So they devoted a large slice of their capital to taking the line three-quarters of a mile beyond the village on a costly extension involving the construction of a swing bridge over the canal and a substantial viaduct over the Oich, as well as pier and station buildings on Loch Ness. At other parts of the system rock cuttings were required, there was one tunnel through hard rock, and there were considerable viaducts spanning the Spean and the Gloy.

THE LAST BATTLE

The advent of the Invergarry & Fort Augustus was the signal for both the North British and the Highland to jettison their treaty obligations. By December 1896 both companies re-entered the field with schemes to link Fort Augustus with Inverness, and they were joined by the Invergarry & Fort Augustus which produced a scheme of its own. The battle was resumed with renewed fury. The contestants poured out money in survey fees, the great trek of witnesses to London was repeated, and some twenty QCs and many lesser legal lights were engaged to represent the respective parties. Mr Pope, who had performed so satisfactorily on behalf of the Highland in the G & NW affair a decade before, was retained again by the Highland. The Highland Railway (Inverness & Fort Augustus Railway) Bill, the Invergarry & Fort Augustus (Inverness Extension) Bill and the North British and West Highland Railway Companies Bill were presented in Parliament on the same day. It was the only time in Parliamentary history that three railway bills all covering the same ground were read on the same day.

The Highland Railway went to London on the defensive; it had little enthusiasm for the line it was promoting. The Great Glen crisis could not have come at a worse time, for the Highland board were beset with troubles. There was a serious domestic situation. For several years the Highland, judged from the standpoint of the dividends it paid, was prosperous, but an inquiry showed that dividends were being paid out of capital, and not out of earnings. When the company was forced into adopting more orthodox bookkeeping methods, its true state of health was revealed. Between 1894 and 1897 the Highland Railway stock fell from 115 to 82½. On top of that the assault up the Great Glen coincided with an attack from the east: the Great North of Scotland Railway chose that moment to make its fifth attempt to obtain running powers into Inverness from its outpost at Elgin. It was a time of travail for the Highland.

Mr Samuel Hoare presided over the committee that considered the three bills. The examination and cross-examination of witnesses went on day after day throughout the spring and early summer of 1897. Mounting legal fees drained away money none of the contestants—least of all the little Invergarry & Fort Augustus—could afford; and there was nothing to show for it. The North British spent £13,449—the equal of ¼ per cent of the dividend—in its efforts to thwart the Highland's attempt 'to occupy the district from Fort Augustus to Inverness in a manner prejudicial to the interests of the company'. Lord Tweeddale considered the money well spent.

Inverness Town Council by a vote of 15 to 3 decided to petition both Houses of Parliament to sanction the Invergarry & Fort Augustus bill. While admitting that it was useful to have the Highland Railway headquarters in Inverness, the business men on the Council thought that they did not get a square deal from that company. Also, the Invergarry & Fort Augustus scheme undertook to run a line to Inverness harbour clearing away some old slum property in the process. Wick Chamber of Commerce, too, opposed the Highland bill. 'We have to pay smartly for whatever benefits we have received from the company,' said their spokesman. 'Until the Highland company has opposition they will extract from their customers pounds instead of pence.'

In the end the Highland won, but it was refused running powers over the Invergarry & Fort Augustus. The bill then went to the House of Lords for consideration by Lord Brougham's committee. The domestic upheaval in the Highland headquarters had produced a new general manager, Charles Steele, and he went to London to plead for the bill in the Lords. Steele made the mistake of threatening the committee:

> If we are not authorised to make the line from Inverness to Fort Augustus, or if it is authorised with concessions to other companies, the Highland Company will not be able to consider any of the contemplated lines north of Inverness which are the only lines that could develop the industries in the North.

Lord Brougham threw out the bill. If the impoverished litigants went back to the Great Glen wringing their hands, they left the London lawyers rubbing *their* hands.

### FRUSTRATION

Now the Invergarry & Fort Augustus Railway proprietors were left in peace to squander their money on their pathetic little railway. They started off boldly on 2 February 1897 with the ceremonial digging of *two* first sods—one at each end of the line. (They had to get Lord Lovat's permission to enter the land where the Fort Augustus sod was cut.) Although the line as planned was single throughout, the optimistic proprietors had bought enough land for double track.

George Malcolm, who had been a co-founder with Mr Boyd of the West Highland, had given his professional services in getting the Invergarry bill through Parliament. When he presented his account amounting to £366 10s 3d the generous proprietors airily wrote a cheque for the nice round figure of £500 and dispatched it to their benefactor. The chief constable of Inverness informed the Invergarry that he had appointed two extra policemen to the district owing to the influx of the railway navvies, and enclosed an account for £21 11s 6d, being the cost of pay and uniform for the two constables. The railway paid up without demur, but refused to pay an account for £12 5s for two 'cabin cells' erected at Fort Augustus to receive recalcitrant navvies.

The line slowly took shape. It started at the west end of Spean Bridge station, curved through a wood and struck north-west to the bank of the Spean, here a wide river flowing in a deep ravine. The passage of the gorge demanded four lattice spans, one of 120 ft, one of 50 ft and two of 60 ft, carried on piers rising 76 ft from the river. Once across the Spean the line passed by Gairlochy through undulating wooded country for 4 miles to the river Gloy, and crossed this on a three-span lattice girder bridge of two 50 ft and one 100 ft spans. The track then climbed gently through a thick forest of pine and fir to emerge on moorland leading to the summit of 370 ft at Letterfinlay. It then dropped down into the Great Glen and ran along the hillside parallel to but above the chain-lochs, Lochy and Oich and the connecting length of Caledonian Canal, to Invergarry village. Then it passed through the 67 yd Oich tunnel, and crossed the four-span Calder Burn viaduct to reach Aberchalder. The final stretch took the track across a patch of moorland and along the shore of Loch Uanagan to Fort Augustus town station, then across the canal and the Oich to the pier station on Loch Ness.

The I & FA spent lavishly and built on a grand scale. The first and last miles absorbed between them one-third of the railway's capital. The tops of the piers of the Oich viaduct were elaborately castellated and the stonework was embellished with a design involving a cross—expensive frills which a wealthier line would have dispensed with. Costly retaining walls were required where the line clung to the hillside above Loch Lochy, one being 338 ft long and from 5 to 25¼ ft high. While it was still being built a massive landslide brought tons of rock, soil and trees down on to the newly-formed permanent way, completely obliterating it.

The hamlet of Gairlochy was provided with facilities that would not have disgraced a small town : in addition to the station there

(37) *Two Glens on a Glasgow train at Fort William about* 1914

(38) *Glens among the mountains in* LNE *days*

(39) *Two Glens prepare to leave Ardlui on a Glasgow —Mallaig train in May* 1959

FORT WILLIAM

(40) K1 *No. 62034 about to leave Fort William for Glasgow, Queen Street,*
24 *May* 1952

(41) *Steam in the shadow of Ben Nevis.* 'Loch Arkaig', 'Loch Treig', 'Glen
Spean' *and* 'Glen Gloy' *at Fort William shed,* 12 *June* 1936

were four lines of sidings and loading banks for goods and cattle.

Invergarry was given an island platform in the Swiss style favoured by the West Highland. A large verandah was provided on the down side and a private waiting room was installed for the use of the occupants of nearby Invergarry House. Generous goods and cattle sidings waited for traffic that was never to materialize; at Letterfinlay summit an unnecessary passing place and signalbox were built and never staffed. Some years later the house at Letterfinlay was listed in an inventory of I & FA property as 'intended for signalman'. Fort Augustus was given two terminal platforms, and a through platform from which the line continued to the pier station.

The North British extended Spean Bridge station and put in a dock platform at the west end for use of the I & FA trains. It also laid the double junction at Spean Bridge at a cost of £303 0s 5d to the Invergarry company. The junction signalling instruments were at first installed in the I & FA box at the junction, but the inspecting officer of the Board of Trade insisted on their removal to the North British booking office in Spean Bridge station. The line was equipped with Webb & Thomson staff with the following block sections:

| | | |
|---|---|---|
| Spean Bridge—Gairlochy | 2 m. | 52 ch. |
| Gairlochy—Invergarry | 12 m. | 24 ch. |
| Invergarry—Fort Augustus | 8 m. | 7 ch. |

The Fort Augustus pier branch was worked by a one-engine-in-steam key controlled by Fort Augustus box. Aberchalder, between Invergarry and Fort Augustus, was novel in being a passing place without signals. All approaching trains had to stop and the driver operated the points by inserting a key token in a one-lever ground frame.

By April 1898 the directors felt confident enough to conduct the press over the works. The man from the *Dundee Advertiser* admired the straight stretches at the eastern end of the line and expressed the opinion that they would 'greatly facilitate matters when the time comes for running at express speed'. In August 1899 the line was inspected by the directors. The North British provided them with a saloon on which they were taken 6 miles from Spean Bridge to the river Gloy. The Gloy viaduct was not complete so the visitors had to de-train and make their own way across the river. On the far side they joined a wagon which the contractors had fitted out with seats, and the contractors' engine took the passengers on to Loch Oich tunnel. Since the tunnel also was unfinished, they had to walk through to where another improvized passenger train was waiting to take them on to Fort Augustus.

It is an odd thing, but on the day before the directors inspected

H

the bits and pieces of their line, it was privately inspected by an officer of the Caledonian Railway and that company's consulting engineer. Nothing more was ever heard of that strange visitation. But what a fire there would have been in the heather if the Caledonian had come to the Great Glen.

The I & FA shareholders were paying for their shares by instalments as the line was built, the company calling for cash as it was required to meet current expenses. A financial crisis broke when certain shareholders refused to answer a periodic call; two prominent former supporters of the scheme, each with £5,000 in partly paid-up shares, decided to cut their losses, and refused the request for further instalments. They forfeited their holdings. Charles Forman had demonstrated his faith in the line by agreeing to take up £20,000 of I & FA stock. But when in 1898 he was called on for a cash payment of £4,000, he asked the company to place that sum against the amount owing to his firm for professional services. Another shareholder who was also a creditor of the I & FA told the secretary to waive his account in lieu of a cash payment. The supply of ready money dried up, and Lord Burton had to provide funds from his private purse—not for the last time.

The Invergarry & Fort Augustus could have offered a service in 1901. That it did not begin for another two years was due to shameless bureaucratic processes which forced the proprietors again and again to go to the courts or to the House of Commons over relatively trivial matters.

The trouble stemmed from the fact that, in spite of private loans, after spending £322,000 on the line the company had no funds left for the purchase of engines and rolling stock. Clearly somebody had to be found to work the line for it, and the obvious candidate was the North British. Of course the Highland Railway objected to that, and the usual Parliamentary circus followed. The North British was not over-anxious to accept the job. Its terms to the Invergarry & Fort Augustus were 60 per cent of the gross revenue subject to a minimum of £3,000 each half-year. 'My company does not feel disposed to work the railway at a possible loss,' said Mr Jackson, the general manager of the North British.

William Whitelaw, the Highland chairman, had no such scruples. At a meeting held in March 1902 the Highland board agreed to work the Invergarry for £2,000 per half-year. Whitelaw was quite prepared to accept a small loss as the price of gaining control of the Invergarry and so keeping the North British out of the Great Glen.

He also made a statement of which the significance was missed at the time. First-class local passenger traffic was then an important source of revenue for railways in the Highlands. The gentry did most of their social visiting by rail; obsequious stationmasters and porters were at hand at all stations to pander to their every need; private waiting rooms and even private stations were not unknown. Whitelaw informed his shareholders that in the previous year there had been a drop of over 1,000 first-class local journeys. 'The loss,' said the chairman,

is almost entirely due to the extraordinary development of motor cars. We are not likely to recover this traffic, but I do not think we will lose much more on long distances through motoring. People are beginning to get a little bit sick of the general squalor of long-distance motoring.

The writing was on the wall.

The North British had conducted negotiations with the I & FA over the use of Spean Bridge station fully expecting to be operating the Invergarry line itself. The arrival of the Highland on the scene changed the atmosphere. When the North British seemed likely to be obstructive, the Invergarry decided to make its own approach road to the station, and build its own separate entrance and station offices. This piece of folly was avoided when the North British, realizing that it was to its own advantage to encourage traffic to and from the West Highland and the Invergarry, not only offered accommodation to the small company but gave it the use of North British staff without charge. (The North British benefited to the extent of £7 17s 6d when a second-hand Highland turntable was consigned from Inverness to Spean Bridge for installation there.) The Invergarry directors voted a £10 annual gratuity to the station-master at Spean Bridge.

The Invergarry & Fort Augustus lost no time in applying for a provisional order to confirm the working agreement with the Highland. The line was ready and waiting to earn money; all that was required was the official stamp on the inter-railway agreement. Alas! the Invergarry & Fort Augustus had filled in its application on the wrong form. It had applied in terms of the Private Bill Procedure (Scotland) Act, whereas it should have proceeded as for an ordinary private bill. It was July before the Parliamentarians reached this conclusion, and the important business of holidays for the legislators brought a halt to further discussion. So the new railway had to lie fallow during the tourist season of 1902.

It was November before the bill was given Parliamentary atten-tion, and it was not passed until 30 June 1903. The Highland Railway just had time to work two engines and rolling stock all the way round by the Caledonian and West Highland to Spean Bridge and set up in business to capture what they could of the summer trade. The Invergarry & Fort Augustus had enough money left to invest in the luxury of a gold whistle, and this was blown cn 27 July 1903 by a local lady who set off the first train. The opening-day luncheon in Fort Augustus was presided over by William Whitelaw, who in a graceful speech wished the new railway well.

Six months later when Whitelaw had the first balance sheet on his desk he realized what he had let his shareholders in for. In its first half-year of operation the railway had produced a total revenue from all sources of £907.

### A HOPELESS STRUGGLE

The first timetable provided four trains each way daily between Spean Bridge and Fort Augustus. Most of the trains were booked to do the journey in one hour exactly, with stops at the three intermediate stations. Two of the up trains originated at Fort Augustus pier station, and one of the down trains terminated there. Unfortunately, the Invergarry & Fort Augustus had obtained its Act too late for the services to be incorporated in the timetables of connecting companies, and at first no through tickets could be issued for journeys between stations on the line and points throughout the country.

To advertise itself the I & FA spent £50 on photographs which were framed in elaborate panels and exhibited at certain stations on the Highland Railway. It offered advertising space free in its first guide, and the guide itself was distributed free. The right to put chocolate and weighing machines at its stations was given to the Sweetmeat Automatic Delivery Company Ltd for a fee of £2 per machine, and the letting of advertising space on the railway was given to Slaughter & Co. of Edinburgh. The I & FA owned the Lovat Arms Hotel at Fort Augustus, and leased it to David Rattray, who promptly complained 'of the loss caused to the hotel by the evening train taking prospective guests away from Fort Augustus'. He wanted the last up train cancelled.

MacBrayne normally withdrew his mid-morning return sailing from Inverness to Fort Augustus in September, but the Invergarry asked him to retain it in September 1903 so that the railway could benefit from any traffic brought by the vessel. MacBrayne agreed, but only after the Invergarry had agreed to subsidize the sailing by

a payment of £100. £50 of this was contributed by the Highland.
Displeased with the arrangement the Invergarry directors instructed
their secretary to 'see the Turbine people' with a view to obtaining
a fast turbine steamer of their own for service in Loch Ness. This
breathtaking command was quite in keeping with a railway that
thought in terms of two first sods and a gold whistle. The Parsons
steam turbine had been applied for the first time to a passenger
vessel only two years previously and was just beginning to
revolutionize water transport.

The more settled traffic pattern of 1904 showed all too clearly
that the railway was to have a struggle to exist. Local people used
it to get to Fort William *via* the West Highland, for the fares were
only half the steerage fare on the Caledonian Canal boats which
had enjoyed a monopoly. But the summer tourist traffic that was to
fill the empty coffers did not materialize in anything like the expected volume. Travellers by choice still went to Banavie and sailed
all the way up the canal; few showed any desire to take the railway
short cut to Fort Augustus.

The 1904 accounts made grim reading for the Invergarry
directors. During the half-year ending 31 July 1904 they spent
£3,776 17s 1d on capital account, mainly for repairs and improvements to the permanent way. Even after deducting £303 13s 2d
obtained from the sale of surplus construction materials, the capital
account still claimed £3,473 3s 11d. That amount, with the half-
yearly £2,000 due to the Highland for working expenses, made a
total outlay of £5,473 3s 11d. The revenue for the half-year, including rents from railway properties, was £976 14s 3d. The Highland
complained that, after all, £2,000 did not cover the cost of working
the line, and asked the Invergarry to make good the deficit. Lord
Burton agreed to pay the Highland £1,000 if it would guarantee to
work the line for ten years and during that time refrain from asking
for additional payments. The Highland refused.

The Highland Railway tried to stimulate trade in 1905 by applying for permission to run steamers from the railway pier at Fort
Augustus to Inverness in connection with the trains. This move was
opposed by David MacBrayne, the sole steamboat operator on that
section of the canal. Incredibly, it was also opposed by the Invergarry & Fort Augustus, on the grounds that if the Highland operated
steamers on the northern section of the canal it might be deprived
of extending its own line to Inverness!

By 1905 it was plain that the tourists preferred the Royal
Route by canal steamer. Contraction, not expansion, became the

policy of the Invergarry & Fort Augustus. At the end of the 1906 summer timetable the service between Fort Augustus town and pier stations was withdrawn, never to be resumed. During its brief service this stretch of line could not have earned more than a few hundred pounds. The heavy investment in bridges, piers and buildings had gone for nothing; they were left to rust and moulder away.

Troubles now assailed the Invergarry from all directions. The factories inspector for Inverness insisted that the company provide life-saving apparatus at the pier it no longer used. (That it hoped to use it again was indicated by the fact that it spent £800 on repairing the pier foundations.) The local sanitary inspector complained that the cesspool at the Lovat Arms was causing offence, and money was spent in providing the appropriate remedy. The Sweetmeat Automatic Delivery Co. struck a blow to morale by removing their machines from the I & FA stations; and in the minute book appeared the plaintive note, 'The Secretary reported that the Assessor had again valued the Railway at Nil.' (It had been valued at £900 while under construction.)

But Slaughter & Co. remitted a cheque for £1 19s 3d to the Invergarry, that being the profit for one year on the letting of advertising sites, and on 1 July 1904 the directors felt confident enough to open a new station and passing place at Invergloy between Gairlochy and Letterfinlay. A belated mail contract signed with the Post Office on 1 August 1905 brought an annual revenue of £75.

Death and desertion had robbed the I & FA of some of its most faithful shareholders, among them Lord Abinger and Charles Forman, and the burden of meeting the crushing annual deficit fell on fewer people. Lord Burton made by far the largest contribution. It was difficult to escape the conclusion that the Invergarry owed its existence, albeit indirectly, to the drinkers of a particular brand of English beer.

The Highland Railway persevered for another year; then on 31 October 1906 it informed the Invergarry it would withdraw its engines and rolling stock on 30 April 1907. Lamenting the decision, William Whitelaw said:

> I think the Highland Company have done all that could reasonably be expected of them. They have worked the line within the estimated cost for four years and given it every possible opportunity. It has not shown any sign of expansion of traffic and we have been experiencing a loss of £2,000 a year.

The Invergarry was forced to go cap in hand to the North British, seeking whatever terms it could get. The agreement between the I & FA and the NB, signed in the head office of Bass Radcliffe & Gretton at Burton on Trent, two clerks employed by the firm acting as witnesses, read like a treaty imposed by the victor on the vanquished. It was to be valid for three years from 1 May 1907. The North British agreed to move in on that date, providing it could move out again on 31 January of any year after giving six months' notice. It had the right to inspect the railway, put it in working order to its own satisfaction and instal additional sidings if considered necessary; all this at the expense of the I & FA. The North British would pay for routine maintenance, but landslides and failures of culverts would be the responsibility of the Invergarry. All I & FA servants would pass into North British control and the NB had the exclusive right to make all future appointments. All monies would be collected by the North British, which would retain 60 per cent and remit 40 per cent to the I & FA within two months of each half-year *provided* that the North British share was not less than £2,000 per half-year. If it fell short of £2,000 the Invergarry would be required to make up half the deficit.

The Invergarry directors found themselves wallowing in a maze of accounts, claims and counter-claims. The Highland Railway sent an account for £2,062 11s, the loss incurred in working the railway for the year ending 31 January 1907. Once again there was a whip-round among loyal shareholders, and money was contributed as follows:

| | | | |
|---|---:|---:|---:|
| Lord Burton | £1,112 | 8 | 9 |
| Forman's Trustees | £234 | 5 | 0 |
| J. C. Cunningham | £139 | 1 | 3 |
| G. Malcolm | £13 | 17 | 6 |
| J. Lambrick | £3 | 2 | 6 |
| Lord Abinger's Trustees | £3 | 2 | 6 |
| G. W. T. Robertson | £2 | 10 | 0 |
| Robert Angus | | 10 | 0 |
| | £1,508 | 17 | 6 |

A cheque for £1,500 was sent to the Highland in part payment of the debt. Next the North British rendered an account for £565 16s 1d, the charge for putting the line in order. The Highland Railway wanted £26 9s 6d from the North British for the tickets, luggage labels and picture postcards it had left at I & FA stations, but the North British maintained they were worth only £6 9s 2d, and that is all it would pay. The luckless Invergarry was presented

with the bill for the difference of £20 0s 4d. By the time the account-
ants had made sense of the financial mess the Invergarry was found
to owe the Highland £400 and the North British £1,027 18s 1d. The
accounts were shared as follows:

|  | H.R. | N.B. |  |  |
|---|---|---|---|---|
| Lord Burton | £260 | £523 | 1 | 1 |
| Forman's Trustees | £80 | £266 | 9 | 6 |
| J. C. Cunningham | £60 | £238 | 7 | 6 |

The North British took over on 1 May 1907, according to the
agreement, although services did not start until 4 May. The agreed
service was four trains each way in summer and two in winter.
The deficit to be shared by Lord Burton and his friends at the end
of the first half-year of NB rule was £627 15s 1d. Burton died in
1909, and the yoke of chairmanship of the I & FA fell on J. C.
Cunningham. Then, at the end of the summer of 1910, the North
British gave notice that services would be withdrawn on 31 January
1911.

The people of the district were fantastically loyal to their railway. They wanted it and were not to blame that their numbers
were too few and their journeyings too infrequent to make it pay
its way. Public meetings were held up and down the Great Glen in
efforts to find ways and means of saving it. On one evening meetings were held simultaneously in Spean Bridge, Invergarry, and
Gairlochy, and at all three assurances of financial support were
given. The money situation had been aggravated by the death of
Lord Burton who had been plugging leaks with his private fortune.
Now the trustees of his estate refused to divert money to the little
railway in the Highlands. The North British under pressure undertook to work it for another summer. On 31 October 1911 it withdrew, leaving the line to its fate.

The Invergarry board resigned themselves to the fact that the
position was hopeless. Following several bitter meetings they took
the sad decision of putting out tenders for scrap. But they were to
find that they had to fight almost as hard to abandon the line as
they had fought to build it. When they tried to sell their property
at its scrap value Inverness County Council moved in with an interdict to prevent the sale. When they took their case to the First
Division of the Court of Session the Lord President reminded them
that they were a main line in their own right and not simply a
branch line that could throw in the towel when it liked. 'Once a
railway has been established,' lectured the Lord President, 'it is to
a certain extent an asset of the public as well as an asset of the

particular company, and this is different from a successful railway company discontinuing an unprofitable branch.' The Invergarry representative was informed that the line could not be sold for scrap in any case, since the proprietors had not taken the statutory steps to abandon it.

The company could not sell the line for scrap, and nobody would lease or buy it. While it lay bound in red tape, private citizens, local and county councils and Government departments haggled over its fate. With an eye on the nearby Mallaig line, the Invergarry pleaded for a Government grant to enable it to give a service to the community; the profit motive was now forgotten.

A long series of letters passed between the Invergarry, the North British and the Board of Trade in an effort to find a solution. The North British made a cash offer of £22,500 for the £344,000 railway. This the Invergarry refused, still hoping to get a better price for the line as scrap. When after nearly two years of negotiations Sir George Younger (Ayr Burghs) asked the President of the Board of Trade what he was doing about the Invergarry & Fort Augustus, the President gave this reply:

> As I think the Hon Baronet is aware, the Board of Trade have for the past two years been in communication both by letters and interviews with the Invergarry Company and the North British Company and various individual bodies (including the County Council of Inverness) who are interested in the matter with the view of arriving at some arrangement for the continuance of the working of the railway. I regret that these efforts have not been successful and I should be glad to do anything in my power to secure the reopening of the line, but I greatly fear that the Board of Trade have exhausted their good offices in the matter.

Meanwhile, the Lochaber District Committee of the Inverness County Council had made an interesting discovery. Their accounts for road repairs in the Spean Bridge—Fort Augustus area had risen by £600 and this they attributed to the increase in motor traffic following the closure of the railway. The Lochaber District Committee suggested to the parent body that a grant of £600 be made to the Invergarry & Fort Augustus to induce it to re-open the line.

The 1913 negotiations resulted in the North British agreeing to work the line again for a trial period, and it was reopened on 1 August. The results were no better than before and the Invergarry directors pressed for it to be scrapped. By this time, however, Inverness County Council had obtained a provisional order to raise £5,000, the difference between the top figure the Invergarry was willing to accept and the £22,500 the North British was prepared to pay for outright purchase. The deal was concluded at Fort Augustus and the man who represented the North British was the same William Whitelaw who had already opened and closed the line on behalf of the Highland. He had become chairman of the North British in the previous year. So in the end it was the ratepayers of the Great Glen who saved the railway. On 28 August 1914 the royal assent was given to the North British Railway (Invergarry & Fort Augustus Railway Vesting) Order Confirmation Act, and the Invergarry became lock, stock and barrel the property of the North British.

By that time the Great War had broken out and in a matter of months the Highland Railway was bending under the burden of wartime traffic it had not been designed to meet. If only there had been a second route to Inverness to share the vital naval traffic to the northern bases! If only the three parties to the 1897 *fracas* had, instead of pouring their money down the legal drain, made a joint-purse pact to build a joint line between Fort Augustus and Inverness, the nation would have had a strategic railway of first importance in the Great Glen. It was easy to be wise after the event.

If anybody deserved to have a railway it was the people in the lower half of the Great Glen. Today railways skirt both ends of the glen, but in the glen itself there is not a foot of line. It would be pleasant to think that somewhere among the quiet alleys of legal London there was a plaque inscribed, 'From the gentlemen of the legal profession to the Railway Promoters of the Great Glen, in gratitude for their munificence.'

# CHAPTER 8

# Trains and Timetables

The main features of the West Highland timetable devised when the Mallaig Extension was opened in 1901 survived and were recognizable 60 years later. The early-morning and mid-afternoon all-the-year-round trains from Glasgow remained, although they had been re-timed. These were the only down passenger trains on the Glasgow—Fort William section in the winter timetable. For a period before 1914 the summer traffic supported two down trains between the early and late trains. These were timed to leave Glasgow at 10.9 and 12.43 but were later consolidated into a single train leaving at 11.23. This train is now recognizable as the 10.5. The first down and the last up trains in the summer ran through from London King's Cross; these served Edinburgh in each direction, but not Glasgow.

The timetable for the Mallaig Extension changed pattern from time to time. Usually there were four trains in each direction daily between Fort William and Mallaig, with an additional service each way on Saturdays. In 1914 a non-stop train ran from Mallaig to Fort William at 6.50 a.m., catering mainly for the outer-islands steamer passengers, followed by a stopping train. The 1925 timetable showed four up trains and two down trains on the Mallaig Extension; both down services were through trains from Glasgow, and three of the up trains went through to Glasgow. In that year an 8.30 p.m. was put on from Fort William to Mallaig.

The original local service from Craigendoran to Garelochhead was extended to Arrochar and Tarbet and included Whistlefield. The basic service on this section was four trains a day each way. They were poorly patronized, largely because of the unfortunate distance of the stations from the villages they purported to serve. By 1964 a railbus was catering for the mere handful of passengers, and services ceased on 14 June that year with the closure of Rhu, Shandon, and Whistlefield stations to passenger traffic. In 1914 an attempt was made to bring Crianlarich into the commuter belt by providing a morning and evening train to and from Glasgow. This was the 8.5 a.m., which worked through to Springburn; the return service left Queen Street (Low Level) at 5.12 p.m.

After the second war an afternoon train was put on from Glasgow to Crianlarich on Saturdays, timed to leave at 3 p.m. or 2.50 p.m. This offered a circular tour, whereby passengers could return from Crianlarich via Callander; they could also alight at Ardlui or Arrochar and Tarbet and return to Glasgow by the Loch Lomond steamer as far as Balloch, and thence by train. Experience showed that few used the train beyond Ardlui and this station was eventually made the terminus. For some years the Loch Lomond circular tour was highly popular and the train was well loaded. In the early sixties the traffic fell away, and in 1964, when Ardlui pier was closed, custom all but vanished.

The establishment of comfortable residential outposts on the shores of the Gareloch, Loch Long and Loch Lomond had been one of the dreams of the original West Highland promoters. It remained a dream.

### THE 'NORTHERN BELLE'

One of the most interesting trains ever to visit the West Highland Railway was the LNE's *Northern Belle*. This made history when it left King's Cross at 11.20 p.m. on 16 June 1933 and cruised for some 4,000 miles before returning to King's Cross at 7.58 p.m. on 30 June. The *Northern Belle* was made up of eight day-cars, six sleeping-cars and a van, and it accommodated 60 passengers and a crew of 20. Included in its amenities were a passenger lounge, a hairdressing saloon, a cocktail bar and two shower baths. The inclusive fare for the cruise was £20.

The *Northern Belle* eventually reached Balloch pier at the foot of Loch Lomond, where the passengers embarked on one of the loch steamers for Ardlui. The night and day portions then left separately for the West Highland line, the day portion arriving at Ardlui station in time to meet the steamer. The train then ran right through to Mallaig. On the return journey a ten-minute stop was made on Glenfinnan Viaduct. One of the passengers kept a log of the cruise, and here is an extract:

> At Ardlui we board the day portion of the *Northern Belle*. But before lunch there is a small ceremony to be performed. For this is Derby Day, and the *Northern Belle* sweep, for which the whole of

the passengers and the staff have entered, has to be drawn. The result of the race comes aboard the train in the afternoon, and the winner of the sweep is announced—one of the train staff. Passengers seem as pleased as if they had won it themselves. On the return from Mallaig the *Northern Belle* stands for ten minutes on Glenfinnan Viaduct. Passengers have heard a good deal about the incomparable views between Fort William and Mallaig and the alternative offered—a motor trip to Loch Ness in search of the Monster—attracted only two passengers, one of these being a Dutch lady who, with kindly forethought, had obtained from the kitchen staff a supply of bread to feed the beast. Alas! she was disappointed. In the evening dinner is served on the train as she stands beside Loch Linnhe.

In April 1935 a similar cruising train organized by *The Scout* magazine took 140 boys to the West Highlands. The train was stabled at Banavie Pier station for two days while the boys climbed Ben Nevis.

### EXCURSION TRAFFIC

On 10 June 1931 the LMS and LNE sent the first-ever train to Oban over the West Highland and Callander & Oban. That year MacBrayne's had introduced the new vessel *Lochfyne* on the Oban to Staffa and Iona run, and a special train was run from Glasgow Queen Street to Oban with passengers for the cruise. The train left Glasgow at 6.10 a.m. and arrived in Oban at 9.27, thus completing the trip in 83 minutes less than the best-timed Glasgow Buchanan Street to Oban train.

In subsequent years joint excursions were operated from Glasgow to Crianlarich *via* the West Highland, returning *via* Callander, but no regular service was established on the short route to Oban until after nationalization. The summer timetable of 1949 contained the first-ever regular return service from Glasgow to Oban *via* Loch Lomond and Dalmally. The train was well advertised and trumpeted as one of the fruits of nationalization. But the public refused to use it, and it was soon withdrawn. It was revived in the sixties as a diesel multiple unit, operating Mondays to Fridays, with an appeal mainly for the tourist traffic.

The LNE and LMS frequently co-operated in running circular tour trains to Crianlarich, out *via* the West Highland and back *via* Stirling or vice versa. These proved very popular, especially when operated as evening excursions at a fare of only 3s for the round trip of 135 miles.

The Six Lochs Rail Cruise was a British Railways variant of the Crianlarich circle. This operated as a diesel multiple unit from

## Edinburgh and Glasgow to Fort-William and Mallaig

| | | | p.m a.m. | | p.m | | Sats only a.m | Sats only a.m p.m | | | p.m | Ex Sats p.m | | Sats only a.m. | Sundays |
|---|---|---|---|---|---|---|---|---|---|---|---|---|---|---|---|
| London (King's X) . lev. | | | 7 E 5 | — | 1030 E | | | 10 0 | | | 1130 | — | | 4 25 | . . . . |
| EDINBURGH (Wav.) . lev. | | | 4a25 | . | 9 a 5 | . | | 10 0 | . | | 2 0 | . | — | 4 p 0 | . . . . |
| GLASGOW { Queen (Low) — | | | 7B50 | | 1032 FB | | 1125 | . | | | 3 46 | 5 B 6 | — | 6 B 7 | . . . . |
| St. (High) . | | | | — | | . | | | | | | | | | . . . . |
| Dumbarton | | | 5 55 6 22 | 8B24 | 11F3 B | | 1154 | 1B38 | — | | 4HB3 | 5B37 | — | 6B36 | . . . . |
| Craigendoran | | | 9 0 | | 1130 | | 12 6 | 2 0 | — | | 4 22 | 5 56 | — | 6 57 | . . . . |
| Helensburgh (Upper) | | 6 39 | 9 6 | | 1136 | | 1213 | 2 6 | | | 4 29 | 6 3 | — | 7 3 | . . . . |
| Rhu | | | 9 11 | | 1141 | | | 2 11 | | | 4 34 | 6 8 | — | 7 8 | . . . . |
| Shandon | | | 9 17 | | 1147 | | | 2 17 | | | 4 40 | 6 14 | — | 7 14 | . . . . |
| Garelochhead | | | 9 25 | | 1155 | | | 2 25 | | | 4 46 | 6 24 | — | 7 24 | . . . . |
| Whistlefield | | | 9 30 | | 12 0 | | | 2 30 | | | 4 52 | 6 29 | — | 7 29 | . . . . |
| Arrochar and Tarbet . | | 7 17 | 9 51 | | 1221 | | 1253 | 2 51 | | | 5 16 | 6 50 | — | 7 50 | . . . . |
| Ardlui (Loch Lomond) | | 7 34 | | | | | 1 10 | | | | 5 38 | | — | — | . . . . |
| Crianlarich . . . arr. | | 7 55 | | | | | 1 31 | | | | 6 0 | . | . | — | . . . . |
| Crianlarich — — lev. | | 8 1 | | | | | 1 37 | — | | | 6 6 | | — | — | . . . . |
| Tyndrum | | 8 14 | | | | | 1 50 | — | | | 6 20 | | — | — | . . . . |
| Bridge of Orchy | | 8 29 | | | | | 2 5 | . | | | 6 35 | | — | — | . . . . |
| Rannoch | | 8 58 | | | | | | . | | | 7 2 | | — | — | . . . . |
| Corrour | | 9 14 | | | | | | . | | | 7 18 | | — | — | . . . . |
| Tulloch (Loch Laggan) | | 9 35 | | | | | 3 8 | . | | | 7 39 | | — | — | . . . . |
| Roy Bridge | | 9 47 | | | | | 3 22 | — | | | 7 51 | | — | — | . . . . |
| Spean Bridge | | 9 57 | | | | | 3 32 | — | | | 8 0 | | — | — | . . . . |
| Fort-William . . arr. | | 1014 | | | | | 3 49 | — | | | 8 17 | | — | — | . . . . |
| Fort-William . . lev. | | 1028 | | | | | | | 4 50 | | 8 30 | | — | — | . . . . |
| Banavie | | 1035 | | | | | | | 4 57 | | 8 37 | | — | — | . . . . |
| Corpach | | 1039 | | | | | | | 5 1 | | 8 41 | | — | — | . . . . |
| Locheilside | | 1052 | | | | | | | 5 13 | | 8 53 | | — | — | . . . . |
| Glenfinnan M (Loch Shiel) | | 11 6 | | | | | | | 5 27 | | 9 7 | | — | — | . . . . |
| Lochailort | | 1127 | | | | | | | 5 48 | | 9 28 | | — | — | . . . . |
| Arisaig | | 1146 | | | | | | | 6 7 | | 9 47 | | — | — | . . . . |
| Morar | | 1159 | | | | | | | 6 21 | | 10 1 | | — | ‑ | . . . . |
| Mallaig ¶ . . . arr. | | 12 6 | | | | | | | 6 28 | | 10 8 | | — | — | . . . . |

*Vertical column notes:* London to Fort-William on Sunday to Friday nights inclusive — RC Glasgow to Glasgow — Sleeping Car (1st and 3rd Class) London to Fort-William — Buffet Car Glasgow to Mallaig Through Train Glasgow to Fort-William — RC Glasgow to Fort-William — TC London to Fort-William

* Saturdays only.    † Except Sats.    § Mondays only.    ‡ Except Mondays
¶ See Ferry Service, Mallaig and Armadale, at foot of Page
B Change Craigendoran    E Sunday to Friday nights inclusive
F From 1st October leaves Glasgow (Queen Street) 10-24 a.m. and Dumbarton 10-58 a.m
H From 15th September leaves Dumbarton 3-2 p.m
M Connection from Glenfinnan Pier to Dalilea and Acharacle off 5-55 a.m. Glasgow to Mallaig
RC Restaurant Car    TC Through Carriage·

For Steamer Sailings to Portree and Stornoway, apply D. MacBrayne Ltd. 44 Robertson St., Glasgow C.2.

### Mallaig—Armadale Ferry Service.

The Ferry service between Mallaig and Armadale (Skye) operated by Messrs. Alexander McLennan (Mallaig) Ltd., will be as under, for the period 16th June to 30th September:—

Mallaig    dep.    9-45 a.m.,    12-20 p.m.,    3-45 p.m
Armadale    dep.    10-45 a.m.,    1-0 p.m.,    ·4-45 p.m

Last LNE summer timetable, 1947

## Mallaig and Fort~William to Glasgow and Edinburgh

| | a.m | a.m | a.m | . | a.m | Sats only p.m | Ex Sats p.m | Sats only p.m | Fort-William to London p.m | . | Sats only p.m | Sundays |
|---|---|---|---|---|---|---|---|---|---|---|---|---|
| Mallaig ¶ lev. | — | 6 35 | — | . | 7 46 | — | — | — | 1 0 | . | — | . . . . |
| Morar | — | 6 46 | — | . | 7 55 | — | — | — | 1 9 | | S 51 | . . . . |
| Arisaig | — | 7 1 | — | . | 8 8 | — | — | — | 1 22 | | 6 8 | . . . . |
| Lochailort | — | 7 24 | — | . | 8 27 | — | — | — | 1 41 | | 6 27 | . . . . |
| Glenfinnan M (Loch Shiel) | — | 7 50 | — | . | 8 52 | — | — | — | 2 2 | | 6 48 | . . . . |
| Locheilside | — | 8 11 | — | . | | — | — | — | 2 17 | | 7 3 | . . . . |
| Corpach | — | 8 30 | — | . | | — | — | — | 2 30 | | 7 16 | . . . . |
| Banavie | — | 8 37 | — | . | | — | — | — | 2 35 | | 7 21 | . . . . |
| Fort-William arr. | — | 8 46 | — | . | 9 24 | — | — | — | 2 42 | | 7 28 | . . . . |
| Fort-William lev. | — | — | — | . | 9 36 | — | — | — | 2 55 | . | 5 20 | . . . . |
| Spean Bridge | — | — | — | . | 9 56 | — | — | — | 3 14 | | 5 39 | . . . . |
| Roy Bridge | — | — | — | . | 10 3 | — | — | — | 3 21 | | — | . . . . |
| Tulloch (Loch Laggan) | — | — | — | . | 1021 | — | — | — | 3 41 | | — | . . . . |
| Corrour | — | — | — | . | 1043 | — | — | — | 4 4 | | — | . . . . |
| Rannoch | — | — | — | . | 1057 | — | — | — | 4 18 | | — | . . . . |
| Bridge of Orchy | — | — | — | . | 1122 | — | — | — | 4 46 | | — | . . . . |
| Tyndrum | — | — | — | . | 1139 | — | — | — | 5 2 | | — | . . . . |
| Crianlarich arr. | — | — | — | . | 1148 | — | — | — | 5 13 | | — | . . . . |
| Crianlarich lev. | — | — | — | . | 1154 | — | — | — | 5 19 | . | 7 36 | . . . . |
| Ardlui (Loch Lomond) | — | — | — | . | 1212 | — | — | — | 5 37 | | — | . . . . |
| Arrochar and Tarbet | 7 18 | — | 10 6 | . | 1231 | 1 0 | 2 45 | 4 50 | 5 55 | | 8 11 | . . . . |
| Whistlefield | 7 42 | — | 1028 | . | | 1 21 | 3 8 | 5 15 | 6 17 | | — | . . . . |
| Garelochhead | 7 47 | — | 1034 | . | 125 | 1 28 | 3 15 | 5 20 | 6 22 | | — | . . . . |
| Shandon | 7 53 | — | 1041 | . | 1 4 | 1 34 | 3 22 | 5 26 | 6 28 | | — | . . . . |
| Rhu | 7 59 | — | 1047 | . | | 1 40 | 3 29 | 5 32 | — | | — | . . . . |
| Helensburgh (Upper) | 8 4 | — | 1052 | . | 1 15 | 1 45 | 3 35 | 5 37 | 6 40 | | — | . . . . |
| Craigendoran arr. | 8 8 | — | 1056 | . | 1 19 | 1 49 | 3 40 | 5 41 | 6 44 | | 8 56 | . . . . |
| Dumbarton arr. | 8E27 | — | 1120 E | . | 1E37 | 2E21 | 4E10 | 6 E 0 | 7EH6 | | 9E29 | . . . . |
| Glas- Queen High L | — | — | — | . | | 2F 4 | | | 7L30 | | 5N40 | . . . . |
| gow Street Low L | 8E59 | — | 1154 E | . | | 3 E 3 | 4E46 | 6E41 | | | — | . . . . |
| Edinburgh (Way.) arr. | 1125 | — | 2B15 | . | 3 50 | 4U47 | 6 23 | 9 8 | 9 26 | | — | . . . . |
| London (King's X) arr. | 9p23A | — | 2a49 | . | 5a15 | 5a5 | 5a56 | a5 | | | 6a50 | . . . . |

☞ For Steamer Sailings from Stornoway, Portree, and Inverness in connection with Trains, apply D. MacBrayne Ltd., 44 Robertson Street, Glasgow, C.2

\* Saturdays only    † Except Saturdays    § Mondays only    ‡ Except Mondays
¶ See Ferry Service Armadale and Mallaig on Page 56
A 9-15 p.m on Fridays and Saturdays    B Saturdays 1-28 p.m    E Change Craigendoran
F Stops Cowlairs 1-55 p.m    H From 15th September arrives Dumbarton 7-17 p.m
L Stops Cowlairs 7-21 p.m    N Stops Cowlairs 9-32 p m
M Connection from Acharacle and Dalilea to Glenfinnan Pier into 1-0 p.m Mallaig to Glasgow
RC Restaurant Car    TC Through Carriage    U 5-11 p.m in October

## Spean Bridge, Invergarry and Fort Augustus.
### (Road Motor Service).

The Train Service has been withdrawn from Gairlochy, Invergloy, Invergarry, Aberchalder, and Fort Augustus, but Parcels and Miscellaneous Passenger Train traffic previously dealt with at these stations will continue to be accepted. The undernoted Motor Service is in operation :—

| | a.m. | . | a.m. | . | a.m. | . | p.m | . | p.m | . | p.m |
|---|---|---|---|---|---|---|---|---|---|---|---|
| Spean Bridge lev. | 8 56 | . | 10 0 | . | 1155 | . | 2 55 | . | 4 25 | . | 8 15 |
| Gairlochy Road End | 8 58 | . | 10 3 | . | 1158 | . | 2 58 | . | 4 28 | . | 8 17 |
| Invergloy | 9 12 | . | 1017 | . | 1212 | . | 3 12 | . | 4 42 | . | 8 32 |
| Invergarry | 9 32 | . | 1037 | . | 1232 | . | 3 32 | . | 5 2 | . | 8 52 |
| Oich Bridge (Aberchalder) | 9 38 | . | 1043 | . | 1238 | . | 3 38 | . | 5 8 | . | 8 58 |
| Fort Augustus arr. | 9 50 | . | 1055 | . | 1250 | . | 3 50 | . | 5 20 | . | 9 10 |

| | a.m | . | a.m. | . | a.m | . | p.m | . | p.m | . | p.m |
|---|---|---|---|---|---|---|---|---|---|---|---|
| Fort Augustus lev. | 8 10 | . | 9 40 | . | 1040 | . | 1 50 | . | 5 25 | . | 6 25 |
| Oich Bridge (Aberchalder) | 8 25 | . | 9 52 | . | 1052 | . | 2 2 | . | 5 37 | . | 6 37 |
| Invergarry | 8 33 | . | 9 58 | . | 1058 | . | 2 8 | . | 5 43 | . | 6 43 |
| Invergloy | 8 58 | . | 1018 | . | 1118 | . | 2 28 | . | 6 3 | . | 7 3 |
| Gairlochy Road End | 9 12 | . | 1032 | . | 1132 | . | 2 42 | . | 6 17 | . | 7 17 |
| Spean Bridge arr. | 9 15 | . | 1035 | . | 1135 | . | 2 45 | . | 6 20 | . | 7 20 |

Glasgow (Buchanan Street) to Glasgow (Queen Street) allowing the passengers time off at Callander, Killin, and Crianlarich, and became one of the most popular trips ever run to the West Highlands. Frequently on Sundays and holidays two six-coach sets, all seats filled, were dispatched, and the 'Six Lochs' also became a favourite with charter parties.

Another variation on the Crianlarich circle was the Amateur Photographers' Excursion run on 25 May 1957. This train allowed stops for photography at Garelochhead, Crianlarich, Killin, and Kingshouse platform and, in addition, it was run slowly at three points to enable photographers to obtain pictures from their carriages. A photographic information bureau was provided on the train, and prizes ranging from photographic equipment to runabout tickets were offered for the best prints submitted to British Railways. A public exhibition of the pictures taken on this excursion was held in Glasgow Central station.

An enterprising excursion involving a visit to Oban and Fort William in one day has been offered on several occasions. A diesel multiple unit was run *via* the West Highland from Glasgow to Crianlarich, where the train divided, one half going to Oban and the other half to Fort William. The Oban passengers sailed to Fort William and the Fort William passengers sailed to Oban. The respective MUs then converged on Crianlarich, where they were united for the return journey to Glasgow.

The Scottish Region Television Train made its first appearance on the West Highland. Its special feature was that each vehicle had a television set mounted above the central gangway door at each end, and passengers were invited to a studio in the van to provide entertainment for their fellow-travellers. The TV train on one occasion was chartered by an education authority, and several hundred children were given a most practical and no doubt palatable West Highland geography lesson.

### THE PATTERN CHANGES

The pattern of passenger and freight traffic changed little in the period between the opening of the line and the mid-twenties. The coming of the British Aluminium Company to Lochaber transformed the scene. The manufacture of aluminium demands above all a supply of cheap electricity. The B A C not only built new plant at Fort William, but created a complex hydro-electric generating system in Lochaber to power the plant. The scheme involved turning

K4's in action

(42) *'The Great Marquess' climbing in Glen Falloch when new*
(43) *No. 3443 heads a Glasgow train out of Fort William in 1939*
(44) *A K4 handles a nine-coach train single-handed on the ascent of Glen Falloch*

NORTH BRITISH CLASSES

(45) *A J36 on a Fort William— Mallaig train near Corpach in 1914*

(46) *A J36 on the Moor of Rannoch in 1938*

(47) *J37s at Mallaig*

Loch Treig into a reservoir from which water was conducted through Ben Nevis by a tunnel which emerged 1,000 ft up the face of the mountain overlooking the Fort William factory. Pipes took the water down to the turbine house at the factory.

For the first time the West Highland found itself with a large industrial enterprise on its territory, and tonnages and revenue reflected the new situation. Freight booked at Fort William, which had been between 10,000 and 15,000 tons a year, and had been as low as 7,428 tons, jumped to 27,114 tons in 1926. By 1928 it was 34,402 tons and by 1931 47,117 tons. Because of the influx of power scheme workers into the district passenger figures showed a corresponding increase. From 23,434 passengers booked at Fort William in 1923 the figure rose to 31,095 in 1926 and 43,250 in 1928. The figures tailed off once the major task of constructing the power scheme and factory was completed, but the new industry brought the railway a substantial permanent gain. In 1934 Fort William booked 27,992 passengers and 42,987 tons of freight. A steady traffic developed in bulk alumina between the Fort William factory and the British Aluminium Company's factory at Burntisland in Fife.

As part of the Lochaber power scheme the level of Loch Treig was raised by 33 ft and the original line at the north end of the loch was submerged, necessitating the construction of a diversion and tunnel. The scheme was serviced from a temporary station at Fersit near the foot of Loch Treig. The contractor's narrow-gauge line passed over the main line at this point on a spectacular wooden trestle bridge. The power scheme changed the lineside scenery. The water that pours through the Ben Nevis tunnel no longer plunges and tumbles down the Falls of Treig and through the gorges of the Spean.

### SUNDAY TRAINS

An outstanding feature of the West Highland scene in the thirties was the development of an intensive Sunday excursion traffic. The first tentative Sunday excursions in the late twenties met with some opposition in Fort William; excursionists found shops closed and house window-blinds lowered as a protest against their intrusion. But a large influx of industrial workers changed the atmosphere in the district and by the early thirties the trading community at least welcomed the excursion trains. On a fine Sunday, upwards of 1,000 people came into the town by train and their arrival had an appreciable impact on the local economy.

The coming of the Sunday trains coincided with the discovery by the masses in the industrial Clyde belt of the glories of the open air. It was the age of the hiker and hosteller. Sunday fares were remarkably cheap even by the standard of the time. The return fare from Glasgow to Fort William was 7s, to Mallaig 9s; nearly enough, 3 miles for a penny. At the height of the season there could be as many as six trains on the line on a Sunday. Glasgow usually dispatched two and sometimes three, one of which went through to Mallaig. Edinburgh accounted for another, and on certain dates West Highland trains originated at miscellaneous points on the LNE, Grangemouth, Peebles, and stations in Fife among them. The Glasgow trains started from Bridgeton Cross and after calling at Queen Street picked up passengers at the Glasgow suburban stations and at Singer and Dumbarton.

But those were also the years of the great industrial depression on Clydeside, and hundreds of hikers could afford to go no further than Arrochar and Tarbet. There was no Sunday winter service on the West Highland or on the Glasgow—Helensburgh line, but one year the regular hiking clientèle induced the LNE to put on a train from Arrochar to Glasgow on Sunday evenings. Engine and stock had to be worked empty from Glasgow, and the line opened throughout for this one train. Since the returning week-enders seldom numbered more than 30, and the fare from Glasgow to Arrochar and back was 3s 9d, the train's earning capacity seldom could have reached £3.

The thirties were certainly happy days on the West Highland. The merry Sunday trains crowded with bronzed, healthy young people will be remembered with pleasure and affection by all who used them. On 3 September 1939, that fateful Sunday, the hikers turned up for their trains as usual. They were running all right, but they were engaged exclusively in the grim business of evacuating schoolchildren from Glasgow. It was the end of an era. No Sunday excursion trains ran on the West Highland again until 1949, and by then a new generation of hikers and campers had been won to road transport. The Sunday trains were withdrawn in 1957, victims in part of a current economy drive.

Before the war the Sunday trains were not in the public timetable; after the war the Sunday service appeared in the timetable.

## THE WAR YEARS AND AFTER

Like railways everywhere the West Highland was transformed with the coming of war. With Southampton and London under constant threat from enemy bombers, alternative safe ports had to be established elsewhere, and the Gareloch was chosen as a site for one of them. The placid beauty of the loch was swept away. Hillsides were sheared of trees, villas were pulled down, every kind of mechanized appliance scooped and clawed at the soil to make way for the docks, cranes, and workshops and all the paraphernalia of a major seaport. This time there could be no plea of destruction of amenity; the country had to have a port to survive. But the older residents of Garelochside must have smiled wryly when they reflected on the fuss that was made fifty years before when the West Highland cut a thin, discreet path along the hillside.

A double line was taken from Croy, between Rhu and Shandon, on a steeply falling gradient to the new port in Faslane Bay. The branch was worked by Royal Engineers railway-operating troops on military principles, and War Department locomotives were used. From the opening of the port in May 1942 until August 1945 the Faslane branch received sixty-five passenger trains and 104,877 loaded wagons from the West Highland. To help in the handling of this traffic a loop and siding accommodation were provided at Faslane Junction, the Helensburgh Upper loops were extended, and a new yard was brought into operation at Craigendoran. The port is now used by Metal Industries Ltd as a shipbreaking centre.

On the outbreak of war the Mallaig Extension was placed in a prohibited zone and travellers had to have a good reason and a special pass to use its trains. A naval base was established at Corpach and new loops and sidings were put in. The capacity of the line was increased by the placing of a new signal box at Camusna-ha, $4\frac{1}{4}$ miles from Mallaig Junction. Fort William's cramped station and yards proved inadequate for the wartime traffic, and the situation was alleviated by the building of additional loops and sidings at Mallaig Junction.

Even the moribund Fort Augustus branch took on a new lease of life. The increased traffic in timber and ammunition from a base set up at Fort Augustus was enough for the sole surviving service, a weekly coal train, to blossom into a daily freight. The military authorities planned to use the Fort Augustus branch as an alternative route to the north in the event of the Highland line being put out of action, and reserve sidings were put in at Spean Bridge and Fort Augustus. The planners must have regretted that the line did not extend to Inverness.

Immediately after the war, the Loch Sloy power scheme brought an increase in traffic to the line. Water had to be piped from Loch Sloy, lying deep in the mountains immediately to the west of Loch Lomond, through the mountains to a point above Inveruglas on Loch Lomond. The pipelines then ran steeply down the mountain face and passed under the railway to reach a turbine house by the lochside. The line was diverted for about a quarter-mile to allow a bridge carrying the track over the pipelines to be built. At the same time Inveruglas station was constructed—close to the site of the turbine house—to serve the camp where a large part of the labour force was quartered. A halt was also established in Glen Falloch. Prisoners of war living at Faslane were picked up at the halt near their camp by the morning work train which then collected British labour at Arrochar and Tarbet, and dropped them all at Inveruglas and Glen Falloch as required. All three stations were removed when the power scheme was completed.

### 'SAVE OUR RAILWAY'

The West Highland remained remarkably intact. The Banavie branch closed on 2 September 1939. The Royal Route had lately fallen from favour, and the Caledonian Canal steamer ran only on alternate days, with the trains from Fort William making a connection. The outbreak of war saw the end of the steamer service, and there was no need for the connecting train. The Fort Augustus branch saw its last passenger train on 30 November 1933. It was the 12.5 p.m. ex-Fort Augustus, and like all passenger trains on the West Highland, it exhibited express headlights. And it took 83 minutes to cover the 23¼ miles! The local people fought hard for its retention, but the figures did nothing to justify the continuance of the service. In the last full year of operation only 1,911 passengers travelled on the branch and the revenue was £179. The once-weekly coal train was run until 31 December 1946 when the line was closed. The track was lifted shortly afterwards, and all that now remains of the Invergarry & Fort Augustus Railway is a shunting neck at Spean Bridge.

When, in the sixties, the era of massive railway closures dawned, the feeling of unease in Fort William changed to alarm when rumour had it that the existence of the whole of the West

Highland line from Craigendoran to Mallaig was threatened. There could not be two railway routes to the Islands, so it was said, and one had to go. It was disconcerting to see chalked on the streets of Fort William the plaintive appeal, 'Save Our Railway'. And these were the same streets along which the good folks of the town had kicked the effigies of politicians who had opposed the railway, the same pavements over which they had carried their torches in triumph when the railway's case was won. Now every foot of railway for which Lochaber had fought was to be swept off the map.

In the nick of time an unprecedented agreement made between British Railways and Scottish Pulp (Development) Ltd saved the railway and guaranteed its continued existence for at least 22 years. Scottish Pulp undertook to set up a large factory at Corpach and lay it out for rail transport. On their part British Railways agreed to maintain the line, deliver locally-grown timber to the mill, and take away the finished products. A traffic of 200,000 tons a year was visualized. 'It is hoped,' said the official announcement, 'that the knowledge that rail facilities will be available on a long-term basis will encourage other industrial development in the area.' The Fort William populace was saved the necessity of kicking along their streets the effigy of the personage most closely associated with the threat to their line.

The position of the West Highland was further strengthened by the closure of the Callander & Oban line east of Crianlarich in the autumn of 1965. All Oban trains now leave Glasgow Queen Street and run to Crianlarich *via* the West Highland. The completely re-cast Oban timetables at long last provide a faster and cheaper service from Oban to Glasgow, although passengers to Edinburgh are faced with increased mileage and fares.

# CHAPTER 9

# West Highland Life

## THE LOCAL SPIRIT

When the West Highland was new the clean, cut rocks were like the raw flesh of a recent wound on the countryside. The fresh earth of the embankments was bare and there were bald spaces where the contractors had hacked their way through woods to gain access to sites. But nature soon reasserted herself. The rocks browned and mellowed and heather and wild flowers in profusion carpeted the embankments. The railway grew into the soil.

Although the West Highland had a separate existence for only fourteen years it soon acquired a spirit of its own, a spirit that amalgamation and nationalization could not quench. The pay envelopes that arrived every week at the West Highland stations might have been inscribed 'N.B.R.' or 'L.N.E.R.', but the men who signed for them thought of themselves as West Highland men. They were a race apart. From the day the railway opened the trains dominated the lives of the people (railway and non-railway) at the places along the line. They turned out then every day to greet the trains and they still do so. Fort William station is almost a community centre where people foregather to gossip and await the arrival of the evening papers by the 4.35 from Glasgow.

The regular traveller on the line knew and appreciated the 'West Highland touches'. There was the late afternoon train rumbling across the Moor of Rannoch in the evening light with the engine now and again emitting gentle pop whistles. That was the driver telling knowledgeable passengers that he had spotted a herd of deer. More often than not if you looked forward you would see an arm pointing from the footplate, and if you followed its direction you would spot the splendid creatures silhouetted against the setting sun. There were the succulent, baked, brown trout that appeared unannounced on the high-tea tables of the friendly West Highland dining-car when the printed menu spoke of nothing more exciting than haddock or sole. There were the Scots firs seen piled at the back of the tender on south-bound runs in the week before Christmas, to say nothing of the odd salmon in the tool box.

There were times when even the most important trains made social stops of which the timetable breathed not a word, when driver, fireman or guard (and maybe all three) gossiped over the fence to an appreciative ganger and his family. They did that on the Mallaig boat connection one morning when someone who mattered was on board. The driver, carpeted, confessed his fall from grace and escaped with a few days' suspension. The fireman, interviewed separately, denied all knowledge of the unauthorized stop and was dismissed.

### LIGHTHOUSEMEN OF THE LAND

When the railway was new, trees were planted round the exposed, isolated cottages by the line to act as windbreaks. To the modern traveller, a clump of trees away ahead is the first indication that he is approaching one of the lonely Moorland outposts. The men of the Moor and their families have intrigued visitors ever since the line was opened. Rannoch was a station in its own right and appeared in the tables. Corrour and Gorton, according to the minutes, were built as passing places and became private stations only incidentally. Corrour was used by the public almost from the beginning: for instance, the navvies for Kinlochleven de-trained there.

Corrour featured in the public timetables from 1934, but the author has been unable to trace any mention of Gorton. It is possible that Lord Breadalbane persuaded the railway to prevent passengers alighting at Gorton, but there is no proof of this. As late as the LNE period, the authorities tried to make a mystery of Gorton, and permission to leave the train there was not readily obtained. A journalist on a Glasgow newspaper who wanted to write a feature on the railway community on the Moor was refused permission. Later, when a writer and photographer entered the forbidden territory uninvited, the published result of their clandestine visit resulted in 'please explain' letters being sent to railway personnel on the spot. A happier result followed an accidental visit by an English journalist who made the acquaintance of Gorton when his train was delayed there. After his account of the settlement appeared in a national paper, innumerable parcels of toys arrived for the children of the line. At one time a special engine and brake made a Christmas visit to the lonely stations and cottages, and a railway official from Glasgow, disguised in the familiar red cloak and white beard, distributed gifts to the railway children.

The education of the children living in isolated houses along the line presented a problem to the authorities, and their solution varied with the school population of the Moor at any given time. At one period the children were picked up from their homes in Argyllshire every school day by the first down passenger train in the morning, and taken all the way across the western corner of Perthshire to their classrooms in Fort William, Inverness-shire. They returned by the last afternoon up train. In a school week they spent sixteen hours travelling and covered some 425 miles.

During the early thirties a school was established in an old passenger carriage on Gorton platform. The Argyll authorities found a lady teacher for it, but there was no place for her to stay in Gorton, so she had to travel up from Bridge of Orchy every morning. At one time there were eleven pupils. Travellers who passed in the trains caught a fleeting glimpse of childish faces lifted momentarily from their books looking curiously at them from the windows of the school. The children of Gorton never set eyes on a motor car for weeks on end, but they had a guard rail in front of their schoolroom door; that was to prevent them tumbling on to the line if they made too exuberant an exit.

The water on the Moor of Rannoch is unsafe, and all Gorton's domestic water has to be imported. It was once the duty of the fireman of the first up train of the day to deliver from his tender twelve bucketfuls for use at Gorton. Now the water comes from Fort William in hygienic containers. Food supplies come in bulk from Glasgow once a week, and are delivered by train to the customer's door. In addition the wives of the railwaymen are provided with market passes which enable them to ride on goods trains to Fort William once a week.

Sudden illness presents another problem for the people on the Moor. They tell tales of an engine dashing in the night with a doctor on the footplate to the succour of a railwayman who was taken suddenly ill. On one such occasion word was received in Fort William late at night that a surfaceman's wife was seriously ill in a lineside house on the north-western edge of the Moor of Rannoch. While the traffic department was opening up the line the locomotive department sent an engine out to Tulloch where arrangements had been made to pick up a doctor. The engine duly delivered the doctor at the house on the Moor and, when he had made his examination, took him back to Tulloch. It was a wild winter night

with a touch of sleet in the air. The engine had to run tender first
—something that is avoided at all costs on the West Highland—and
the chilling blast of the icy mountain air tore through the cab. All
on the footplate were chilled to the marrow, and the fireman's
hands were so numbed that he could hardly hold the shovel.

The spiritual needs of the railwaymen were not forgotten. When
the railway came to the West Highlands it entered tracts of country
where the Reformation had never penetrated. The first Protestants
in the district were the men who came from the south to work on
the line. Churches were improvized in station waiting-rooms, the
local signalman acting as beadle for the minister, who came often
long distances perhaps one Sunday in four to preach to his small
railway flock. Later as the Protestant population increased the
station churches were attended by any civilians who could reach
them.

The relief man on the West Highland had to be a 'lad o' pairts',
able to turn his hand to anything. His standard equipment consisted
of a portable bed, a cooking outfit, a fishing rod and a snare wire.
Thus equipped he could answer an emergency anywhere on the line
and be able to live in tolerable comfort.

There is a story told about the relief man who was sent to one
of the settlements on the Moor of Rannoch to take over from a
family who were going on holiday. The train which set down the
relief also picked up the holiday family, and there was time only
for a brief exchange of words. The newcomer had a free run of the
house and when he went into the kitchen he found a note containing instructions—not for handling the railway's business, but for
tending the animal population of the place, which consisted of
miscellaneous poultry, a few cats, a dog and three goats. On the
first day the goats escaped on to the Moor and attempts by the
relief man to retrieve them met with hostile demonstrations.

There used to be a celebrated goat at Gorton. Its peculiarity was
that it found the grass that grew on the track much sweeter than
anything offered on the Moor or in the patch of garden beside the
house. Drivers got into the habit of watching for it, and time and
again they saw the beast making hair-raising escapes from under
their wheels. Then one night the last down passenger arrived at
Fort William and when the driver was looking round the fore end
he found a tuft of shaggy hair adhering to the wheel guard. He was
wondering just what he had hit when he remembered the Gorton
Goat. The damage was not mortal but the goat ever after displayed
a bald patch on its hindquarters.

Tablets are exchanged manually on the West Highland, often at spectacular speeds. There have been few accidents to personnel, although the first signalman to come to Ardlui was pulled under the wheels of a train and killed while exchanging a tablet. The sweep of a train along an island platform, the flash of hoops as nimble hands effect the change is a characteristic sight on the line. It is not uncommon to see a railway family gathered at the door of their cottage to watch one of their members change the tablet.

In steam days the practice was for firemen to hang the tablet carriers by the hoop on the handle of the hand brake while they were in section. There was an occasion when the last train of the day arrived at a signal box on the Moor of Rannoch without a tablet. The driver reported that the carrier had swung off the hand-brake handle with the swaying of the engine and had fallen on to the track. It was a Saturday night and darkness had fallen; there was no point in searching the line immediately. The signalman decided to wait until Sunday when the line would be closed to all traffic and he could stroll up the track at his leisure keeping an eye open for the tablet. When he woke on Sunday morning he found the landscape with an even covering of deep snow!

A fireman tells the story of how he came to Glasgow on holiday and treated himself to the unaccustomed luxury of a visit to the cinema. As he was taking his seat in the darkened auditorium he heard a voice behind the screen say 'and the train cannot leave a station without it'. When he looked at the screen there was a signalman standing on a station platform holding up a tablet. 'I nearly put my hand out for it,' said the fireman, relating the tale afterwards.

### 'THE GHOST'

A casual visitor to Fort William might well have overheard an engine-driver's wife complain that her husband was 'on *The Ghost*'. She would have been referring to the only regular named train the West Highland has known, and even that name has never appeared in a timetable. *The Ghost* is the express freight that leaves Sighthill, Glasgow, about 2.15 a.m. and runs through to Fort William. Its time of departure and intermediate stops have varied over the years, but it was common in steam days for it to stop only at Crianlarich for water. It regulates the domestic scene in railway houses up the length of the West Highland Railway. The working day begins for many West Highland signalmen when the bells offering *The Ghost*

ring out, for all the boxes are switched in at its approach. As the
train makes its way north the railway rouses itself for the work of
the day.

Many are the tales they tell in West Highland bothies about
*The Ghost* and its journeyings. The Inspecting Officers of the Board
of Trade would have been happy to have issued reports about some
of the things that happened to it if only they had learned about
them. But there was a feeling on the West Highland that what
happened on the line was no business of Glasgow's, let alone
London's. What on a more orthodox railway would have produced
a stodgy printed report became on the West Highland the stuff of
legends passed from mouth to mouth.

There was the morning about daybreak when *The Ghost* came
panting up off the Moor and the driver shut off to let his fireman
pick up the tablet at Corrour. When he saw the fireman toss the
hoop over the handbrake handle he opened up smartly, and with
the gradient falling in front of him had put on a bit of speed by
the time the wagons at the back end of the loose-coupled train took
up the slack. The brake van was given a nasty tug. It was sharp
enough to snap the coupling between the van and the rest of the
train, but not sharp enough to waken the guard who was sound
asleep in the van. Now, although most of the train was over the
summit and on a falling gradient, the detached van was still on the
rising gradient. It followed its train for a second or two, then
slowed and stopped, and gently began to run back the way it had
come. The last the Corrour signalman saw of it was as it fast
disappeared down the line in the direction of Rannoch.

The van was next seen bounding out of the rock cutting above
Rannoch station and soaring on to the viaduct. Plainly, it was, as
they say of ships in distress, not in command. The rule book was
explicit about such a situation : the Rannoch signalman was duty-
bound to derail the runaway. But when he saw it charging down
off the viaduct at speed he knew that to do so would mean killing
the guard. Any grand notion he had of leaping aboard had to be
abandoned when he saw the speed at which it rattled through the
station. So he let it alone.

Gorton was duly warned that the runaway was approaching, but
the signalman there, too, could not bring himself to cause its
deliberate derailment. It swept through at upwards of 35 miles an
hour. Now it was on the long descent to Bridge of Orchy. The
stationmaster concluded that if it negotiated all the curves and was
still on the rails by the time it reached him, the rising gradient

south of the station would check it. He, too, let the van run through, but he followed it on foot and found it at a dead stand about two miles along the line. The still slumbering guard responded to a sound shaking. 'Do you know where you are?' asked the stationmaster. 'No,' admitted the guard, peering about him. 'You're at Bridge of Orchy,' the stationmaster informed him. 'Ach, don't be daft,' said the guard, 'we were there two hours ago.' 'Well, you're back again!' replied the stationmaster.

The van had run back 25 miles.

There is an old joke about the West Highland train that was late 'because she had the wind against her'. It was a joke that sometimes fell flat; the younger generation of footplatemen scoffed when they heard the old-timers' tales of minutes lost because of wind. It was not until the early days of the diesels that dramatic visual proof of the effect of wind on a locomotive's performance was offered. On a March day in 1962 the afternoon up passenger had threaded its way round the Horse Shoe and was emerging on to the length of track leading up to the summit at the county march. A full gale was blowing from the west, and as the train came out of the shelter of the Horse Shoe the driver saw the speedometer needle drop back from 35 to 15. His first thought was that the communication cord had been pulled, but a glance at the vacuum gauge revealed that vacuum was being maintained. The wind, pressing on the sides of the coaches and grinding the wheel flanges against the rails, was the culprit.

### ACCIDENTS

In spite of the natural hazards of operating the West Highland accidents have been rare and the few that have occurred were relatively minor. The 8.40 a.m. Sighthill—Crianlarich goods came to grief in a rock fall on Loch Lomondside about mid-day on 8 August 1906. It had been raining heavily all morning and the rocks must have loosened and plunged on to the line after the passing of the forenoon up passenger. Andrew McKinnon, the driver of the goods, never had a chance. He had just passed through Craigenarden tunnel and was nosing round a blind curve near the Pulpit Rock when the obstruction appeared almost under his buffer beam. The engine struck the rocks heavily and the wagons piled up against it and were smashed to pieces. McKinnon was badly hurt, and had to be taken by motor car to hospital in Helensburgh. The line was blocked for 24 hours, during which time passengers were shuttled between

Arrochar and Tarbet and Ardlui by the Loch Lomond steamers.

The West Highland has witnessed two head-on collisions between trains; both took place in stations, but neither was serious. About 7 a.m. on 6 December 1909 the first up local from Arrochar and Tarbet to Craigendoran collided with a down freight that had been held to cross it at Glen Douglas. The driver was slowing down to make a conditional stop, otherwise the impact would have been greater than it was. Two coaches, both empty, were telescoped, but because of the absence of casualties the accident received little attention.

The other head-on collision occurred at the north end of Bridge of Orchy station on 17 April 1954. A K1 No. 62012 on a southbound goods struck B1 No. 61064 heading a northbound goods. There was extensive damage to the front ends of both engines, and the north end of the station was completely blocked by derailed wagons. The block occurred at one of the most critical points on the line, for there was no parallel road beyond Bridge of Orchy on which to organize the customary bypass bus service. Moreover, it was Easter Saturday and the morning train from Glasgow, double-headed and with ten coaches, was following the down goods. With the north end points at Bridge of Orchy out of action, there was no way of running an engine round a ten-coach train. The down passenger was, therefore, sent forward from Crianlarich with one engine and seven coaches, a formation that could be handled in the down sidings at Bridge of Orchy. The passengers were conducted round the wreckage and entrained in a special which departed for Rannoch hauled by a K4 running tender first.

On 27 January 1931 the 4.5 passenger train from Fort William to Glasgow met with a peculiar mishap on the Moor of Rannoch. The train, a heavy one, was double-headed and had six fish vans at the rear. The last vehicle, a 9-ton van, carried only 22 cwt of fish. When the train left Corrour on the falling gradient of 1 in 200 both engines were steaming, but some 600 yd south of the station Driver McIntosh on the train engine shut his regulator. Driver Young on the pilot engine kept his regulator open until the train had breasted a short stretch rising at 1 in 83 about 3 miles out from Corrour. The train then coasted briskly across the Moor on a falling gradient of 1 in 86.

At that part of the Moor the track wound in easy curves round pools and rocky outcrops. Only 11 minutes were allowed for the 7¼ miles between Corrour and Rannoch, and it was here that southbound trains whipped up speeds substantially in excess of the

40 m.p.h. maximum permitted on the line. By the time the 4.5 had run three-quarters of a mile down the slope the speed was climbing into the 50s and Young made a brisk brake application. The sudden check caused two wheels of the last van to lift momentarily off the rails.

In the 7¼-mile section there were only 70 yd of imperfect track, and the van was on the bad patch at that moment. There was an irregularity of curvature amounting to no more than a quarter of an inch, and the wheels, instead of settling back on the rails, dropped on to the sleepers. The derailed vehicle bumped along behind the train for 3½ miles as it wove round the reverse curves, rattled through the Cruach Rock snow-shed and dropped down the 1 in 53 into Rannoch station. The drivers knew nothing about the incident until they looked back after stopping at Rannoch : here the rear van had become completely derailed at the points and pulled the next vehicle with it.

The accident was attributed to the effect of the sudden brake application on a lightly loaded four-wheel vehicle riding on imperfect track. In future the railway company made a point of attaching fully-loaded six-wheeled vans at the rear of trains.

On Saturday 18 July 1953, the start of the annual Glasgow Fair holiday, traffic on the West Highland was exceptionally heavy. The 3.46 from Glasgow to Mallaig was made up of nine coaches and one large van in charge of K1 No. 62011 and B1 No. 61277. Southbound traffic was equally heavy, the 2.52 from Fort William to Queen Street having ten coaches and two vans. The trains were booked to cross at Ardlui. The appropriate tablets were picked up at Arrochar and Tarbet and Crianlarich respectively, and as one train steamed along Loch Lomondside and the other rumbled down Glen Falloch towards the rendezvous it did not seem to have occurred to anybody that *both* trains were too long for the Ardlui loops. The 3.46 was the first to arrive, and the stationmaster made the disconcerting discovery that the train overlapped the points at both ends of the station. Meanwhile, the even longer 2.52 had turned up and was being held at the up home.

The B1 was uncoupled from the front of the down train, run up over the points at the north end of the station, and set back into the up siding. That left space for the 2.52 to squeeze into the up side of the island platform. The train was brought in under caution, and the engine was stopped halfway along the platform. The next move was to have the K1 cautiously edge its train along the down platform until the buffers were almost touching the carriages of the up train. It was then found that the rear van had just cleared the fouling point at the south end of the station by inches. The 2.52 was able to run through; once it was clear the B1 was restored to the down train. Both engines then took water and left 39 minutes late.

**Note, added with the fourth edition (1998)**

Many aspects of life in the West Highlands have changed since this was written. The people of Fort William no longer turn out to meet every train; Gorton is now uninhabited, and *The Ghost* ceased to run in the early 1980s. However, we have retained this chapter unaltered and without addition as a true record of times past.

CHAPTER 10

# Locomotives and Rolling Stock

### NO WORKSHOPS

The writer who sets out to record the history of the West Highland Railway locomotives is faced at the outset with the daunting fact that the railway had no workshops, no locomotive superintendent, and in all its history only two classes—comprising 30 engines—were designed specifically for use on its metals. To give an account in detail of all the classes that ran on the railway would be to produce a re-hash of North British locomotive history. For all that, there is much that is worth mentioning about the engines that served there.

### THE WEST HIGHLAND BOGIES

Matthew Holmes was in command at Cowlairs when the North British Railway was called on to produce motive power for the West Highland Railway. A light machine capable of handling modest loads at modest speeds on continuous heavy gradients and severe curves was what was required. Holmes simply took his standard highly successful inside-cylinder 4—4—0 and adapted it to the needs of the West Highland. The result was NBR Class N—the West Highland bogie. The engine weighed 43 tons 6 cwt in working order. The standard 6 ft 6 in. driving wheels were reduced to 5 ft 7 in. and the wheel base of 9 ft 1 in. was cut to 8 ft 2 in. Two brake blocks were fitted to each driving wheel. The cylinders were 18 in. by 24 in., and a boiler of new design was used.

Six of these engines were built in 1893 (693—698), and by the time the railway was opened six more were ready for service—55, 393, 394 and 699-701. Twelve more were turned out in 1896 —227, 231, 232, 341-346 and 702-704. Not all were sent to the West Highland. A modification of the standard engine that Holmes might well have considered eminently suitable for a West Highland engine was an improved cab. The Holmes cutaway cab did not quite fit in

(48) *C.R. No. 123 in a blizzard at Glen Douglas in 1963*
(49) GNSR *'Gordon Highlander' with Caledonian coaches and observation car in Glen Falloch*

## MORE NORTH BRITISH LOCOS

(50) *A West Highland bogie and train of West Highland stock at Rhu in the early days*

(51) *C15s for the Craigendoran — Arrochar local service at Craigendoran. Note the express head-lamps*

(52) *Farewell to steam on the West Highland. Enthusiasts' special hauled by 'Glen Douglas' and J37 at Bridge of Orchy 1 June 1963*

with the Moor of Rannoch on a night of wind and rain. Yet the old drivers swore that the Holmes cab was more comfortable than the enclosed Drummond cab and the Reid cab of later days.

The West Highland bogies worked freight as well as passenger trains. Some of the freight trains were worked by Holmes Class C 0—6—0s which were almost new in 1894. The class was associated with the West Highland for 70 years; as Class J 36 some of their number were still at work at the demise of steam on the line. Of the West Highland bogies, seven survived to become Class D35 of the LNE, the last but one going to the breaker in October 1924. The odd man out was No. 695, one of the 1893 batch. This engine was enlarged and rebuilt by W. P. Reid in 1919, and became the sole representative of LNE Class D36. As rebuilt it was given a new boiler with Robinson superheater, new 19 in. by 26 in. cylinders with piston valves, and a side-window cab. It far outlived its fellows; it continued to do interesting work on and off the West Highland until it was scrapped in 1943, with 50 years of toil in difficult terrain behind it.

As new designs came from Cowlairs for general use on the North British system, some were tried out on the West Highland and if their performance was acceptable they were given regular duties. Two new classes were introduced to the line in 1906. One was Reid's Class K 'Intermediate' 4—4—0, and the other was his Class B 0—6—0. Both were more powerful than the two classes that had monopolized traffic since the opening of the line. The 4—4—0s were useful in saving double-heading of trains that had become marginally too heavy for a single West Highland bogie.

In 1913 came the engine whose class name is synonymous with West Highland—Reid's 'Glen'. The 'Glen' was not designed as a West Highland engine. It was a mixed-traffic design, but the happy decision to name it after West Highland glens, and the fact that many—though not all—of the engines made their way to the line at some part of their existence, left it with the reputation of being *the* West Highland class. For more than twenty years the 'Glens' bore the brunt of the passenger duties, and for many more years they were to be seen assisting engines of a later generation.

Also at work on the West Highland were some of Drummond's famous express passenger 4—4—0s of 1877, the 476 class. These had been built principally for service on the Waverley route, and their 6 ft 6 in. driving wheels were considered by some to be unsuitable for the West Highland terrain. Nevertheless they were useful engines, and on busy summer Saturdays when locomotive

K

power was scarce they could take over a train single-handed and give a good account of themselves. The last of the class was scrapped in 1923.

### The 'Glens' with North British numbers

| | | | |
|---|---|---|---|
| 34 | Glen Garvin | 298 | Glen Shiel |
| 35 | Glen Gloy | 307 | Glen Nevis |
| 100 | Glen Dochart | 405 | Glen Spean |
| 149 | Glenfinnan | 406 | Glen Croe |
| 153 | Glen Fruin | 407 | Glen Beasdale |
| 221 | Glen Orchy | 408 | Glen Sloy |
| 241 | Glen Ogle | 490 | Glen Dessary |
| 242 | Glen Mamie | 492 | Glen Gour |
| 256 | Glen Douglas | 493 | Glen Luss |
| 258 | Glen Roy | 494 | Glen Loy |
| 266 | Glen Falloch | 495 | Glen Mallie |
| 270 | Glen Garry | 496 | Glen Moidart |
| 278 | Glen Lyon | 502 | Glen Fintaig |
| 281 | Glen Murran | 503 | Glen Arklet |
| 287 | Glen Gyle | 504 | Glen Aladale |
| 291 | Glen Quoich | 505 | Glen Cona |

No. 256 Glen Douglas has been preserved and restored to North British livery. Until 1925 No. 492 was called Glen Gau.

The 'Glen' was followed in 1915 by Reid's superheated Class S, and this class too, as J 37, remained at work on the line until steam was withdrawn in 1963. The local trains between Craigendoran and Arrochar and Tarbet were handled for the most part by Class L and Class M 4—4—2 tanks, later Class C16 and C15. Class C15 also shared the working of the Fort Augustus branch with Drummond R Class 4—4—0 tanks. In 1940, 9135 (later 67460) was fitted for push-pull working and in the 1950s 67475 and 67474 followed suit.

During the Highland occupation of the Fort Augustus line the traffic was handled by Highland Railway Skye bogie No. 48 and 4—4—0 tank No. 52.

In early LNE days the names Doncaster and Gresley meant little to the West Highland old hands. Railway politics notwithstanding, the West Highland was still the West Highland. English innovations were not welcomed. If an engine arrived from the south with a newfangled footplate fitting, there was always an understanding relative in the works who would provide a good old North British counterpart to be fitted surreptitiously at Fort William. Visiting inspectors *had* to pass Craigendoran, and as soon as their presence was noted on West Highland metals the news was flashed to Fort William. Then there was brisk activity at the shed as the orthodox fittings were retrieved and the forbidden North British parts hidden under the coal—along with the hastily removed 'Jemmies'.

The West Highland Jemmy usually consisted of a short length of wire with a fishplate fastened to each end. The wire, when set across the orifice of the blastpipe and weighed down with the fishplates, was said to be a wondrous aid to steaming. But the sharp blast thus induced did not do the tubes any good, and the Jemmy tended to cause back pressure. The more fastidious driver, by answering a Peterborough firm's advertisement that appeared in the railway press at one time could, for the modest outlay of 1s 6d, avail himself of 'The Driver's Friend', a professionally made Jemmy guaranteed to improve the steaming of any locomotive. The device, claimed the advertisement, 'will fit any blast pipe, and can be put in or taken out in two seconds'. That 'taken out in two seconds' was significant; trouble awaited the driver whose engine was found to be equipped with a Jemmy, whether hand-made or mass-produced.

### THE COMING OF THE K'S

By the early thirties passenger-train loads had increased, and in the height of summer double-heading was almost universal. By then the vast resources of the LNE were behind the West Highland, and from the varied stock of locomotives under his control Gresley decided that his H2 class built for the Great Northern Railway would be the most likely to solve the West Highland's problems. As Class K2, thirteen of the engines were allocated to the West Highland. These humble, mixed-traffic machines had conferred on them the dignity of Gaelic nameplates, and in deference to the climate in their new territory they were taken to Cowlairs and given single-window cabs. They were named and numbered as follows:

| 4674 | *Loch Arkaig* |
| 4682 | *Loch Lochy* |
| 4684 | *Loch Garry* |
| 4685 | *Loch Treig* |
| 4691 | *Loch Morar* |
| 4692 | *Loch Eil* |

4693   *Loch Sheil*
4697   *Loch Quoich*
4698   *Loch Rannoch*
4699   *Loch Laidon*
4700   *Loch Lomond*
4701   *Loch Laggan*
4704   *Loch Oich*

The 'Lochs' could take 220 tons compared with the 'Glens'' 180 tons. One result was that the normal five-coach passenger train which had had to be double-headed when a string of fish vans was put on its tail was now handled by one 'Loch'. The K2s were particularly useful on the Mallaig Extension, where they soon supplanted the 'Glens' on the passenger trains. On the Craigendoran —Fort William section the heaviest trains were worked by K2s assisted by 'Glens'.

The K2 was to some extent a stop-gap engine; plainly something still more powerful was required. A K3 would have done the job if its axle-load had not been too heavy for the West Highland. Gresley had produced an engine to meet the special traffic demands on the East Coast route between Edinburgh and Aberdeen. Now, in 1936, he turned his attention to producing a special engine to cope with the peculiar demands of the West Highland. The result was the K4.

The first K4, 2—6—0 No. 3441 *Loch Long*, emerged from Darlington Works and was sent to King's Cross for tests early in May 1937. The following table compares some of the features of the K3 and K4.

|  | K3 | K4 |
|---|---|---|
| Dia. of coupled wheels | 5 ft 8 in. | 5 ft 2 in. |
| Wt of engine | 72 tons 10 cwt | 68 tons 8 cwt |
| Wt of tender | 52 tons | 44 tons 4 cwt |
| Heating surface | 2,308 sq. ft | 1,732 sq. ft |
| Grate area | 28 sq. ft | 27.5 sq. ft |
| Tractive effort at 85 per cent boiler pressure | 30,031 | 32,939 |

No. 3441 had three cylinders of 18½ in. by 26 in., which were cast in one piece. Walschaerts valve-gear was employed in the outside cylinders and Gresley's system for the inside cylinder. The boiler barrel was 5 ft 6 in. in diameter and 11 ft 7 in. between tube plates. The boiler pressure was 180 p.s.i. A Robinson 24-element superheater was provided, and narrow firebars gave 56 per cent air space.

*Loch Long* was put to work on the West Highland in the summer of 1937 on both passenger and freight trains, and the drivers soon realized that they had been given a tool of unprecedented quality.

The K4 became the talk of Eastfield and Fort William sheds, and there was keen competition among the men to get their hands on the regulator. *Loch Long* could take 300 tons unassisted, and it used no more water than a K2 with two-thirds of the load.

The success of *Loch Long* prompted Gresley to put five more K4s in hand at Darlington. With an eye to public relations, the policy of naming the engines after Highland lochs was discontinued in favour of the more romantic practice of naming them after clan chiefs. All the engines were turned out in apple green. The first of the five, No. 3442, appeared from Darlington Works in June 1938 and arrived at Fort William in time to help with the summer traffic.

To appreciate the story of 3442's name plate you have to know something of Lochaber history. The new engine was serviced at a shed within sight of Inverlochy Castle, and it was there in 1645 that James Graham, Marquess of Montrose—the one they called The Great Marquess—soundly defeated a Campbell army under their chief, the Duke of Argyll. Montrose had been away in Campbell country killing Campbells and looting their property, and while he was so engaged word came to him that the Duke of Argyll had invested Inverlochy. Montrose hurried back to Lochaber, swooped on the castle and put two thousand Campbells to the sword.

When No. 3442 arrived at Fort William the local folks were puzzled to find that the engine bore the name *Mac Cailein Mor*. Mac is Gaelic for 'son of', Mór is 'great'. *Cailin* (the spelling is that of Innes of Learney, Lord Lyon King at Arms) was the founder and chief of the Clan Campbell. The new engine might well have been named *Duke of Argyll*. Why on earth had the LNE chosen to honour a man who had been no friend of Lochaber? The tale that went round Fort William was that the railway company had intended all along to honour the Marquess of Montrose but that some Sassenach (and the word can mean a Lowland Scot as well as an Englishman) had told them that *Mac Caelien Mor* was Gaelic for *The Great Marquess*. Anyway, the plate as it stood was wrong: there was a vowel too many in *Cailien* and the accent was missing over the vowel in *Mor*. No. 3442 disappeared into the shops and duly emerged safely named in *English—The Great Marquess*. The vanquished of Inverlochy had become the victor, the villain the hero. No. 3445 of the class was named *Mac Cailin Mór* and the erstwhile rival clan chiefs joined forces to improve the services on the West Highland line.

There were those who were not reconciled to a Campbell being commemorated in Lochaber. Clan history apart, had it not been a

Campbell who had done his utmost to keep the railway out of his part of the Highlands? But *Cameron of Lochiel* was a happy choice for No. 3443, for a Cameron of Lochiel had put his weight behind every railway scheme in the history of Lochaber. No. 3444 was named *Lord of the Isles*, and No. 3446 took the title *MacLeod of MacLeod*. It is perhaps a pity that the name-pickers did not go the whole hog and call it *Sir Rory Mór, MacLeod of MacLeod*. That would have been an engine name to remember.

In 1945 No. 3445 was rebuilt at Doncaster by Edward Thompson as a two-cylindered engine with cylinders 20 in. by 26 in., and the boiler pressure was increased to 225 pounds. The engine became the prototype of the K1 class which was turned out from 1949 in large numbers for mixed traffic duties by Peppercorn. *Mac Cailin Mór* as Class K1/1 spent some two years in East Anglia before returning to Eastfield where it was joined by a batch of March K1s. The engines of this class associated with the West Highland were 62011, 62012, 62031, 62034 and 62052. *Mac Cailin Mór*, 62031, 62032 and 62052 were transferred from Eastfield to Fort William in June 1954.

The K4s did away with some, although not all, of the double-heading. They always worked alone; they were not allowed to be piloted. The Sunday excursion trains were often loaded to nine vehicles, the maximum for a K4. The engines came to the West Highland about the same time as the LMS Class 5s were introduced on the Oban road. The maximum load for a Class 5 on the Oban line was then 265 tons. West Highland drivers must have felt much satisfaction when they climbed out of Crianlarich with nine vehicles behind their K4s and caught sight of a Class 5 running parallel with them on the other side of Strathfillan with a lighter train—and piloted by an ex-Highland 'Castle'. The K4s in their shining green looked magnificent against the majesty of the West Highland landscape. The sight of one of them fighting its way up Glen Falloch with nine LNE teak coaches behind it, or winding round the wooded slopes above Loch Long with a train of LNE green and cream special excursion stock, was a memory to treasure for a lifetime.

After nationalization Fort William became a sub-shed of Perth, and LMS Class 5s from the parent shed began to appear on the West Highland. The earliest members of the class to arrive were in poor shape, and some lamentable performances were recorded. But it is only fair to add that when Class 5s, both LMS and Standard, were put on the line in tip-top condition they gave excellent results.

The advent of the 4—6—0 saw the older classes relegated to

minor duties, and some entirely disappeared from the West Highland. The K4s no longer handled passenger traffic south of Fort William, but west of the town they continued to perform feats that were entrusted to no other engine. On 26 July 1954 *MacLeod of MacLeod* took over at Fort William the 5.15 ex-Glasgow, a train of eight coaches and two vans that had arrived double-headed some 45 minutes late, and ran it to Mallaig with a loss of no more than five minutes. The tare load of that train was 291½ tons, and with its passengers it must have been 20 tons over the permitted maximum for a K4.

In May 1953 an attempt was made to replace the K2s on the Mallaig road with four Ivatt 2—6—0s—43132, 43133, 43135 and 43137—but the experiment failed. The engines were withdrawn in June of the same year. By the middle 50s the 'Glens' were making only fleeting appearances on the West Highland, but in May 1959 *Glen Falloch* and *Glen Loy* returned to stage a glorious swan-song. For a week they worked between Glasgow and Fort William, their exploits providing material for a most enjoyable television film.

By the early 1960s once-famous West Highland classes were vanishing, not only from the West Highland, but from human ken. The last of the C15s was withdrawn in April 1960, to be followed in March 1961 by the last C16. Before the year was out the 'Glens' (except for the preserved *Glen Douglas*), the K4s and the unique K1/1 had disappeared from the scene; *Mac Cailin Mór* was condemned in June; *Loch Long*, *Cameron of Lochiel*, *MacLeod of MacLeod* and *Lord of the Isles* were condemned in October; *Glen Loy* was withdrawn in November. The very last of the K4s, *The Great Marquess*, was condemned in December, but was preserved privately. Of the old guard two 'Lochs' remained—*Loch Arkaig* and *Loch Rannoch*—pottering about on Cowlairs ballast trains; but their days were numbered.

## STRANGERS WITHIN THE GATES

On 10 May 1956 an unusual visitor to the West Highland was Class 6 No. 72001 *Clan Cameron*. This engine headed the 3.46 from Glasgow Queen Street to Fort William and returned with the 9.31 a.m. from Fort William the following day. The exercise was a rehearsal for a special, due to be run on 16 June from Glasgow to Spean Bridge in connection with the gathering of the Clan Cameron at Achnacarry. The driver, fireman and guard on that occasion all had the surname Cameron. In spite of a start ten minutes late, and twenty minutes lost on the road, the 'Clan' had its seven coaches in Spean Bridge on time. In case of accidents the railway authorities stationed K4 *Cameron of Lochiel* at Crianlarich ready to take over.

In the closing years of steam, the enterprise of the railway societies was instrumental in bringing several interesting strangers to West Highland metals. Perhaps the most incongruous visitor was Caledonian Railway No. 123—a 7 ft single on the West Highland gradients! This grand old veteran made one of its trips in a raging blizzard. On an earlier occasion No. 123 partnered No. 256 *Glen Douglas* on a trip from Glasgow to Oban *via* the West Highland and the Callander & Oban. That was the first time a 'Glen' had tasted Callander & Oban metals. In their day, of course, the 'Glens' had been prohibited, a fact apparently forgotten by the powers that be. Another interesting combination on the West Highland was GNS No. 49 *Gordon Highlander* hauling the two Caledonian restored coaches. In 1961 *Cameron of Lochiel* was retrieved from mundane duties in Fife and performed excellently on a last K4 run from Glasgow to Fort William.

Other classes that appeared on the West Highland from time to time were J38 and J39 0—6—0s and V1 2—6—2 tanks, the latter on Arrochar local trains. During the second war Class 07 2—8—0s helped out with the heavy freight. The special workings from Glasgow to Oban *via* Dalmally raised some problems for the operating department, for the 'Glens' were prohibited from using the Oban road. The odd pairing which gave the combination of power and route availability was an ex-Great Eastern B12 4—6—0, No. 8502, and the rebuilt West Highland bogie No. 695 (in LNE days, 9695). These engines handled the pioneer trip to Oban in 1931 and were subsequently employed on Crianlarich circular excursions. When the regular daily train from Glasgow (Queen Street) to Oban was instituted in 1949 it was hauled throughout by a B1.

The LMS Class 5s and Standard Class 5s were joined by ex-LNE B1s, and in the last days of steam these engines took most of the traffic on the Craigendoran—Fort William section. It was pleasant to see the final 4—6—0 designs of two great pre-grouping companies in partnership, lifting a heavy train away from Ardlui to begin the ascent of Glen Falloch. Such entertainments were short-lived. In December 1961 the railway authorities announced that it was hoped within a few months to replace the forty-five steam engines on the West Highland railway system—and this included the Callander & Oban as well as the West Highland—with twenty-three Type 2 diesel-electrics and four diesel shunting engines.

## LOCOMOTIVE PERFORMANCE

On the West Highland the speed of a train is governed by the nature of the line rather than by the power at the head end. Train timing loses much of its excitement if the timer knows in advance that over large tracts of territory speed will not climb out of the 30s and in 100 miles may never reach 50. For that reason logs of West Highland runs are rare. The following extracts from two logs meticulously recorded by A. J. S. Paterson in the last decade of steam are of particular interest.

The first log records part of a run from Glasgow to Fort William by the 10.21 a.m. on 6 August 1954. The engine was Class 5 No. 44908, and the five coaches weighed 167¾ tons tare, 180 tons gross. After an average run from Glasgow to Craigendoran Junction, the train left Craigendoran station 2 min. 05 sec. late. Uninspired footplate work brought the deficit to 4 min. 10 sec. by Garelochhead and 5¼ min. by Arrochar and Tarbet. The Fort William crew who took over from the Eastfield crew at Ardlui faced a challenge; because of the late running of the up train the 10.21 left Ardlui 19 min. 39 sec. late.

The new crew showed more spirit than their predecessors. The train left Crianlarich 16 min. 16 sec. late, and this was down to 14 min. 11 sec. by Tyndrum. It was at Bridge of Orchy that the fireworks started. From a dead stand at the station, 44908 was climbing steadily at 40·9 m.p.h. a mile out, and this on gradients of 1 in 80 and 1 in 170. The following mile, with gradients of 1 in 240 and 1 in 114, was taken at a top speed of 50 m.p.h. Then followed a 3-mile stretch of 1 in 60 and 1 in 66 with speed falling in the first mile to 42·9, in the second to 37·5 and finally to 32·2 at milepost 55.

A recovery to 45 m.p.h. at milepost 57 brought the train to Gorton showing a gain of 1 min. over scheduled time on the difficult 8-mile section. A further minute was clipped off the time from Gorton to Rannoch and 2 min. were picked up between Rannoch and Corrour. A detailed log of the run from Bridge of Orchy to Corrour Summit follows.

A fast run down Lochtreigside and through the Spean gorges, plus smart station work, had the train in Fort William only 4 min. 28 sec. late.

The second log records a run on 7 August 1954 from Mallaig to Glenfinnan Summit. The train was the 2.45 p.m. Mallaig to Glasgow (Queen Street) made up of 5 coaches weighing 168 tons tare. The

## LOG 1

| Station | M.P. | Sched. | Actual | Speed | |
|---------|------|--------|--------|-------|---|
| Bridge of Orchy  *dep* | | 28.00 | 26.39 | | 14 m. 55 s. late |
| | ½ | | | 24·3 | |
| | 50 | | 29.57 | 29·0 | |
| | ½ | | 30.51 | | |
| | ¾ | | 31.14 | 39·1 | |
| | 51 | | 31.36 | 40·9 | |
| | ¼ | | 31.56 | 45·0 | |
| | ½ | | 32.14 | 50·0 | |
| | ¾ | | 32.34 | 45·0 | |
| | 52 | | 32.52 | 50·0 | |
| | ¼ | | 33.09 | 52·9 | |
| | ½ | | 33.29 | 45·0 | |
| | ¾ | | 33.49 | 45·0 | |
| | 53 | | 34.10 | 42·9 | |
| | ¼ | | 34.32 | 40·9 | |
| | ½ | | 34.56 | 37·5 | |
| | ¾ | | 35.20 | 37·5 | |
| | 54 | | 35.44 | 37·5 | |
| | ¼ | | 36.10 | 34·6 | |
| | ½ | | 36.38 | 32·2 | |
| | ¾ | | 37.05 | 33·3 | |
| | 55 | | 37.33 | 32·2 | |
| | ¼ | | 38.01 | 32·2 | |
| | ½ | | 38.29 | 32·2 | |
| | ¾ | | 38.55 | 34·6 | |
| | 56 | | 39.19 | 37·5 | |
| | ¼ | | 39.42 | 39·1 | |
| | ½ | | 40.04 | 40·9 | |
| | ¾ | | 40.24 | 45·0 | |
| | 57 | | 40.44 | 45·0 | |
| Gorton *pass* | | 44.00 | 41.31 | | 13 m. 47 s. late |
| | 57¾ | | 41.59 | | |
| | 58 | | 42.19 | 45·0 | |
| | ¼ | | 42.39 | 45·0 | |
| Rannoch *pass* | | 55.00 | 51.39 | 45·0 | 12 m. 44 s. late |
| | 64¾ | | 51.57 | | |
| | 65 | | 52.32 | 25·7 | |
| | ¼ | | 53.09 | 24·3 | |
| | ½ | | 53.46 | 24·3 | |
| | ¾ | | 54.23 | 24·3 | |
| | 66 | | 54.57 | 26·5 | |
| | ¼ | | 55.57 | 26·5 | |
| | ½ | | | | |
| | ¾ | | 56.22 | | |
| | 67 | | 56.45 | 39·1 | |
| | ¼ | | 57.09 | 37·5 | |
| | ½ | | 57.34 | 36·0 | |
| | ¾ | | 57.59 | 36·0 | |
| | 68 | | 58.24 | 36·0 | |
| | ¼ | | 58.50 | 34·6 | |
| | ½ | | 59.17 | 33·3 | |
| | ¾ | | 59.42 | 36·0 | |
| | 69 | | 60.05 | 39·1 | |
| | ¼ | | 60.29 | 37·5 | |
| | ½ | | 60.54 | 36·0 | |
| | ¾ | | 61.17 | 39·1 | |
| | 70 | | 61.40 | 39·1 | |
| | ¼ | | 62.04 | 37·5 | |
| | ½ | | 62.27 | 39·1 | |
| | ¾ | | 62.52 | 36·0 | |
| | 71 | | 63.14 | 40·9 | |
| | ¼ | | 63.37 | 39·1 | |
| | ½ | | 64.00 | 39·1 | 10 m. 40 s. |
| Corrour *pass* | 71 54c. | 70.00 | 64.24 | | late |

## LOG 2

| Station | M.P. | Sched. | Actual | Speed | |
|---------|------|--------|--------|-------|---|
| Mallaig  *dep* |  | 00.00 | 00.00 |  | 43 s. late |
|  | 39 |  | 02.03 |  |  |
|  | 38¾ |  | 02.57 | 16·67 |  |
|  | ½ |  | 03.42 | 20·0 |  |
|  | ¼ |  | 04.22 | 22·5 |  |
|  | 38 |  |  |  |  |
|  | ¾ |  | 05.35 | 24·0 |  |
|  | ½ |  | 06.03 | 32·2 |  |
|  | ¼ |  | 06.29 | 34·6 |  |
| Morar    *arr* |  |  | 07.43 |  |  |
| Morar    *dep* |  | 09.00 | 08.17 |  | Time |
|  | 36 |  |  |  |  |
|  | 35 |  | 12.09 |  |  |
|  | ¾ |  | 12.29 | 45·0 |  |
|  | ½ |  | 12.47 | 50·0 |  |
|  | ¼ |  | 13.07 | 45·0 |  |
|  | 34 |  | 13.27 | 45·0 |  |
|  | ¾ |  | 13.47 | 45·0 |  |
|  | ½ |  | 14.12 | 36·0 |  |
|  | ¼ |  | 14.42 | 30·0 |  |
|  | 33 |  | 15.18 | 25·0 |  |
|  | ¾ |  | 16.02 | 20·5 |  |
|  | ½ |  | 16.48 | 19·6 |  |
| Arisaig   *arr* |  |  | 18.07 |  |  |
| Arisaig   *dep* |  | 22.00 | 19.51 |  | 1 m. 26 s. |
|  | 31 |  | 22.35 |  | early |
|  | 30 |  | 25.07 | 21·5 |  |
| Beasdale | 29 |  | 26.47 |  |  |
| *pass* |  |  | 27.27 |  |  |
|  | 28 |  | 28.32 |  |  |
|  | 27 |  |  |  |  |
|  | 26 |  | 32.16 |  |  |
|  | 25 |  | 34.29 |  |  |
|  | 24 |  | 36.34 |  |  |
| Lochailort |  |  | 37.16 |  |  |
|   *arr* |  |  |  |  |  |
| Lochailort |  |  | 38.58 |  |  |
|   *dep* |  | 41.00 | 41.55 |  |  |
|  | 23 |  | 43.33 |  |  |
|  | 22 |  | 45.10 |  |  |
|  | 21 |  | 45.32 | 40·9 |  |
|  | ¾ |  | 45.55 | 39·1 |  |
|  | ½ |  | 46.17 | 40·9 |  |
|  | ¼ |  | 46.39 | 40·9 |  |
|  | 20 |  | 47.02 | 39·1 |  |
|  | ¾ |  | 47.29 | 33·3 |  |
|  | ¼ |  | 47.57 | 32·2 |  |
|  | 19 |  | 48.32 | 25·5 |  |
|  | ¾ |  | 49.10 | 23·5 |  |
|  | ½ |  | 49.50 | 22·5 |  |
|  | ¼ |  | 50.34 | 20·5 |  |
|  | 18 |  | 51.17 | 20·9 |  |
|  | ¾ |  | 52.01 | 20·5 |  |
| Summit |  |  | 52.57 |  |  |

engine was K4 2—6—0 No. 61998 *MacLeod of MacLeod*. From a late start of about ¾ min. the engine got away smartly and was doing 22-23 m.p.h. at the first summit 2 miles out, after negotiating gradients ranging from 1 in 50 to 1 in 150. Departure from Morar was on time. The engine, driven over Keppoch Moss at 45-50 m.p.h., rushed into the ½ mile of 1 in 90 followed by a stretch of 1 in 50 beset with severe reverse curvature. Speed had dropped to 19·6 by the next summit, although an excellent climb had put the K4 1½ minutes to the good by Arisaig.

The 8 miles to Kinlochailort, packed as they are with sharp curves and steep gradients (including two miles of 1 in 48), were taken with the usual caution. The engine quickly reached 40 m.p.h. on the 3 miles of level track east of Lochailort, but soon it was battling with stretches of 1 in 50 and 1 in 48 by the side of Loch Eilt. Speed never fell below 20½ m.p.h. and Glenfinnan Summit was cleared in 13 min. 59 sec.

The start from Glenfinnan station was over 12 minutes late due to the late arrival of the down train. Some brisk running along the easy length beside Loch Eil brought the train into Fort William only 7 min. late.

### ROLLING STOCK

The carriages specially designed and built at Cowlairs for the opening of the West Highland Railway were imaginative and ambitious vehicles for their time. Matthew Holmes had the idea of giving as many passengers as possible a window seat while at the same time catering for those who preferred orthodox compartment-type accommodation. The vehicles had single compartments at each end with a large saloon in the middle. Each compartment seated four passengers on one side and three on the other, the space usually allocated to an eighth passenger being occupied by a door leading into the saloon. In the first-class vehicle the compartments were 7 ft deep and the intervening saloon was 21 ft long. The saloon itself was sub-divided by a light partition in which was a swing door.

The outstanding feature of the carriage was the space given to windows. The first-class saloon windows were 4 ft 6 in. long by 2 ft 4½ in. deep. Walnut mouldings and gold beading were much in evidence. 'The fittings,' said a contemporary description, 'include a folding basin with water tap and mirror and a carafe and tumbler arranged in the manner adopted in the best of steamship cabins.'

Contractors' photographs of the new railway decorated the walls. Messrs Laycock of Sheffield installed the brown spring blinds, the torpedo ventilators and the Gold system of carriage heating. In the third-class coach the end compartments were 5 ft 10 in. deep, and the central saloon was 24 ft long. The observation windows were somewhat smaller—4 ft by 2 ft 4½ in. The first-class coach seated a total of 42 passengers, the third class 60 passengers.

The vehicles weighed 22 tons, were 50 ft 1 in. over the buffers, 8 ft 0¼ in. wide and 11 ft 9 in. high above rail level. They were mounted on standard North British four-wheel bogies. They compared very favourably with the six-wheel 15-ton East Coast Joint Stock vehicles that catered for the through passengers from King's Cross to West Highland destinations. In 1895 an East Coast bogie composite was introduced for the West Highland service. A peculiarity was that it had coupé ends. During the first North British occupation of the Invergarry & Fort Augustus one of these coaches was used in winter only to provide the passenger service. Main line comfort including steam heating and lavatory accommodation was offered to 12 first-class and 25 third-class passengers.

The West Highland saloon carriages were not entirely successful in their original condition. The trouble stemmed from the fact that none of the windows was designed to open, and the torpedo ventilators sent a thin jet of fresh air into the vehicles almost at roof level. The result was that the interiors became uncomfortably hot. The observation windows were broken by opening half-lights which, if they improved the temperature, spoiled the appearance of the coach and impeded the view.

In 1906 the North British built large, handsome corridor carriages with which to challenge the Caledonian's *Grampian Express* for the Glasgow—Aberdeen traffic. Seven years later a modified version of this vehicle was designed for the West Highland. It had side corridors but no vestibules; this was to allow gable windows to be fitted in the end compartments. On the trial run of these vehicles to Fort William on 24 April 1913, William Whitelaw and directors and friends joined the train. The idea of the coupé compartment was good, but only a very limited number of passengers could enjoy a rear view of the receding scenery. As recently as 1951 one of these carriages was used daily to transport railway employees from Queen Street to Cadder yard and back. The staff train appeared in the public timetable as far as Bishopbriggs and railway enthusiasts made a ploy of occupying the coupé compartment for the trip up Cowlairs Incline. The view across the tender on to the footplate as the engine—sometimes a J36—blasted its way up through the tunnel could be enthralling. It was not until the rebuilt ex-LNE beaver-tail cars from the Coronation sets were sent to the West Highland in the late fifties that an observation car worthy of the name was seen on the line.

Dining-cars were late in coming to the West Highland. The first ones—old Great Northern vehicles—began operating on 8 July 1929. Their advent meant the curtailment of one of the West Highland's most delightful customs. During the servicing stop at Crianlarich passengers could have a snack at the dining-room on the platform, or they could collect a meal basket which the guard had ordered for them in advance. The Crianlarich basket became an institution. Some of the travellers took their baskets to the seclusion of their compartments, but others preferred to explore its mysteries in the open air. Many a passenger who had entrained the previous night in London enjoyed his first Scottish breakfast sitting on a platform seat at Crianlarich, his appetite whetted by the pure, crisp air of a Perthshire morning. The stopping time at Crianlarich varied between 5 and 11 minutes. The demand for the famous baskets became less as the dining-cars grew in popularity, but breakfast, luncheon, and tea baskets were still being offered at the outbreak of war in 1939. The arrival of the trains was greeted with enthusiasm by the Crianlarich hens. The sound of an approaching train was the signal for every fowl in the railway cottage gardens to go squawking and clucking over the rails, oblivious of the danger of churning wheels, to solicit crumbs from the open-air diners. The dining-room still functions at Crianlarich, but the 4-to-6-minute stop of the diesel-hauled trains puts some restriction on its use.

### EPILOGUE

Now the diesels are in the glens. Glen Falloch no longer echoes to the crack of twin exhausts as a double-header roars across the Dubh Eas. No more do the sparks patter like hail on the carriage roofs. No more does the shriek of a K2, responding to a lineside 'whistle' board, rise to the rocky tops of the mountains. No longer can a traveller stand on Rannoch platform of an evening and hear the thin whistle of a 'Glen' far away out on the Moor.

These were sounds to remember.

# CHAPTER 11

# *Postscripts*

One summer day a few years ago I found myself sharing a compartment in a West Highland train with an elderly American couple and a young lady from Kent. It was a sparkling morning, and our English traveller frequently poked her camera at the passing scene. Eventually she opened her bag, extracted a book and handed it to me with the query, 'Have you read this?' I would have answered with a simple *yes* had not the Americans (who were in the know) broken into broad grins which demanded an explanation. The book I had been offered was my own *The West Highland Railway*. 'This has made my day,' declared my lady reader, and I could see she meant it.

It is very gratifying for an author to be told that he has achieved precisely what he set out to achieve. My aim in writing the book had been to try to capture the peculiar magic of the West Highland Railway in print, and when the book first appeared in the shops I was not convinced that I had done so. Then came a steady and continuing flow of letters from people who had experienced the West Highland's magic and were at pains to tell me that they had found it again in the pages of my book.

A church organist wrote from Surrey, 'I would like to send a few lines to say how much pleasure your book has given me over the past two years—so much so that I recently bought another copy in the Pan edition for conveniently slipping in the pocket.' 'Thank you very much for giving such a great deal of pleasure,' wrote Lord Garnock. 'Having been brought up in a part of the world traversed by that remarkable line it gave me a great deal of pleasure to read a whole book devoted to the West Highland and certainly brought back many memories.' A retired passenger guard who had seen 51 years of service with the GNR and LNER wrote to say how in his young days he had been fascinated by a nameboard he had seen on a north train leaving King's Cross: *Edinburgh, Glasgow, Fort William, Mallaig*, but it was 1972 before my correspondent, by then a widower, set off to see the West Highland. 'I was thrilled by all I saw on the whole journey,' he wrote. 'I was lucky enough to meet two ex-railwaymen and their wives who had done the trip after reading your book.'

One West Highland tale I encountered but did not use in my book for want of corroboration was the story of the West Highland baby. It appeared that this legendary infant had been born in a West Highland train and had been named after the guard, the fireman or the driver according to which version you chose to accept. I was more than interested to receive a letter from Dorset written by the doctor who had delivered the baby. He described how he and his wife were returning to England, after spending a fortnight tramping in the West Highlands, when the guard, in an agitated state, inquired through the train if there was a nurse on board. On being asked by the doctor what was wrong the guard replied, 'Oh sir, we're going to have another passenger.' Investigation proved that this was indeed the case. The train was running between Roy Bridge and Tulloch and there was nowhere to put off the mother-to-be. She was taken to a first class compartment. The doctor explained what happened next. 'In the next compartment were the Marquess and Marchioness of Bute. The former had a painful condition for which he had some analgesic tablets. He gave me a number of these. The marchioness and my wife acted as my helpers. They collected all the lavatory towels, kept me supplied with boiling water from the diner and stood guard at the door of the compartment. I was amazed at the contents of the railway first-aid box—everything essential.'

At Crianlarich there was a stroke of luck when a Scots Canadian nurse on her way back to Canada boarded the train. She was nicely in time to assist at the birth. The baby was born about 40 minutes out of Glasgow. The doctor concluded, 'My one regret was that in the excitement I did not take a photograph of my wife at Queen Street attired in tramping kit carrying the baby wrapped in triangular bandages to the ambulance.' The baby was named Evan McLeod Nicholson after the nurse and the doctor.

But what of recent events? The most significant change in the West Highland since the book was first published has been the re-siting of Fort William station. The railway, of course, had cut off the town from Loch Linnhe, a piece of deplorable planning which the townspeople had recognised too late and had been a bone of contention in local politics for 80 years. The new station at the east end of the town was opened on 13 June 1975. The original station and approach lines disappeared within a week. The engine shed and associated yard and sidings likewise disappeared and were replaced by a motive power depot and marshalling yard at Tom-na-Faire near Mallaig Junction. Gorton platform and

LATTER DAYS STEAM

(52)   *Two Stanier Class 5 4–6–0s crossing the Fillan viaduct at Crianlarich, against the background of Ben More in 1959*

(53)   *K1 No. 62012 on Mallaig–Fort William train on the ascent from Keppoch Moss to Arisaig in the summer of 1954*

(54) *Class 27 D5382 passes the engine shed at Crianlarich in April 1968 with a freight from Glasgow*

(55) *The old station at Fort William: Class 27 D5356 waits to leave on 8 October 1971. A road now covers the site of the delightfully positioned original station*

signal box have vanished, Ardlui has lost its platform buildings due to subsidence and Glen Douglas public platform no longer functions. On the signalling side tokenless block has been installed between Crianlarich and Rannoch to control movements on the single line sections between these places, and foreshadowed the end of yet another traditional facet of railway operation, the exchange of tokens at crossing places.

## POSTSCRIPT TO THE THIRD EDITION
### by Alan J.S. Paterson

It is eight years now since the second edition of this popular book appeared and, but for the much lamented death of its author, there is no doubt that he would have had much to narrate regarding the many changes in the West Highland scene in recent times. In adding these notes to bring the story up to date it occurs to me that the reader may be interested in a personal view of the many alterations north of Craigendoran as they appeared to me during a recent journey over the whole route to Mallaig. During the 1950s and up to the end of steam traction in the early sixties, I had been a frequent traveller on the West Highland, gaining an intimate knowledge of the railway itself as well as the districts which it served. The departure of the steam engine, however, meant for me and many other railway enthusiasts the end of one of the principal attractions of this fascinating line, and other interests claimed my attention thereafter. My journeys, therefore, to Fort William and Mallaig after 1961 were rare, and ceased entirely after 1972. Consequently, it was with a feeling of keen anticipation that I arranged to make a return trip to Mallaig during late May, 1984 for I knew that much had changed in the dozen years since my last run.

### THE SOUTHERN SECTION

It is still necessary to rise at an early hour to make the return journey in one day with a reasonable time at Mallaig, and I joined the train from Glasgow (Queen Street) at its first stop at Dumbarton. Although all modern timetable references are, of course, on the 24-hour system, the habits of a lifetime make it difficult to think of the early morning departure from Glasgow as anything but 5.50 a.m. Older times were recalled when the train was notified as running over half an hour late—so often were the timekeeping faults south of the border reflected in long delays on the single line sections of the West Highland, and the problem still seems to exist today, to some extent.

The train arrived behind type 37 diesel electric locomotive No. 37027 *Loch Eil*, bearing on her side panel the West Highland terrier motif which is now widely used to identify and advertise the line's services—it appears, for example, on the public timetable leaflets. This is an ingenious and attractive publicity feature and, as with so many good ideas, one wonders why nobody thought of it before. The name *Loch Eil* recalled vividly the Gresley K-2 which, thirty years earlier, might well have appeared on the corresponding train but there was nothing then in service similar to the second 'engine'—No. 97252 *Ethel 3*—one of the older and now obsolete diesel electric locomotives of which three have been specially adapted to provide electric heating for the carriages. (The apparent 'name' is, in fact, compounded of the initial letters of the words 'Electric Train Heating ex-Locomotive'). At a fairly moderate cost, each of these former type 25 diesels was altered to become a generator vehicle supplying the modern Mark 3 sleeping carriages and Mark 2 daytime coaches, thus ensuring the continued provision of sleeper facilities over the Fort William line, for the type 37 diesel electric engines, fitted only with steam heating, could not cope with the most modern coaches. The train itself consisted of two Mark 3 sleeping carriages, which now run via the West Coast main line from London, another change from the years when the West Highland connections were identified exclusively with the East Coast route from King's Cross. Two Mark 2 day coaches and three older vehicles made up the remainder of the seven-coach train.

It is probably true to say that most of the obvious changes in the West Highland line have taken place on the section south of Arrochar, and to one who knew the railway in earlier times it was depressing to note the absence of the stations at Craigendoran Upper, Rhu, Shandon and Whistlefield, which have now been demolished, leaving few traces of their existence. At Helensburgh Upper the up loop line has been taken out and the station—now unstaffed—looks unkempt and neglected, to a great extent abandoned to the undergrowth now encroaching upon it. This part of the line, running mostly beside and above the Gareloch, is vastly different from what it was thirty years ago, for the suburban sprawl now extends as far as Garelochhead itself. Much of it has been built for defence personnel who have moved into the area to serve the extensive NATO installations, which can be seen at their most obtrusive at the once peaceful wayside crossing of Glen Douglas. But all this housing came too late to save the once familiar 'push-and-pull' train service which ran for many years from Craigendoran to Arrochar and Tarbet in connection with the Helensburgh suburban trains. The new population on the Gareloch depends wholly upon road transport, and the hillside echoes no longer to the scream of a North British whistle as the handsome little tank engine with its two carriages rattles amongst the trees high above the loch.

Garelochhead station, largely untouched, is the first sign that the older West Highland still survives, although the buildings are painted nowadays in a combination of shades of green—not, perhaps, entirely successfully. Nevertheless, as the train swung round the curve out of the station loop and started on the first long climb, to Glen Douglas, all the old thrill was there, of the slowly-changing panoramic views, the fresh scent of highland vegetation, the magnificent sight of primroses and bluebells in veritable cascades down the hillsides. May is a lovely month to see the line at its very best, and in fine weather there is no other route in Britain to compare with its scenic glories. On the occasion of my journey, however, the morning was dull, with a fine, misty rain, and *Loch Eil* was in some trouble getting her train under way on the sharp climb to Whistlefield, slipping continuously and noisily on the wet rails before finally getting a grip.

There are obvious changes on this section, which is now covered with the large-scale plantings of the Forestry Commission, and a landscape once very bleak is well on the way to being heavily wooded. The work of the Commission is also evident further north, most notably on long stretches of Rannoch Moor. Despite criticisms in some quarters as to the visual impact of seemingly endless tracts of evergreens, there is no doubt that the planting of these trees is bringing fresh prospects to an area which badly needs work, and in the long run they will help the railway to remain in being. Whatever may be said of trees, however, they are infinitely preferable to the sinister clutter of military equipment and installations now disfiguring the hillside at Glen Douglas, a dreary reminder in this otherwise peaceful spot of the continuing political tensions under which we all live.

### THE CENTRAL SECTION

From Arrochar & Tarbet the original stations are practically intact, with two or three notable exceptions. The impressive buildings at Ardlui, once the largest of any intermediate station on the line, have finally succumbed to subsidence and have long since been swept away. At Craianlarich, fire destroyed the old structure several years ago and a more modern, and much smaller, building has been substituted. Happily for West Highland *aficionados*, the tearoom of long tradition and happy memory was spared the conflagration and survives.

Crianlarich engine shed remains as a prominent feature of the erstwhile steam operating facilities, but the old turntable has gone now. Apart from this, however, the sidings are all *in situ* and Crianlarich is obviously a centre for local permanent way repair work. The original signals remain much as before, save only that here, as elsewhere over the whole route, the original Stevens pattern lower quadrant signal arms have at long last been replaced by upper quadrants. Most, however, are mounted on the lattice posts of North British design. More modern signalling has replaced the older type at Tyndrum (Upper) and Bridge of Orchy, where the station loops have been arranged for double direction running. At the former station the train ran through the down side in the normal way, passing an up goods train headed by one of the un-named type 37 locomotives, but at Bridge of Orchy we ran through the up side, although passing no other train at that point.

There is much evidence of new planting by the Forestry Commission all the way from upper Glen Falloch, through Tyndrum and on past Bridge of Orchy. This is, of course, the district so closely identified in Gaelic literature with the celebrated bard Donnchaidh Ban—Duncan Macintyre (1724–1812)—whose poetry sang the praises of Glen Orchy as none other. It is a scene dominated by the striking outline of Ben Doran, a mountain closer to the poet's heart than all others—'An t-urram thar gach beinn aig Beinn Dobhrain' (pre-eminent over every mountain is Ben Doran)—and whose natural beauties he extols in many lovely verses. Descending slowly round the Horse Shoe Bend towards Bridge of Orchy one is constantly reminded of the old bard as the whole splendid panorama unfolds. It is one of the great moments of the railway journey to Fort William.

On Rannoch Moor the old crossing place at Gorton has now wholly vanished, but at Rannoch station the passing loop still remains and all is much as it used to be in former days. The long climb up to Corrour, the summit of the railway, is still distinguished by snow fences—now much eroded by time, fire, and the weather, it must be admitted—and the unique snow shed in the Cruach rock cutting continues as before to draw comment from uninformed passengers. At Corrour there is still a passing loop, where *Loch Awe*, yet another of the ubiquitous type 37 engines, headed the 4-coach 08.40 train from Fort William to Glasgow. This engine carries a name new to the West Highland, for Loch Awe lies in former Caledonian Railway territory on the Oban route and it was never used by the London & North Eastern Railway as a title for one of its engines. Nevertheless it is now an appropriate and attractive addition to the list of named locomotives running to the western highlands.

THE NORTHERN SECTION

The descent to Fort William down Loch Trieg and on through Glen Spean is as attractive as ever, with the dramatic passage of the Monessie Gorge remaining one of the highlights of the entire journey. Tulloch station is practically unchanged, but in contrast Roy Bridge is now no more than an unkempt halt, all its operating facilities having been removed. However, at Spean Bridge the scene was quite different— station buildings renovated, the passing loop still in use, and sidings obviously carrying local freight traffic—generally an atmosphere of activity in pleasing distinction to the closed and unstaffed stations further south. Yet another type 37—No. 37081 *Loch Long*—headed an up goods here, its name recalling an old favourite of steam days, the pioneer Gresley K-4 2-6-0. Just west of the station is to be seen one of the few surviving relics of the ill-fated Invergarry & Fort Augustus Railway in its former engine shed, still intact, and now used for private purposes by a local owner.

Fort William presents probably the greatest changes to one familiar with the old terminus. John Thomas drew attention to how the railway had cut off the town from Loch Linnhe, but in truth it is difficult to see how, in Victorian days, the demand for a centrally situated station could have been met otherwise. The site of Fort William rises steeply from the water's edge to a height of three or four hundred feet and the only flat ground available for the railway was on the loch side. What gave rise to a demand for the removal of the station to another spot in later years was the burgeoning road traffic which, every summer, jammed up the town's main thoroughfare. Present-day planners therefore abolished the old station and replaced it with a by-pass road and roundabouts. While these facilities were much needed and long overdue, it can hardly be said that the aesthetic result has been much of an improvement, the exposed frontage to the loch being bleaker than ever. I was fond of the old station, which was admittedly not a classic architectural feature, but it was pleasant to walk from it along the lineside to the engine shed at the old military fort on a fine summer evening, an innocent pleasure, alas!, now denied to the railway enthusiast. The new station, about half a mile short of the former terminus, is clean and smart, without being outstanding, but it has good facilities for passengers and remains quite conveniently placed for the town.

## THE MALLAIG EXTENSION

I found the Mallaig line adequately served by a three-coach train hauled by the inevitable type 37 engine, this time No. 37192, but it was pleasing to note quite heavy passenger traffic. All stations on the extension remain in use in some shape or form, but Banavie, Corpach, Locheilside and Morar have been reduced to unstaffed halts, as has also Lochailort, which has lost its passing loop and sidings. The stations at Glenfinnan and Arisaig retain full operating provisions. The entire line is unquestionably the finest scenic section on the whole of the British Rail network, and has lost little of its charm for those whose principal interest lies in railway operation. In the summer of 1984 it has been the scene of an imaginative experiment by British Rail, in which preserved steam locomotives, beautifully restored to original condition, have been used to haul regular trains during the peak months. Initial public response appears to be gratifyingly favourable, and this marvellous section of railway once again witnesses the sight of a North British goods engine, No. 673 *Maude*, in her pre-1923 livery, in service over the line on which this class was one of the first to be employed when it was opened at the turn of the century. Accompanying her will be two LMS Stanier Class 5 4–6–0s and these, although never used on the Mallaig line in steam days, were nevertheless latterly the mainstay of the traffic south of Fort William.

Morar station, reduced to an unstaffed halt, has an unusual feature in the operation of its level crossing, where the gates are now opened and closed, as required, by the train crew. This very practical solution has allowed station staff to be dispensed with, permitting economies to be made on a route where reduction of overheads is as important as the generation of fresh traffic.

Mallaig station nowadays presents a rather forlorn appearance, having lost its overall canopy roof and most of its sidings. The engine shed is derelict, the turntable removed, and no traffic is now taken to and from the pier at the harbour. But the Caledonian–MacBrayne ferry to Armadale still reminds us of the steamer connections of former days, and the cry of seagulls remains a feature of this remote outpost of the railway system. Here you are on the doorstep of the Hebrides, the Isle of Skye beckons from across the Sound of Sleat, the western seas shimmer as always, and somehow one is aware that, in spite of much change, the West Highland Railway is still the same in spirit.

PROSPECTS IN 1984

What is the present position of the line? As a result of recent decisions by British Rail, through which a considerable degree of commercial autonomy has been given to local managers, the prospects are surprisingly good. Passenger traffic has increased in the last two years and freight appears buoyant. Large-scale planting of timber along the route appears to offer longer-term prospects and the possibility of reopening the pulp mill at Corpach where closure of the original plant caused grave local unemployment. Bulk alumina for the Fort William factory is also a probable source of increased traffic from the south. But the development of tourist traffic, possibly in conjunction with circular tours from the Kyle of Lochalsh line, certainly offers one of the best opportunities of increased revenue, justifying the long-term retention of the Mallaig line, always the most commercially vulnerable part of the West Highland system. Besides the experimental use of steam traction, a well-tried feature from earlier years was reintroduced in 1983 in the form of observation cars, nostalgically turned out in LNER varnished teak livery and named *Lochaber* and *Loch Eil*, resulting in a welcome boost to traffic on the Mallaig extension. Sunday excursions were experimented with on that section during the same summer, with encouraging results, while on that part of the route between Craigendoran and Crianlarich a Sunday service was also given by Edinburgh–Oban through trains. Although not perhaps strictly a West Highland service, it is possible that its success may pave the way for an eventual reintroduction of the former Fort William Sunday excursion trains, last run in 1957.

# The West Highland Up-to-Date

When the late John Thomas wrote this book in the 1960s the West Highland Railway had been running for about seventy years. It has now been running for half as long again, and for the book to go to a fourth edition is a remarkable testimony both to the enduring fascination of its subject and to the quality of the original text.

For the second edition, in 1976, the original author added a short introduction, which has been left unaltered. For the third, A.J. Paterson provided a postscript largely describing how the line appeared in 1984 to a traveller more familiar with it in the 1950s. Most of this too re-appears, the principal omissions being paragraphs which dealt mainly with the lineside scene. To be asked to provide material to update the book yet again is no small honour.

Since more, and more fundamental, changes have arguably taken place on the WHR in the thirty-five years since the mid-sixties than in the seventy years previous, it now seems time to attempt some sort of chronological record of them. Although the greatest change would have been the one that thankfully has not taken place: in the late 1990s the line is still open, and trains still run to Fort William, and Mallaig, and Oban – and that is something which in the mid-1960s one would not have predicted with any confidence at all. But while successive governments weighed profitability against social need, the fortunes of the West Highland Line had their downs and ups along the way.

When John Thomas completed his text two big changes had just taken place: with progressive closure of the Callander & Oban line east of Crianlarich, Glasgow-Oban trains had been diverted to run over the West Highland as far as Crianlarich (freight trains in the autumn of 1964, passenger a year later); and steam locomotives in general had been replaced by diesels. The unsatisfactory North British type 2 locomotives (class 29) were used during their short lives; the much more satisfactory Sulzer type 2s of class 27 became a familiar feature of the West Highlands.

In other respects it was still very much a traditional railway. Trains continued to be locomotive-hauled and diesel multiple units appeared only on rare occasions. Semaphore signals prevailed, points were worked by rods from signal boxes, tablets authorised entry to single-line sections.

Exceptionally, the block trains of pulpwood between Crianlarich Lower (retained for loading them) and Corpach, which kept the line busy between 1965 and 1980, were on two stages of their journey propelled rather than pulled by their locomotives – something very rare in British practice. These stages were the Crianlarich spur, which had by then become the main line, and between Fort William and Corpach.

Although the surviving section of the Callander & Oban, west of Crianlarich, had become a branch of the West Highland, the passenger train service between Glasgow and Oban seems to have been superimposed (complete with the 01.00 mail from Glasgow, which survived until about 1981) on the existing West Highland service with very little attempt to amalgamate them. This meant an increase in the train service south of Crianlarich from two or three trains each way daily to five or six, which must have helped to compensate the inhabitants of Arrochar for the loss of their local service from Craigendoran the previous year. It also gave passengers for Oban, and the isles beyond, a train service from Glasgow which was substantially quicker than before. But travellers from further afield had to change at Glasgow, and for those travelling from the South that meant changing between Central and Queen Street stations.

Despite this, Oban was still being shown a decade later in West Coast Route timetables as served from Euston. There had indeed been, until 1965, a through overnight train service from Euston with sleeping cars, but when Oban trains were diverted over the West Highland no replacement was provided: no through coaches or sleeping cars for Oban appeared in the overnight Fort William service from Kings Cross, nor was any connecting train provided from Crianlarich, where passengers attempting to change trains were faced with a wait of a couple of hours or more. Regrettably, this situation has persisted to the present day: to be deprived thus of Oban line traffic cannot have helped the Fort William sleeper during its recent battle for survival.

On the positive side, some excellent colour brochures to encourage travel over the West Highland lines were produced in the 1970s, and such promotional material, both in print and on video, and in French and German as well as English, has become a continuing feature.

In 1982 British Rail established market-based sectors initially called InterCity, Freight, London & South East, and Other Provincial Services (all but the second being concerned with passenger traffic). These became responsible for specifying and marketing train services while the geographically-based regions continued to run the railways. Details of responsibility and nomenclature saw many confusing changes over the years which followed: specifically, Scottish Region eventually acquired Provincial sector responsibility for passenger train services within Scotland, and adopted the name ScotRail. It was therefore responsible for running the West Highland

lines, and for their local passenger train services; but freight was the responsibility of the freight sector, and the overnight train from London, like all
sleeping car services, went to InterCity. This put the InterCity sector in the
position of providing a train service to Corrour, which so far from being a
city is probably the most remote station on the system – evidence perhaps
both of the difficulty of establishing a perfect administration for a railway, and
of how what best suits the system as a whole may not suit individual lines
within it.

In 1983 the 'Friends of the West Highland Line' were formed: the
Government-sponsored Serpell Report on railway finances envisaged widespread closures, and railways in the West Highlands seemed particularly
under threat. The society was, and is, dedicated to promotion and development of facilities and services on the West Highland Line. From the start it
included the Crianlarich-Oban section within its sphere of activity, and to
formalise this adopted in 1995 a slight change of name to 'Friends of the West
Highland Lines'. The society's newsletters are a fruitful source of information, and I am indebted to them.

In the summer of 1984 British Rail instituted a regular steam train service
between Fort William and Mallaig. It became both successful and unique, the
only regularly scheduled steam trains, using preserved locomotives, on BR.
As such it found its way into the public timetables. InterCity, responsible for
steam excursions on British Rail, became the sector responsible for the
Mallaig steam trains.

Locomotives were hired from preservation groups – the Scottish Railway
Preservation Society, Steamtown Carnforth, the North Eastern Locomotive
Preservation Group, and others – and manned by British Rail crews. At the
end of the 1987 summer season, steam returned to the main West Highland
line when the locomotives which had been hauling the Mallaig trains were
able to haul special trains as far as Craigendoran on their return journeys
South. This became a regular event.

The locomotives used were mostly Class 5 4-6-0s, although the North
British 0-6-0 *Maude* was also used during the first season on short workings
to Glenfinnan. The LNER-designed K1 class 2-6-0 no. 2005 appeared, followed in 1989 by 2-6-0 no. 3442 *The Great Marquess* which had been built for
the West Highland in 1938. On eventual withdrawal she had been bought by
Lord Garnock, who later became Lord Lindsay and whose enjoyment of the
first edition of this book is mentioned on page 159. The locomotive had been
based in the South: by the late eighties she was on the Severn Valley Railway
and in need of a major overhaul. It had been the owner's ambition that the
locomotive should return to the West Highland and this was tentatively
planned for 1990. However, when it became known that Lord Lindsay had
become terminally ill, the SVR locomotive department pulled out all the

stops to get no. 3442 ready for 1989: successfully, for they were in time for him to ride her footplate from Fort William to Banavie on 15 July, a fortnight before his death.

On regular locomotive-hauled train services, both passenger and freight, the type of locomotive most closely associated with the West Highland since 1980 has been the class 37 1,750 hp Co-Co diesel-electric. In 1985 Sunday trains reappeared in the timetable and a new station, Loch Eil Outward Bound, was opened on the Mallaig line. Some fish traffic was carried from Mallaig in 1987, after an interval of twenty five years, and the loop at Gorton was reinstated the same year.

A big development, throughout the West Highland lines, was the installation of Radio Electronic Token Block signalling. In this, the token (or tablet) takes the form of a cab display and is issued by radio from a central computer. Physical tokens, semaphore signals, and their associated signal boxes are superseded. The West Highland installation was attended with many problems but was commissioned on 19 May 1988. It cost £1,850,000. The signalling centre is at Banavie, in a new building in the same architectural style as the old signal boxes. Some semaphore signals were retained at Fort William.

With the introduction of RETB, staff were withdrawn from all stations except Fort William, Oban and Mallaig. Subsequently tickets from intermediate stations have been issued on the trains by conductors, who accept cheques and credit cards as well as cash, and issue tickets to stations beyond Glasgow as well as stations served by the West Highland trains themselves.

In 1988 Railfreight, as the freight sector was named, signed a ten-year contract to carry alumina to Fort William for British Alcan's smelters. Although some freight traffic had been lost (coal to Oban, in 1983, for instance) business was generally buoyant: aluminium, china clay, paper, oil and timber were all being carried.

SuperSprinter DMUs of class 156 took over all ScotRail passenger services on the West Highland lines on 23 January 1989. There were, of course, snags – the wheels squealed abominably on curves until a cure was found, and there was limited space for bikes and baggage. But the SuperSprinters knocked 24 minutes, on average, off the journey time from Glasgow to Fort William, and 15 to Oban. The frequency was increased to an unprecedented four trains each way daily, and the service became at last a truly integrated one, with trains from Glasgow dividing at Crianlarich into portions for Oban and for Fort William/Mallaig. This was in addition to the overnight London-Fort William train, which was by then originating at Euston and calling at Birmingham, but had ceased to call at Glasgow.

The London train continued of course to be locomotive-hauled, and in 1990 added to its load a Motorail service for cars, their drivers and passengers between London and Fort William. The West Highland lines had also become popular routes for long-distance excursions and touring trains, including some promoted by InterCity's own charter train unit, and others, such as the luxury Royal Scotsman, using privately-owned rolling stock. On occasion such trains have been steam-hauled over the Mallaig line.

Buildings at some unstaffed stations have seen constructive re-use under lease. Those at Glenfinnan became the Glenfinnan Station Museum, opened in 1991 with historic artefacts and interpretive material relating to the West Highland lines. Notable, in due course, were operational block instruments with tablets, bells and gongs, and reduced admission fees for visitors arriving by train. Spean Bridge with its restaurant was ScotRail's 'Best Unstaffed Station of 1997'.

In the summer of 1989, the newsletter of the Friends of the West Highland Line recorded that the cost of running the West Highland was, roughly, £4 million a year, and that it took £2 million in revenue.

Freight traffic declined rapidly in the early 1990s. Railfreight, required by the Government to act commercially, closed its loss-making Speedlink wagonload service in July 1991. Part of the oil traffic to the Oban line was lost in September 1991 and the remainder, including important traffic to Connel, in 1993. (The village which is home to the contributor of these notes lies astride the road between Grangemouth and Connel: it has had to put up with frequent bulk oil tankers thundering through it ever since.) Oil traffic to Fort William and Mallaig also disappeared, and fish and timber traffics had ceased. Crianlarich Lower, used intermittently for freight during the 1980s, was closed and the site subsequently sold. By 1994 the only remaining freight was that carried under contract to the aluminium and paper industries at Fort William, and the Ministry of Defence at Glen Douglas.

Meanwhile, in the summer of 1992 the overnight trains to and from London had lost their ordinary coaches and in common with all overnight trains between Scotland and England catered for sleeping car passengers only. What this meant for local travellers on the West Highland line was that, except during high summer, the last southbound train left Fort William at 17.42: even though another train left at 19.55 and called at all stations to Helensburgh, *they* were not allowed to use it.

In September 1992 the basic SuperSprinter service over the West Highland lines was reduced to three trains each way daily, although in high summer most of these ran separately to and from Glasgow and until 1994 locomotive-hauled trains were provided as well. The 'West Highland Railcard' offering a discount for local residents was introduced in 1993.

Fundamental changes to the railway industry came into force on 1 April 1994. Ownership of infrastructure, track and signalling, and responsibility for operating these, passed to Railtrack, a public sector body privatised as

Railtrack Group PLC in 1996. Responsibility for freight train services passed to freight companies, and for passenger train services to train operating companies (TOCs) using rolling stock leased from rolling stock owning companies. These companies, initially subsidiaries of British Railways Board, were all eventually to be privatised either by sale or, in the case of the TOCs, by franchise.

So in 1994 responsibility for running the West Highland was divided between ScotRail and InterCity West Coast as TOCs, several freight companies and Railtrack. The SuperSprinters had passed into ownership of Angel Train Contracts. All this seemed initially to have little effect, however, and attention was concentrated on celebrating the centenary of the opening of the railway between Craigendoran and Fort William. During August there were exhibitions at Helensburgh, Fort William and Crianlarich, and a local DMU train service between Helensburgh and Arrochar. Sunday 7 August saw a steam special of SRPS (Scottish Railway Preservation Society) coaches, which originated from Edinburgh and was hauled between Cowlairs and Fort William by nos. 3442 and 2005.

The actual centenary on 11 August was celebrated by a near-re-enactment of the original celebrations described in chapter one: a special train from Glasgow brought the VIPs to Fort William, where an ornamental archway had been erected over the railway. *The Great Marquess* and a single coach passed ceremonially beneath the archway, and the present Marchioness of Tweeddale unveiled a commemorative plaque.

There had been rumours of cuts in sleeper train services for some months when on 14 December 1994 the Director of Passenger Rail Franchising, the official charged with laying down the minimum level of train services to be provided by franchisees, announced that the Fort William sleeper, the Scotland-West Country sleeper and all Motorail services would be excluded on the grounds that they were disproportionately uneconomic.

At that date the Fort William sleeper was running from Euston combined with the Inverness sleeper as far as Edinburgh, where they were separated. The announcement that it was to be withdrawn provoked months of fierce controversy, protests by user groups based in Scotland and London, newspaper campaigns, parliamentary debate and governmental vacillation. But above all, seemingly, it provoked Duncan McPherson, convenor of Highland Regional Council who had earlier received three successive Government assurances that all trains in that region would be retained.

Amongst all the to-ing and fro-ing, two important points became clear. One was that the figure quoted by the Government of £450 for the subsidy per passenger was, even if accurate, far higher than the saving to be made by withdrawing the train: much of the subsidy was needed to meet fixed costs which, if the sleeper were taken off, would have to be re-allocated to other trains. The other was that on its way from Edinburgh to the West Highland line the sleeper traversed three sections of line used by no other passenger trains. To withdraw it would be in effect to close these sections, and to evade lengthy statutory consultation procedures British Rail intended to divert a Sunday Glasgow-Inverness train over one of them, and to run short-distance trains over the other two in the middle of the night. The press promptly called these 'ghost trains'.

It was this technicality which enabled Highland Region on 8 May 1995 to obtain from the Court of Session an interdict, later upheld on appeal, which prevented withdrawal of overnight passenger services to Fort William without proper consultation. It was only just in time, as withdrawal had been announced for 28 May. Omitted from the public timetable, the Fort William sleeper continued to run, though Motorail was lost. The sleeper had been transferred from InterCity to ScotRail in April 1995, and when it reappeared in the timetable in September an un-subsidised seating coach had been added between Edinburgh and Fort William. The train arrived at Fort William too late however to make a convenient connection for Mallaig and the isles (although it did, on certain dates, connect with the steam train). The Fort William sleeper was eventually included in the Passenger Service Requirement for the West Highland Line.

While all this had been going on, the Mallaig steam trains too had come under threat of withdrawal. The intended operator under privatisation had looked at the costs and pulled out. Happily the West Coast Railway Co. Ltd stepped into the breach. This company, based at Carnforth, has as its main activities charter train operation and traditional railway engineering. It continued the Mallaig steam train operation as *The Jacobite*, using locomotives nos. 75014 (BR standard class 4) and 48151 (LMS Class 8F), both of them new to the line. The latter, despite its long fixed wheelbase, gave no trouble, and the former, although of a class not previously used in the line, proved well suited to it. The locomotives are hired – others have also been used – but coaches come from West Coast's pool of charter train stock. The train is marketed to the general public as a steam run over one of the great railway journeys of the world, and it pays its way.

Timber traffic recommenced from Fort William in 1995 and subsequently from Arrochar. Freight operations were privatised during 1996–7: Freightliners Ltd which carries paper over the WHR was the subject of a management buy-out, and the other freight companies concerned were purchased by Wisconsin Central Transportation Corporation and incorporated into the latter's subsidiary English Welsh & Scottish Railway (EW&S). This new undertaking has proved to be vigorous in pursuit of business, and timber traffic began to flow also from Crianlarich and Taynuilt in 1997; in the latter case it was the first freight over the Oban line for four years.

An outer suburban train leaving Garelochhead at 07.32 for Glasgow was introduced with the support of Strathclyde Passenger Transport on 1 October 1996. ScotRail was privatised by franchising to National Express Group PLC for seven years from 1 April 1997.

The seating coach attached to the sleeper between Edinburgh and Fort William had proved regrettably erratic in its presence in the train. On the occasion of the FWHL annual general meeting at Rannoch on 24 May 1997, for instance, it had not been attached and at one stage some twenty fare-paying passengers were standing in the luggage van. From September 1997 it was, amid protests, withdrawn. Happily, while this chapter was being prepared, ScotRail announced that a new leasing and maintenance agreement would enable it to be reinstated.

A move towards offsetting the disadvantage of fragmented responsibility for the West Highland Railway, and other railways in the Highlands, came in December 1997 with formation of Highland Rail Developments. This group includes in its partners Highlands & Island Enterprise, local enterprise companies, local authorities, Railtrack, ScotRail, EW&S, FWHL and other 'Friends of...' societies. The task of its development officers is to identify opportunities to develop use of railways and then progress them. A specific opportunity on the West Highland is to aid development of heritage travel by reinstating turntables for steam locomotives at Fort William and Mallaig.

The saga of the West Highland lines is not finished yet. But the nearest airports to Fort William are Glasgow and Inverness, and it is no hyperbole to suggest that for the inhabitants of the districts served, and the isles beyond, the railway remains a lifeline. For city dwellers, whether from Glasgow, London or elsewhere, it remains the wide open gateway to a day, a week, or a fortnight free from the pressure of urban cares. Long may it last.

Many people have kindly helped to provide the facts needed to piece together this final chapter; John Yellowlees of ScotRail and Robert Gardner of the Friends of the West Highland Lines have been particularly helpful.

(57)   *The* Royal Scotsman *luxury tour train is headed by a class 37 Co-Co diesel electric as it climbs from Tyndrum towards County March summit on an August evening in 1993.* [P.J.G. Ransom]

(58)   *Two two-car SuperSprinters in multiple leave Bridge of Orchy en route from Fort William to Glasgow in August 1993.* [P.J.G. Ransom]

## CONTRASTS AT CRIANLARICH

The top photograph shows another double-headed train with two Glens, No. 9221 Glen Orchy and No. 9100 Glen Dochart, on an up express in 1926. Many passengers would be taking refreshment in the famous tea room that is still open while the locomotives' tanks are replenished. In the 1971 photograph by Derek Cross (below) No. D5369 heads an Oban–Glasgow train which has just joined the West Highland line from the truncated Callander & Oban while No. D5355, which has just arrived from the Scottish Pulp works at Corpach, waits to reverse down the spur to the Callander & Oban to enable the wagons to be reloaded with logs

# *Appendix*

## 1: WEST HIGHLAND CHRONOLOGY

| | |
|---|---|
| 12 August 1889 | West Highland Railway Act passed |
| 23 October 1889 | First sod cut near Fort William by Lord Abinger |
| 20 July 1890 | Banavie branch authorised |
| 5 September 1893 | Last spike driven on Rannoch Moor by Mr Renton |
| 31 July 1894 | West Highland Railway (Mallaig Extension) Act, 57 & 58 Vict., passed |
| 3 August 1894 | Final inspection of line by Board of Trade |
| 7 August 1894 | Public opening Craigendoran to Fort William |
| 11 August 1894 | Ceremonial opening |
| 4 September 1894 | Derailment at Woodend Farm crossing |
| 1 November 1894 | Refreshment baskets available at Arrochar and Tarbet |
| 1 January 1895 | Inverlair: name changed to Tulloch |
| 27 May 1895 | Glen Douglas siding opened |
| 1 June 1895 | Banavie branch opened |
| July 1895 | Refreshments available at Crianlarich |
| 1 May 1896 | Whistlefield station opened |
| 6 May 1896 | Derailment at Mallaig Junction |
| August 1896 | West Highland Railway Act, 1896 (Extension to Ballachulish) |
| 14 August 1896 | West Highland Railway Mallaig Extension (Guarantee) Act, 59 & 60 Vict., passed |
| 21 January 1897 | First sod of Mallaig Extension cut at Corpach by Lady Margaret Cameron of Lochiel |
| 20 December 1897 | Crianlarich spur to Callander & Oban opened |
| 8 February 1901 | Death of Charles Forman |
| 1 April 1901 | Mallaig Extension opened |
| 22 July 1901 | First sleeping-car service from King's Cross—Fort William. Summer only |
| 8 August 1906 | Accident at Pulpit Rock |
| 21 December 1908 | North British Railway (Confirmation) Act |
| 31 December 1908 | North British took over West Highland Banavie branch and Mallaig Extension by terms of above Act |
| 6 December 1909 | Accident at Glen Douglas |
| 1 January 1923 | The grouping: North British Railway, including West Highland Railway, becomes part of London & North Eastern Railway |
| 1 June 1924 | Row: name changed to Rhu |
| 1 May 1926 | Gortan: name changed to Gorton |
| 8 July 1929 | Restaurant-cars first introduced on 4.30 a.m., 5.45 a.m. and 11.23 a.m. down and 12.10 p.m., 4.5 p.m. and 5.12 p.m. up trains |

| | |
|---|---|
| October 1929 | Sleeping-cars start operating throughout year |
| 27 January 1931 | Rannoch Moor derailment |
| 6 July 1931 | Loop put in at Rhu |
| 1 August 1931 | Fersit opened |
| 7 August 1932 | Loch Treig diversion brought into operation |
| 31 August 1933 | Buffet cars on 9.52 a.m. up and 3.36 a.m. down trains |
| 15 September 1934 | Corrour, formerly private, opened to public |
| 1 January 1935 | Fersit closed |
| 2 September 1939 | Last passenger train on Banavie branch |
| 2 October 1939 | Sleeper service withdrawn |
| 27 April 1941 | Faslane Junction opened |
| 21 December 1941 | New signal box and extended loops brought into operation at Helensburgh Upper |
| 4 January 1942 | Craigendoran yard opened |
| 15 November 1942 | Camus-na-ha signal box opened |
| 26 March 1943 | Corpach naval sidings completed |
| 5 April 1944 | Withdrawal of restaurant-cars |
| 26 August 1945 | Faslane platform (temporary) opened |
| 29 October 1945 | Inveruglas (temporary) opened |
| 10 April 1946 | Glenfalloch (temporary) opened |
| June 1946 | Restoration of restaurant-cars |
| 1 January 1948 | Nationalisation: West Highland Railway becomes part of British Railways, Scottish Region |
| 23 May 1949 | First regular train Glasgow—Oban via West Highland and Crianlarich spur |
| 17 April 1954 | Collision at Bridge of Orchy |
| 9 January 1956 | Rhu closed (first closure) |
| 24 September 1956 | Television train, first in Britain, runs over West Highland |
| 4 April 1960 | Rhu re-opened as unstaffed halt |
| 14 June 1964 | Craigendoran (West Highland), Rhu, Shandon, Whistlefield and Glen Douglas closed. Last day of local service Craigendoran—Arrochar and Tarbet |
| 7 September 1964 | Oban freight trains diverted to run over West Highland south of Crianlarich |
| 27 September 1965 | Oban passenger trains diverted to run over West Highland south of Crianlarich |
| 13 June 1975 | New Fort William terminus opened, replacing original station in the town |
| 1980 | Closure of pulp mill at Corpach with adverse effect on rail freight traffic |
| 1982 | Responsibility for traffic passes to BR's InterCity, provincial and freight sectors |
| 1983 | Observation cars restored to Mallaig extension—summer service only |
| 1983 | Sunday excursions reintroduced on West Highland line |
| 1984 | Steam engines return to service as a tourist attraction on the Mallaig route |
| 19 May 1988 | Radio Electronic Block Token working commissioned |
| 23 January 1989 | Class 156 SuperSprinter DMUs introduced: faster and more frequent train services |
| 14 May 1990 | Motorail to Fort William introduced |

| 1 April 1994 | Ownership of West Highland Railway passes to Railtrack; train services provided by BR subsidiary train operating and freight companies |
| 14 December 1994 | Director of Passenger Rail Franchising announces withdrawal of Fort William sleeper |
| 8 May 1995 | Highland Region obtains inderdict against withdrawal of sleeper; sleeper subsequently included in Passenger Service Requirement |
| 28 May 1995 | Motorail withdrawn |
| 27 June 1995 | Operation of Mallaig steam trains by West Coast Railway Co. Ltd commences |
| May 1996 | Railtrack privatised as Railtrack Group plc |
| 1996–7 | Freight companies privatised. Freight subsequently carried by Freightliners Ltd and English Welsh & Scottish Railway |
| 1 April 1997 | ScotRail TOC privatised by franchise to National Express Group plc |
| December 1997 | Highland Rail Developments group formed |

*Heading south after a season on the Mallaig line, Class 5 4–6–0 No. 44871 crosses the larger of the two viaducts on the Horseshoe Curve on 16 October 1993. Who would have thought, when steam was superseded in the 1960s, that such a scene would be possible thirty years later?*

## 2 : MILEAGES

|  | Miles | Chains | Opened | |
|---|---|---|---|---|
| Craigendoran Junction | 0 | 0 | | |
| Craigendoran | 0 | 17 | 7 Aug. | 1894 |
| Helensburgh Upper | 2 | 8 | ,, | |
| Rhu | 3 | 70 | ,, | |
| Faslane Junction | 5 | 20 | 27 April | 1941 |
| Shandon | 6 | 48 | 7 Aug. | 1894 |
| Garelochhead | 8 | 76 | ,, | |
| Whistlefield | 10 | 30 | 1 May | 1896 |
| Glen Douglas | 15 | 21 | 7 Aug. | 1894 |
| Arrochar and Tarbet | 19 | 47 | 7 Aug. | 1894 |
| Inveruglas | 23 | 26 | 29 Oct. | 1945 |
| Ardlui | 27 | 47 | 7 Aug. | 1894 |
| Glenfalloch | 30 | 33 | 10 April | 1946 |
| Crianlarich | 36 | 23 | 7 Aug. | 1894 |
| Crianlarich Junction | 36 | 31 | ,, | |
| Crianlarich Junction to C & O | | 39 | ,, | |
| Tyndrum | 41 | 24 | ,, | |
| Bridge of Orchy | 48 | 68 | ,, | |
| Gorton | 57 | 40 | ,, | |
| Rannoch | 64 | 36 | ,, | |
| Corrour | 71 | 54 | ,, | |
| Tulloch | 81 | 60 | ,, | |
| Roy Bridge | 87 | 34 | ,, | |
| Spean Bridge | 90 | 57 | ,, | |
| Mallaig Junction | 98 | 70 | ,, | |
| Fort William | 99 | 70 | ,, | |
| Fort William Pier | 99 | 72 | ,, | |
| Fort William | 0 | 0 | ,, | |
| Mallaig Junction | 1 | 0 | ,, | |
| Banavie Junction | 2 | 26 | 1 April | 1901 |
| Banavie Pier | 2 | 68 | 1 June | 1895 |
| Banavie | 2 | 49 | 1 April | 1901 |
| Corpach | 3 | 52 | ,, | |
| Camus-na-ha | 5 | 18 | 15 April | 1942 |
| Locheilside | 10 | 25 | 1 April | 1901 |
| Glenfinnan | 17 | 4 | ,, | |
| Lochailort | 26 | 14 | ,, | |
| Beasdale | 30 | 76 | ,, | |
| Arisaig | 34 | 29 | ,, | |
| Morar | 39 | 5 | ,, | |
| Mallaig | 41 | 66 | ,, | |

## NOTES

Most of the dates given in this table and elsewhere in the book are British Railways' official dates. Occasionally, when the official date seems suspect, a second source is used. For instance, the official date for the opening of Whistlefield conflicts with the date given in the contemporary local press. All the mileage points listed are stations, with the exception of Faslane Junction, Mallaig Junction and Camus-na-ha. Glen Douglas and Beasdale were opened as private stations. Gorton and Corrour were established as passing places and no mention was made in the Act of their function as stations. They were in fact used as private stations by local landowners. Glen Douglas and Corrour eventually appeared in the public timetable (see Chronology) but Gorton never did so. Passengers apparently experienced no difficulty in alighting at Glen Douglas and Corrour in their 'private' days, but visitors were not encouraged at Gorton. Beasdale, on the other hand, catered for the public from its opening, and was the only one of the four private stations to keep its own accounts. The traffic books show that there was steady custom all the year round.

In the West Highland Railway Act of 1889 the station subsequently named Arrochar and Tarbet was listed as Ballyhennan after a nearby hamlet.

## 3: PASSENGERS AND FREIGHT BOOKED AT FORT WILLIAM
### 1913—1934

| Year | No. of Pass. | Goods Tons | Minerals Tons | Total Tons |
|---|---|---|---|---|
| 1913 | 31,708 | 6,773 | 5,618 | 12,391 |
| 1914 | 26,624 | 5,346 | 5,276 | 10,622 |
| 1915 | 29,745 | 5,581 | 5,294 | 10,875 |
| 1916 | 14,889 | 7,165 | 5,223 | 12,388 |
| 1917 | 13,751 | 4,833 | 3,232 | 8,065 |
| 1918 | 16,645 | 4,181 | 3,247 | 7,428 |
| 1919 | 24,450 | 9,009 | 7,987 | 16,996 |
| 1920 | 28,194 | 7,516 | 5,719 | 13,234 |
| 1921 | 22,184 | 8,607 | 5,053 | 13,660 |
| 1922 | 25,364 | 9,957 | 6,292 | 16,249 |
| 1923 | 26,434 | 11,083 | 6,275 | 17,358 |
| 1924 | 26,011 | 11,934 | 5,443 | 17,377 |
| 1925 | 35,851 | 20,463 | 6,651 | 27,114 |
| 1926 | 31,095 | 16,507 | 7,841 | 24,348 |
| 1927 | 41,200 | 19,539 | 10,575 | 30,114 |
| 1928 | 43,250 | 24,322 | 10,080 | 34,402 |
| 1929 | 41,013 | 33,815 | 13,805 | 47,720 |
| 1930 | 33,478 | 34,103 | 8,501 | 42,604 |
| 1931 | 32,048 | 37,119 | 9,998 | 47,117 |
| 1932 | 31,737 | 32,811 | 8,889 | 41,770 |
| 1933 | 32,743 | 30,390 | 7,777 | 38,167 |
| 1934 | 27,992 | 34,582 | 8,405 | 42,987 |

## 4: NUMBER OF PASSENGERS BOOKED AND PASSENGER RECEIPTS FOR ALL WEST HIGHLAND STATIONS, 1930

| Station | No. of passengers | Passenger receipts |
|---|---|---|
| Helensburgh (Upper) | 8,113 | £3,224 |
| Rhu | 3,065 | £762 |
| Shandon | 1,272 | £196 |
| Garelochhead | 3,367 | £450 |
| Whistlefield | 3,819 | £274 |
| Arrochar & Tarbet | 10,917 | £1,802 |
| Ardlui | 887 | £161 |
| Crianlarich | 2,253 | £957 |
| Tyndrum | 1,358 | £359 |
| Bridge of Orchy | 3,215 | £916 |
| Rannoch | 11,106 | £3,807 |
| Tulloch | 1,075 | £425 |
| Roy Bridge | 1,665 | £415 |
| Spean Bridge | 5,959 | £2,004 |
| Fort William | 33,478 | £12,841 |
| Banavie | 2,229 | £220 |

| Banavie Pier | 115 | £5 |
|---|---|---|
| Corpach | 2,829 | £251 |
| Locheilside | 2,974 | £186 |
| Glenfinnan | 2,641 | £884 |
| Lochailort | 2,478 | £421 |
| Beasdale | 562 | £55 |
| Arisaig | 5,735 | £1,067 |
| Morar | 6,207 | £548 |
| Mallaig | 16,842 | £8,242 |
| Gairlochy | 1,948 | £295 |
| Invergarry | 1,020 | £604 |
| Fort Augustus | 4,301 | £1,852 |

## 5: INVERGARRY & FORT AUGUSTUS RAILWAY CHRONOLOGY

| | |
|---|---|
| 14 August 1896 | Invergarry & Fort Augustus Act passed |
| 2 February 1897 | First sod cut |
| 14 July 1903 | Final Board of Trade inspection |
| 21 July 1903 | Highland and Invergarry & Fort Augustus Railway Act passed allowing Highland Railway to operate the line |
| 22 July 1903 | Line opened by Mrs Ellice of Glengarry |
| 1 July 1904 | Invergloy platform opened |
| 30 September 1906 | Fort Augustus pier closed |
| 30 April 1907 | Highland Railway withdrew its engines and rolling stock |
| 1 May 1907 | North British took over |
| 4 May 1907 | North British ran first trains |
| 30 October 1911 | Invergloy platform closed |
| 31 October 1911 | Line closed to all traffic. North British withdrew |
| 1 August 1913 | Line re-opened by North British |
| 28 August 1914 | North British Railway (Invergarry & Fort Augustus) Vesting and Confirmation Act passed. North British purchased line |
| 1 December 1933 | Line closed to all traffic except one weekly coal train |
| 31 December 1946 | Final closure. Track lifted |

## 6: INVERGARRY & FORT AUGUSTUS RAILWAY

*Directors at opening, 22 July 1903*

Rt Hon Lord Burton, chairman
Cpt. Edward Charles Ellice, M.P. of Glengarry
Rt Hon Lord Abinger
J. C. Cunningham
George Malcolm, Esq., of Invergarry
John Lambrick, Burton-on-Trent

## 7: INVERGARRY & FORT AUGUSTUS RAILWAY: MILEAGE

|  | Miles | Chains |
|---|---|---|
| Spean Bridge | 0 | 0 |
| Gairlochy | 2 | 52 |
| Invergloy | 8 | 15 |
| Invergarry | 15 | 6 |
| Aberchalder | 19 | 27 |
| Fort Augustus station | 23 | 9 |
| Fort Augustus pier | 24 | 6 |

Engine turntables and water columns were provided at Spean Bridge and Fort Augustus. There was a water column at Invergarry.

## 8: INVERGARRY & FORT AUGUSTUS RAILWAY: PASSENGERS
## CARRIED AND TRAIN MILES
### Highland period

| Six months ending | Passengers carried | Passengers miles run | Goods miles run | Total |
|---|---|---|---|---|
| Jan 1904 | 12,829 | 16,923 | 4,607 | 21,530 |
| Jul 1904 | 11,133 | 14,389 | 4,246 | 18,636 |
| Jan 1905 | 12,625 | 16,502 | 3,825 | 20,327 |
| Jul 1905 | 9,917 | 13,305 | 3,821 | 17,126 |
| Jan 1906 | 12,362 | 16,154 | 3,858 | 20,012 |
| Jul 1906 | 8,948 | 12,840 | 3,974 | 16,814 |
| Jan 1907 | 12,395 | 15,304 | 4,514 | 19,818 |
| First North British period | | | | |
| Jul 1907 | 7,784 | 10,194 | 2,563 | 12,758 |
| Jan 1908 | 13,226 | 16,186 | 3,626 | 19,812 |
| Jul 1908 | 10,111 | 13,435 | 3,792 | 17,227 |
| Jan 1909 | 12,113 | 14,801 | 4,316 | 19,117 |
| Jul 1909 | 9,575 | 13,167 | 4,112 | 17,279 |
| Jan 1910 | 11,704 | 15,228 | 4,324 | 19,552 |

## 9: INVERGARRY & FORT AUGUSTUS RAILWAY: PASSENGER
## AND FREIGHT REVENUE
### Highland period

| Six months ending | Passenger | Goods |
|---|---|---|
| Jan 1904★ | £848.16.4 | £190.11.6 |
| Jul 1904 | £696.10.9 | £143.9.5 |
| Jan 1905 | £911.4.3 | £194.6.9 |
| Jul 1905 | £681.3.9 | £142.6.1 |
| Jan 1906 | £933.14.9 | £221.6.5 |
| Jul 1906 | £665.6.9 | £147.8.11 |
| Jan 1907 | £907.6.1 | £220.7.2 |

★ Includes 10 days in June 1903

|          | First North British period |             |
|----------|---------------|-------------|
| Jul 1907 | £660.18.7     | £142.12.10  |
| Jan 1908 | £963.13.9     | £224.6.11   |
| Jul 1908 | £672.1.3      | £142.8.7    |
| Jan 1909 | £909.5.0      | £205.14.9   |
| Jul 1909 | £700.18.4     | £176.19.11  |
| Jan 1910 | £883.9.3      | £202.19.3   |

## 10 : 'LOST ON RANNOCH MOOR'

There is an interesting tailpiece to the story of the survey party lost on Rannoch Moor. In 1927 an article entitled 'Benighted on Rannoch Moor' was published in *Blackwood's Magazine*. It gave a full account of the episode, but mentioned the participants by profession only, and not by name. In 1937 Lt.-Col. the Rt Hon A. C. Murray, director of the LNE, had a copy of the *Blackwood* article bound and presented to the company's museum in Edinburgh. At the same time Murray asked W. A. Fraser, engineer, Scottish Area, LNE, if he could identify the people in the story. Fraser got in touch with J. E. Harrison, who had been Forman's young assistant in 1889, and in his letter of reply dated 27 November 1937 from Skelmorlie, Ayrshire, Harrison gave full particulars of all the men who had taken part in the Rannoch Moor walk. He concluded his letter,

I always like hearing of others being interested in the story and it is extraordinary how many have written to me about it. The Scottish Mountaineer Club had it in the recent issue of their Journal—by request. I was glad to hear from you and hope you are well—as I am myself—though scarcely feeling equal to another such trip across the Moor.

Yours very sincerely,
J. E. Harrison
(only survivor! !)

Ten years later, in April 1947, interest in the episode was again revived when Lt.-Col. Murray sent the article to Sir Robert Burrows, chairman of the LMS. Burrows commented :

I took it home with me last night and read it with great relish. I know most of the country, but I must confess I have never done the walk. If the walk had been in summer and by young men there would be nothing much in it. The idea of Victorian middle-aged men setting off with umbrellas and ordinary civilised garments to attempt the feat in January is the maddest thing I ever heard of, but very amusing.

# 11: SCOTRAIL TRAIN TIMES, 24 MAY UNTIL 26 SEPTEMBER 1998

## RAIL SERVICES   GLASGOW–OBAN–FORT WILLIAM–MALLAIG

### MONDAYS TO SATURDAYS

| Station | C | SX BK | A | D | | J |
|---|---|---|---|---|---|---|
| Edinburgh d | — | 0505 | 0700 | 0730 | 1130 | 1700 |
| Glasgow Queen St. d | 0555c | — | 0812 | 0842 | 1242 | 1812 |
| Dalmuir d | 0629 | — | 0827 | 0857 | 1257 | 1827 |
| Dumbarton Central d | — | — | 0837 | 0907 | 1307 | 1837 |
| Helensburgh Upper d | 0656 | — | 0855 | 0925 | 1325 | 1855 |
| Garelochhead d | 0710 | — | 0906 | 0936 | 1336 | 1907 |
| Arrochar & Tarbet d | 0733 | — | 0926 | 1000 | 1357 | 1927 |
| Ardlui d | 0747x | — | 0943 | 1013 | 1412 | 1948 |
| Crianlarich a | 0810 | — | 0959 | 1029 | 1427 | 2003 |

*Crianlarich to Oban*

| Station | D | | J | |
|---|---|---|---|---|
| d | 1034 | 1433 | | 2009 |
| Tyndrum Lower d | 1041 | 1440 | | 2016 |
| Dalmally d | 1058 | 1457 | | 2033 |
| Loch Awe d | 1103 | 1502 | | 2038 |
| Falls of Cruachan d | 1107x | 1506x | | 2043x |
| Taynuilt d | 1117 | 1516 | | 2052 |
| Connel Ferry d | 1128 | 1527 | | 2103 |
| Oban a | 1140 | 1539 | | 2115 |

*Crianlarich to Fort William*

| Station | BK | A | | J |
|---|---|---|---|---|
| d | 0816 | 1005 | 1439 | 2015 |
| Upper Tyndrum d | 0830 | 1016 | 1450 | 2026 |
| Bridge of Orchy d | 0850 | 1030 | 1504 | 2040 |
| Rannoch d | 0917 | 1051 | 1525 | 2106 |
| Corrour d | 0930x | 1103x | 1537 | 2118 |
| Tulloch d | 0951 | 1119 | 1553 | 2134 |
| Roy Bridge d | 1001x | 1130 | 1603 | 2144 |
| Spean Bridge d | 1009 | 1136 | 1609 | 2150 |
| Fort William a | 1025 | 1149 | 1622 | 2203 |

*Fort William to Mallaig*

| Station | | K | A | | J |
|---|---|---|---|---|---|
| Fort William d | 0845 | 1035 | 1200 | 1627 | 2210 |
| Banavie d | 0851 | — | 1207 | 1633 | 2216 |
| Corpach d | 0856 | — | 1212 | 1638 | 2221 |
| Loch Eil O.B. d | 0902 | — | 1218 | 1644 | 2227 |
| Locheilside d | 0907x | — | 1223x | 1649x | 2232x |
| Glenfinnan d | 0919 | 1130b | 1234 | 1702 | 2242 |
| Lochailort d | 0935x | — | 1250x | 1717x | 2258x |
| Beasdale d | 0944x | — | 1259x | 1726x | 2307x |
| Arisaig d | 0951 | — | 1306 | 1734 | 2315 |
| Morar d | 1000 | — | 1315 | 1742 | 2323 |
| Mallaig a | 1007 | 1225 | 1322 | 1749 | 2330 |

### NOTES — GLASGOW–OBAN–FORT WILLIAM–MALLAIG

A   Starts from Stirling at 0718 on Mondays to Fridays (except Glasgow Public Holiday Mondays 25 May and 20 July)
B   From 22 June
C   Sleeping car accommodation only from London Euston, depart 2130 Mondays to Fridays, 2110 Sundays. Sleeping car reservations compulsory. Limited seating accommodation also available from Edinburgh only – reservations recommended.
D   Starts Falkirk Grahamston 0756 on Saturdays.
E   From 28 June
F   28 June to 30 August
G   Until 21 June
H   26 July to 6 September
J   From 27 June to 8 August also stops Westerton 1824.
K   The Jacobite steam train. Reservations recommended. Operated by West Coast Railway Company Ltd., telephone 01524 732100 for confirmation of days and dates of operation.
SX   Saturdays excepted
a   Arrival time.
b   Arrives 1112.
c   Glasgow Queen Street Low Level. Change at Dalmuir. Does not run on Glasgow Public Holiday Mondays 25 May and 20 July.
d   Departure time.
x   Stops on request. Customers wishing to alight must inform the on-train staff and those wishing to join must give a hand signal to the driver.

Catering available on all services, except those marked ●

## RAIL SERVICES   MALLAIG–FORT WILLIAM–OBAN–GLASGOW

### MONDAYS TO SATURDAYS

| Station | SX C● | B | J GK | | B | SX A |
|---|---|---|---|---|---|---|
| Mallaig d | — | 0600 | 1030 | 1410 | 1610 | 1815 |
| Morar d | — | 0607 | 1037 | — | 1617 | 1822 |
| Arisaig d | — | 0616 | 1046 | — | 1626 | 1831 |
| Beasdale d | — | 0622x | 1052x | — | 1632x | 1837x |
| Lochailort d | — | 0631x | 1101x | — | 1641x | 1846x |
| Glenfinnan d | — | 0648 | 1118 | — | 1701 | 1903 |
| Locheilside d | — | 0657x | 1127x | — | 1712x | 1912x |
| Loch Eil O.B. d | — | 0703 | 1133 | — | 1718 | 1918 |
| Corpach d | — | 0709 | 1139 | — | 1724 | 1924 |
| Banavie d | — | 0713 | 1143 | — | 1728 | 1928 |
| Fort William a | — | 0720 | 1152 | 1610 | 1737 | 1937 |

| Station | B | J GK | B | SX A |
|---|---|---|---|---|
| Fort William d | 0730 | 1203 | 1742 | 1950 |
| Spean Bridge d | 0743 | 1216 | 1755 | 2007 |
| Roy Bridge d | 0749 | 1222 | 1801 | 2014x |
| Tulloch d | 0801 | 1233 | 1812 | 2027 |
| Corrour d | 0817 | 1250 | 1829 | 2048x |
| Rannoch d | 0828 | 1301 | 1840 | 2107 |
| Bridge of Orchy d | 0849 | 1320 | 1859 | 2132 |
| Upper Tyndrum d | 0905 | 1336 | 1915 | 2150 |

*Oban to Crianlarich*

| Station | SX C● | | B | |
|---|---|---|---|---|
| Oban d | 0805 | 1300 | 1810 | |
| Connel Ferry d | 0816 | 1331 | 1821 | |
| Taynuilt d | 0827 | 1342 | 1832 | |
| Falls of Cruachan d | 0835x | 1350x | 1840x | |
| Loch Awe d | 0841 | 1357 | 1846 | |
| Dalmally d | 0847 | 1402 | 1852 | |
| Tyndrum Lower d | 0905 | 1421 | 1910 | |
| Crianlarich a | 0919 0919 | 1347 1428 | 1923 1923 | 2201 |

*Crianlarich to Glasgow/Edinburgh*

| Station | SX C● | B | J GK | | B | | SX A |
|---|---|---|---|---|---|---|---|
| d | — | 0925 | 1353 | 1432 | 1929 | — | 2203 |
| Ardlui d | — | 0944 | 1413 | 1447 | 1947 | — | 2223x |
| Arrochar & Tarbet d | — | 0959 | 1428 | 1501 | 2001 | — | 2240 |
| Garelochhead d | — | 1018 | 1449 | 1521 | 2020 | — | 2304 |
| Helensburgh Upper d | 0744 | 1030 | 1501 | 1533 | 2032 | — | 2318 |
| Dumbarton Central d | 0800 | 1045 | 1514 | 1546 | 2045 | — | — |
| Dalmuir d | — | 1054 | 1523 | 1555 | 2054 | — | 2340 |
| Glasgow Queen St. a | 0836 | 1114 | 1545 | 1614 | 2114 | — | — |
| Edinburgh a | 0950 | 1220 | 1650 | 1720 | — | 2220 | 0048 |

### NOTES — MALLAIG–FORT WILLIAM–OBAN–GLASGOW

A   Sleeping car accommodation only to London Euston, arrive 0745. Sleeping car reservations compulsory. Limited seating accommodation also available to Edinburgh only – reservations recommended.
B   From 27 June to 8 August also stops at Singer 1526, Drumry 1528, Drumchapel 1531 and Westerton 1534.
C   Does not run on Glasgow Public Holiday Mondays 25 May and 20 July. Runs via Singer and Maryhill.
D   Until 21 June
E   From 28 June
F   28 June to 30 August
G   From 22 June
H   26 July to 6 September
J   From 27 June to 8 August also stops at Singer 1557, Drumry 1600, Drumchapel 1602, Westerton 1605, arrives Glasgow Queen Street 1617.
K   The Jacobite steam train. Reservations recommended. Operated by West Coast Railway Company Ltd., telephone 01524 732100 for confirmation of days and dates of operation.
SX   Saturdays excepted
a   Arrival time.
d   Departure time.
x   Stops on request. Customers wishing to alight must inform the on-train staff and those wishing to join must give a hand signal to the driver.

Catering available on all services, except those marked ●.

Whilst no Sunday services were listed for the summer of 1947 (see pages 125 and 126), the summer 1998 timetable included a regular Sunday service (though less frequent than that for weekdays) which is not shown here.

# Author's Notes

The main sources used in the writing of this book are contained in two great storehouses of railway knowledge, the British Transport Historical Records Office, Edinburgh, and the Mitchell Library, Glasgow. All the relevant Acts are available to show exactly what the promoters had in mind. The minute books of the companies unfold in detail the story of the railways as it developed. But the minute books, important as they are, present neither a complete nor a balanced picture. It is easy to conclude from an inspection of the West Highland minutes that there were times when the directors 'forgot' to minute items that they did not want publicised. For instance, the minutes barely mention the trouble between the railway and the contractor in 1891, and certainly nothing of the magnitude of the crisis emerges. The researcher has to go to the court records as reproduced in *The Glasgow Herald* and *The Scotsman* for the technical details, and to the excellent reporting of *The Oban Times* for an impression of the impact on the West Highland community of the stoppage of work.

The annual Board of Trade (and later Ministry of Transport) inspections and resulting reports on the condition and conduct of the Mallaig Extension (mandatory under the Guarantee Act) provide first-class source material. Seldom has a line in this country been the subject of public scrutiny year by year for thirty years of its life. The Invergarry & Fort Augustus Railway minutes were in four volumes; unfortunately, the final and vital volume, which told the Invergarry's own story of the eclipse, is missing. But the most important features of the episode can be gathered from the proceedings of the North British Railway and Inverness County Council. After the passing of the North British Railway (Confirmation) Act of 1908 the affairs of the West Highland tended to become lost amid the business of the North British, and patience and diligence are required to disentangle purely West Highland material from the mass of matter available. NBR and LNE traffic note books give details of traffic at all stations on the system, and by abstracting statistics from the West Highland stations it has been possible to give a picture of the traffic pattern on the line over the years.

The West Highland is our most photogenic line, yet it has been neglected by photographers. The reasons are not hard to seek. The railway is largely inaccessible to travellers on foot. (Let the doubter try to make his way to the track through the neck-high tangle of bracken, boulders and bog to be found even in such civilised spots as Loch Lomondside.) Sections are long and trains are few. For a considerable part of the year the only two up and down trains traverse most of the line in the hours of darkness, daybreak or dusk when photography is impossible. Hence most West Highland pictures are taken from moving trains or at stations. The few taken in section are usually obtained at the rare places where the railway can be viewed at close quarters from the public road. The pictures in this volume have been selected for their West Highland flavour. The West Highland is above all a *scenic* railway and photographs, to do it justice, must illustrate its scenic attractions. A book of this kind is no place for the stock view of a locomotive posed against a coal dump.

# BIBLIOGRAPHY

Minute books of the West Highland Railway.
West Highland Railway Accounts and Reports to Shareholders.
The West Highland Railway Act, 1889.
The West Highland Railway (Mallaig Extension) Act, 1894.
The West Highland Railway (Guarantee) Act, 1896.
The West Highland Railway Act, 1896.
North British Railway (General Powers) Act, 1902.
North British Railway (Confirmation) Act, 1908.
NBR and LNER Traffic Note Books.
NBR, LNER and BR public and working timetables.
Records of the House of Commons.
Invergarry & Fort Augustus Railway minutes.
Invergarry & Fort Augustus Railway Accounts and Reports to Shareholders.
*The Story of the West Highland*. (G. Dow.) 1947.
*Lochaber in Peace and War*. (W. T. Kilgour.) 1908.
*Concrete Bridges and Culverts*. (H. G. Tyrrell.) 1909.
*Loyal Lochaber and its Associations*. (W. D. Norrie.) 1898.
*Kilkumein and Fort Augustus*. (O. Blundell.) 1914.
*Romantic Lochaber*. (D. B. McCulloch.) 1939.
*The Glory of Scotland*. (J. J. Bell.) 1932.
*The Land of Lochiel*. (T. R. Barnett.) 1927.
Newspapers and periodicals: *Railway Gazette, Railway Magazine, Railway Times, Railway Engineer, Railway Herald, LNER Magazine, The Engineer, Engineering, Journal of Transport History, Blackwood's Magazine, The Scots Magazine, The Green Man, Journal* of the Stephenson Locomotive Society, *The Glasgow Herald, The Glasgow Argus, Glasgow News, The Scotsman, The Oban Times*.

# Index

Illustrations are indicated by **heavy** type